CAROLINGIAN PORTRAITS

carolingian portraits

A STUDY IN THE NINTH CENTURY

by Eleanor Shipley Duckett

ANN ARBOR PAPERBACKS

THE UNIVERSITY OF MICHIGAN PRESS

THIS BOOK IS DEDICATED TO
CORNELIA AND THOMAS CORWIN MENDENHALL
OF SMITH COLLEGE
for their interest in medieval studies
and in those who work therein

First edition as an Ann Arbor Paperback 1969
Reissued as an Ann Arbor Paperback 1988
Copyright © by The University of Michigan 1962
ISBN 0-472-09157-3 (cloth)
ISBN 0-472-06157-7 (paper)
Library of Congress Card Catalog No. 62-18441
Published in the United States of America by
The University of Michigan Press
Manufactured in the United States of America

1991 1990 1989 1988   4 3 2 1

FOREWORD

The ninth century on the Continent of Europe was an age of darkness: of constant strife between the sons and grandsons of Charles the Great; of unending descents for raid and plunder by pirates upon the coasts of France and Italy, of Germany, Belgium, and the Netherlands; of long and often tedious quarrels among theologians and philosophers.

Its records lie in Latin annals, letters, treatises, very largely as yet untranslated into English. Scholars of distinction—of England, America, Germany, Holland, France, and Belgium, especially of France and Belgium—have gathered from these their clear and deeply probing narratives and interpretations of the history of Church and state in this time; others have told us of the lives and writings of individual men.

Yet, compared with other centuries, the ninth of our era seems to lack some simple story of its leaders. The student who is not a specialist, the general reader interested in medieval European history, is familiar with Charlemagne, with Einhard, perhaps with Amalar of Metz. But he does not know much, I venture to think, about Lupus of Ferrières, or Hincmar of Reims, and possibly not a great deal concerning even Louis the Pious or Pope Nicholas the Great.

The century, nevertheless, is one of importance and interest. It saw not only the rise, but the gradual decline and the fall of the Empire founded by Charlemagne. It saw, in the years between the reign of this Emperor and that of his grandson, Charles the Bald, a significant change in the relation between thrones and sees, the powers secular and ecclesiastical. It saw a new concept of Papal authority in the mind of Nicholas the Great; a new domination in the purpose of the great Metropolitans of the Church; a struggle of their bishops against this will to dominate.

It saw the forging of the False Decretals and the writing of a famous medieval biography. It saw a lasting contribution to the progress of the Roman liturgy. It held within itself a passion for scholarship which was not sterile, but constructive. Finally, it held men and women of that humanity which has happily, and often unhappily, been common to all ages of the world.

It has therefore seemed to me worth while to try to bring back into life here seven of these men, placed for better understanding against the background of their own turbulent time. My apology for including the more familiar figure of Charlemagne among them must be that my story of an Empire had to have a beginning before it could draw toward its end.

For the errors in my story I alone am responsible. I would, however, thank especially Harold Pink, of the Cambridge University Library, whom I consulted in regard to manuscripts connected with Lupus of Ferrières; and Philip Grierson, reader in medieval numismatics, University of Cambridge, professor of numismatics, University of Brussels, for his extraordinary generosity in allowing me to borrow, carry across the Atlantic, and keep as long as I wished seven rare volumes from his own private collection.

E. S. D.

July 1962
Northampton, Massachusetts

CONTENTS

Chapter I

THE RISE OF THE CAROLINGIAN EMPIRE
CHARLES THE GREAT

1

On January 28, 814, at nine o'clock in the morning, Charles the Great, "Most Serene Majesty, crowned by God, Emperor great and pacific, governing the Roman Empire and by God's mercy king of the Franks and of the Lombards," died of pleurisy in his Palace at Aachen in West Germany, between the Meuse and the Rhine. He was seventy-one years old. For forty-six of these years he had been king of the Franks; thirteen had now gone by since Pope Leo III had crowned him Emperor in St. Peter's, Rome, since he had heard the Litany of Praises chanted to God in his honor by the multitude assembled for the High Mass of Christmas Day. In his last weeks, as he lay failing in body but ever active in mind, reading Latin texts of the Bible with an eye still alert for errors, he must sometimes have turned his thoughts back over what he had done in his world.

He had entered into the rule of a great kingdom, won partly by inheritance in 768 from his father, King Pippin the Short, partly by a determined seizure, which took no account of other heirs, of his brother's portion when that brother, Carloman, appointed with him joint-king by their father, had ended their uneasy partnership by his death in 771. Then Charles had held under his power lands extending from Frisia in the northeast to Provence and the Gothic Septimania on the border of Spain in the south. He was king over Neustria, with its cities of Paris, of Soissons, and of Rouen; over Austrasia, country of the Rhine and the Moselle, with its cities of Cologne and Mainz and Metz; over the forests and mountains of Thuringia; over Alemannia, country of the Rhine and the Danube; over Aquitaine and Burgundy.

But he had looked beyond even these wide bounds. There had been Italy. In 773 he had answered the appeal of Pope

Hadrian I and had marched to defend the Papal See of Rome from Lombard menace. He had laid siege to Pavia, capital city of the Lombard king, Desiderius; he had captured it in 774 and had sent Desiderius and his queen as prisoners of war to Frankland. Henceforward, he himself had been king of the Lombards in northern Italy and proudly bore the title of Patrician of the Romans. Two years later he had again marched into Italy, to put down Lombard rebellion, and had returned only when its leader, the Lombard Duke of Friuli, was dead and when the rebel cities, Friuli and Treviso, were in his own hands. In 781 he had seen his son, Pippin, then four years old, anointed at Rome as king of Italy by the same Pope Hadrian; as ruler supreme he had entrusted this kingdom's increasing territory to the care of loyal Frankish governors. For nearly thirty years Pippin and his counselors had held their Court in the north and central lands of Italy, always under the dominant control of Charles. After Pippin's early death at the age of thirty-three, Charles had given his crown to Pippin's son, young Bernard, and once more had fortified its rule by the presence of two able advisers of his own appointing. Nor had Italy in the south lain untouched by him. In 786 he had marched with an army to win control over the Duchy of Benevento; he had received the homage of its Duke and had held in his keeping the Duke's younger son as a guarantee of good faith.

Charles, then, had conquered in Italy. Had not the Papal See needed his hand? At the same time he had already put this hand to another war of conquest, which he also held to be good and timely as a Christian crusade. North of Austrasia and Thuringia lived countless savage Saxon tribesmen, by old tradition heathen worshippers of strange gods. Was not he a Christian ruler, whose divine vocation it was to further the spreading of the Christian faith? It was for him, he had felt convinced, to conquer these heathen for the glory of Christ and the saving of their benighted souls, and also to conquer them for the protection and the extending of his Frankish kingdom. Saxon raiders were always eager and ready to descend for plunder on Frankish fields; Saxon people, too, as a great and mighty force were standing implacable in the path of Frankish progress and growth.

Year by year he had gone out on campaign against these free, warrior Saxons, who for thirty-three years, from 772 until 804, stubbornly resisted his will to conquer their freedom and their land. He had destroyed their sacred Irminsul, symbol of their pagan creed; he had pursued them on the Weser and the Ocker and the Eder, on the Rhine and the Elbe and beyond the Elbe. He had ravaged their harvests; he had deported their men, women, and children from their homes to foreign settlements in Frankland; when they had dared to fall upon his army in bold retaliation, he had massacred them in thousands. Again and again they had seemed to surrender. They had submitted, time after time, to the hated rite of Christian baptism, only to rise again the next year in fresh defiance. For eight years, from 777 until 785, he had pursued their chieftain Widukind, who fled before him to the wilds north of the Elbe. In the end Widukind, too, had been brought in subjection to the font, received as son in the Lord God and laden with gifts by his conqueror. When Charles had judged the time to be ripe, he had ordered for all Saxons in formal Edict the strict observance of Christian tradition, only to hear that once more they had risen in all the force of their will, ready to die rather than to give of their substance for payment of tithes to the Church of this Frankish king. "As a dog that returns to its vomit," wrote the pious Frankish recorder of these years, so the Saxon returned from his Christian baptizing to fight anew for the faith of his fathers. At last they could fight no more; and Saxony had become a Frankish land, divided out by Charles among his Frankish counts for its rule.

East of Alemannia lay Bavaria. On Bavaria the Frankish crown had already placed its mark; a vassal of King Charles, its Duke Tassilo, held it under oath of loyalty. At Worms in 781 he had sworn to keep this oath. But, so Bavarian men themselves declared, he had broken his word. He had, indeed, given his son to Charles as hostage. Then, through the urging of his wife, Liutberga, he had stirred up his neighbors, the unconquered Avars, to rise against this king of the Franks. Liutberga hated Charles; she was a daughter of the Lombard Desiderius, whom he had driven from a throne into exile. In 787 Charles had set out for Bavaria; he had met Tassilo near Augsburg and the river

Lech and had forced him by overwhelming power to pray for mercy. In 788 a general assembly of Franks and Bavarians had condemned him to death. His conqueror had spared his life, but sent him and his son to live within monastic walls. As he was to do in Saxony, so the Frankish king now distributed this Bavarian Duchy in portions among nobles of his people as reward for service done.

The Avars dwelt east of Bavaria. They were a nomad people who had come originally from Asia and had moved from land to land until they had settled in the modern Hungary and Yugoslavia. There in the course of years they had become a menace to Frankish Bavaria and northern Italy. The Saxon war was pressing Charles hard. But in 791 he had marched to the Avar borders; he had encamped there for three days while litanies were chanted and mass was offered for his cause and for the conversion of these barbarians; he had defeated them and stripped bare their homes on the Danube and the Raab. Four years later Eric, now Duke of Friuli in the Frankish kingdom of Italy, had forced his way far within their land to their great fortress, the *Ring*, sacred center of their fighting power, and had beaten down its outer walls; in 796 Pippin, king of Italy, had completed its destruction. The Avars had submitted; led by their *tudun*, their chieftain, they had given their homage to the Christian Church and to Charles. Huge wagons of booty traveled from the ruins of their citadel to the Frankish king, who forwarded from it a large portion as offering to the Holy See at Rome.

These were the campaigns of high satisfaction in the king's memory. Nor were they all. On the western coast the Bretons still maintained a measure of independence, though they saw their fields ransacked in punishment for revolt against his power; in 786, 799, and 811, at least for the moment, they, too, had felt the force of his hand. Over the southern coastlands of Septimania Charles ruled by inheritance. Beyond Septimania and the Pyrenees lay new scope for his desire. There he had gained the "Spanish March" and held it in control. In 785 Gerona had surrendered to his army; in 795 his troops were in Vich; in 801 Barcelona was captured. By this time the Frankish tide of power was advancing toward the Ebro. In 799 the governor of Huesca had offered Charles the keys of the city; in 811 Tortosa had given up its walls. Neither place, however, remained securely under Frankish rule; the victory was only partial. Amid the mountains and passes of the Pyrenees the Basque fighters fiercely held their freedom; Charles always carried in mind the slaughter in 778 of his men, distinguished officers among them, in the narrow defile famous to later centuries as Roncevaux. They had been returning, called back by a crisis of the Saxon war, from a rash attempt of the king to possess himself of Spanish land held by Arab chieftains. The constant quarrels between Muslim governors had tempted him to seize a chance of profit.

Finally, there were the peoples of regions far north, across the Elbe. Among these the Abodrites were for the most part his friends, ready to aid his ambition, conscious of his strength in war. In 789 he had received homage from the leader of the Wiltzi, neighbors of the Abodrites, after scouring their lands; he had subdued, also, Sorbs and Slavs beyond the river, at least for the time being. Farther north stretched the unknown distance, held by Scandinavian Vikings, hunters and warriors. Already Charles had felt their menace and had lived in uneasy peace with a Viking king of Danes, Godfrid. Both rulers had diligently fortified their borders, on shore and inland. In 810 Frisia and its islands had been attacked by raid and plundered. For Charles, however, the outbreak of Viking storm and devastation was still too far away to cause him serious trouble; his thought was of defense against a time possibly to come.

Over this vast territory, an Empire in all but name and thus built up from many peoples, he had watched and had ruled with a zeal equal to his lust for conquest. His representatives, his *missi,* chosen from men of marked ability, bishops and lay nobles, had carried his instructions and commands when they went out from his Councils and his Court to administer justice and to keep the peace far and wide. Regularly year after year he had presided over the General Assemblies held in the centers of his dominion, in the various Palaces of his crown. For the educating of his ignorant Franks he had called to his Court scholars from Italy, from Spain, from England. From York in England he had brought to Aachen the most renowned master of the time, Alcuin, to

direct the work which by long-established custom made the
Frankish Court a "School" of training for the boys and youths
of high rank who were in later years here and there to govern
and to defend their king's realm. To Alcuin and to his writings
many Frankish leaders owed their introduction to the liberal arts.

Above all, with constant vigilance Charles had provided for
the forming, the ordering, of the life of the Frankish Church.
Abbeys and churches he had built and endowed without cease.
Episcopal centers he had founded and enriched. Missions had
been sent out to the distant heathen. Through Alcuin he had
gained a text of the liturgy of his Church which was to carry
its influence down the centuries, as far as Rome itself. Revision
had been made of the text of the Latin Bible, and of the Lection-
ary or Book of Lessons to be read at Mass. His great aim and
desire had been uniformity of custom and of usage in Frankish
discipline, ecclesiastical and spiritual; reverence for the Church
of Rome and her tradition; one pattern of worship, based on
Rome, for all whom he ruled. To further the making of copies
of Missals, Bibles, Books of Hours, he had stimulated the develop-
ment and practice of the beautiful and clear script known as the
Carolingian minuscule, in the *scriptoria*, the rooms set apart for
writing, of many Frankish abbeys. For the quickening of study
in these abbeys he had written, probably between 794 and 800
and with the aid of Alcuin, a personal Letter of admonition, addressed to Baugulf, abbot of the royal monastery of Fulda in
Austrasia, who afterwards circulated its warning words among
his brother rulers of cloistered monks. For lay people, one and
all, Charles had required of his clergy diligent teaching of the
elements of the Faith, as expressed in the Creed and the Lord's
Prayer. Heathen rites he had vigorously attacked; heresy, especially the Adoptionist error of Felix of Urgel, he had pursued until
its upholders were silenced; in the long struggle of the Iconoclastic
Controversy he had taken notable part—condemning alike the
undue adoration and the unseemly contempt of pictures and
statues venerated by the faithful—in the writings which bear
the name of the *Caroline Books,* compiled under his own command. Debate on matters theological, Biblical, liturgical was

his particular joy. Against the counsel of the Pope himself he had insisted upon the public chanting in his Palace Chapel of the *Filioque* clause in the Creed; we still have the lively dialogue in which the envoys of Charles, sent to hold discussion at Rome— among them were Adalard, abbot of Corbie, and Jesse, bishop of Amiens—respectfully argued the matter with the Holy Father. Frequently he forwarded to his bishops and clergy his request for his own informing on knotty points of Church doctrine or ritual. Manner was only next in importance to matter; the very mode of chanting in his Chapel was governed by his sure sense of decorum and harmony.

2

And so his power and fame had grown. Supreme in his own headship as king of the Franks, a king who ordered and appointed his bishops as he did his lay ministers, who gave and dispensed the tenure and the revenues of his Frankish abbeys, who presided over the Synods of his Frankish Church as he did over the Assemblies of his Frankish state, he had risen in his realm and in foreign lands to a standing which was his alone. The trouble and tragedy of other powers had aided his advance. In 797 Constantine, Emperor of the East at Constantinople, had been blinded and deposed by Irene, his own mother, who had then as Empress assumed the throne. In 799 Pope Leo III, who on his succession four years before had sent to Charles the keys of St. Peter's Confession and the standard of the City of Rome, now wounded by the brutal force of his enemies in the streets of that city, had been welcomed with all honor by Charles at Pader- born in Saxony. There into the king's ear Leo had poured out his griefs; the following year Charles had gone to Rome to spend three weeks of winter in inquiring into this outrage, and seen its leaders condemned. In 799 Alcuin had written to his Frankish ruler: "As greatly as you rise above other men in the power of your kingship, so greatly do you excel all in honour of wisdom, in order of holy religion. Happy the people who rejoice in such a Prince. . . . With the sword of devotion in your right hand you purge and protect the churches of Christ within from doctrine of traitors; with the sword of your left hand you defend them without from the plundering raids of pagans. In the strength of God you stand thus armed."

But, putting into words the thought of other men, Alcuin had dared further: "There is one power of the Papacy, of the Vicar of Christ. There is another, the lay power of Imperial Constantinople. There is a third, of your own kingship, through which the Lord Jesus Christ has made you ruler of Christian people, excelling in your strength the two which I have named, more renowned in wisdom, more exalted in the dignity of your realm. See! on you alone all hope for the churches of Christ leans for its support."

Alcuin and his friends, Arno, archbishop of Salzburg, Candidus, and Fridugis, had gradually led on the mind of their King Charles to the same thought. When, however, on Christmas Day, 800, Pope Leo III had crowned him in St. Peter's as Emperor of the Romans, he had been taken by surprise and his mind had immediately rebelled. The Pope might, indeed, bless this honor, but it was not for him to bestow it on his own initiative, for his own purpose thus to magnify his benefactor, Charles, without the concurrence of Constantinople. The time had not yet come; the Court at Constantinople had not yet acknowledged Charles as colleague and brother in Christian imperial rule.

He had waited; he had worked with diplomacy and with bold force of arms for yet another eleven years. In 802 Irene in her turn had been thrust from her throne, and Nicephorus, controller of the Public Treasury at Constantinople, had become Emperor. In 811 Nicephorus had been killed in battle. Strong and ready partisanship then had given the crown to Michael Rangabé, a ready son-in-law. Michael was no strong character, and promptly had yielded to coercion from Frankish source, adroitly applied. The following year Michael's envoys from the East had at last acclaimed Charles in the Palace of Aachen with the words of salutation customary for those of imperial dignity, crying to him in the Greek tongue as "Emperor and Basileus."

On his own side, it is true, Charles had made concession; he had abandoned his claim of hold over territories around the head of the Adriatic: Venice, and cities which lay near the coast in Dalmatia.

The Pope's words, unwelcome as they had been in 800, the homage of the multitude in St. Peter's, the recognition at Aachen, had finally reconciled the Frankish king to the responsibility of imperial rank. It was pleasant that in 800 the Patriarch of Jerusalem had sent to him in Rome the keys of the Lord's Sepulchre and of Calvary's sacred enclosure, with the standard of Jerusalem's city. It was pleasant that in 802 and in 807 gifts had arrived for him from the caliph of Baghdad. In 802 an elephant, a wonder unknown in Frankland, had been dispatched to the Court. Its name was Abul Abaz, and it lived nine years, until it fell as it marched with Charles against the pirates of the North in 810. The offerings of 807 were truly magnificent: tents of silk, wrought in various colors; perfumes and unguents; candelabra; a clock which rang out the hours and at each striking sent forth knights in armor from twelve windows, windows which opened for the marching out of these knights and closed again, each hour, as they returned. One can see King Charles delighting in this gift of precision and mechanical skill.

But recognition had not really changed a fact already true. Charles had been king of an empire before he was thus doubly acclaimed. And his rule, he firmly believed, had been destined for him by the will and providence of an all-wise God. It was for him to govern through this divine authority, given him by Heaven's grace, and to leave it at his death in the hands of his sons.

Only, however, in 812, upon the recognition by Constantinople of his imperial standing in the West, was the matter of succession to this title of Emperor in the West decided by Charles. No mention of this had been made when, in accordance with Frankish tradition, in 806 he had divided out by formal act the lands of his rule for government among his three sons. This act would come into final force only after his death. As long as he lived, it was he who was Emperor in the West. To which of his sons, if any, he would bequeath the imperial title, he had left for the time being undecided. Then his two elder sons—Pippin,

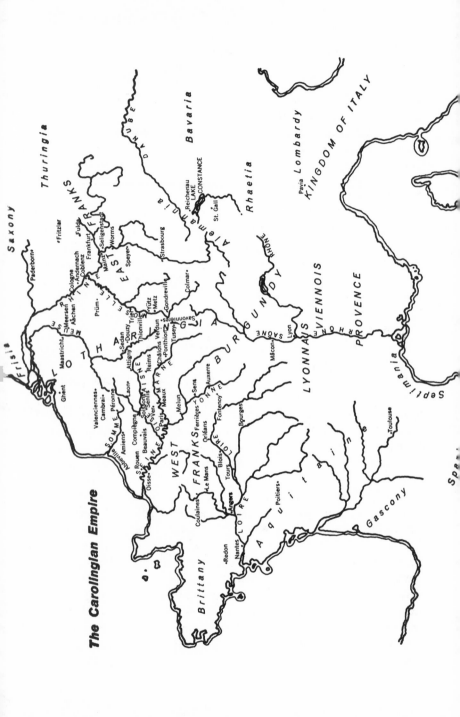

The Carolinglan Empire

Frisia

Saxony

Thuringla

Paderborn

Fritzlar

Ghent

Maastricht

Meersen

Aachen

Cologne

Andernach

Coblenz

Fulda

Seligenstadt

Frankfurt

Mainz

Worms

Speyer

Prüm

EAST FRANKS

Strasbourg

Colmar

Reichenau

LAKE CONSTANCE

St. Gall

Bavaria

DANUBE

RHINE

ELBE

LOTHARINGIA

Sedan

Attigny

Douzy

Trier

Thionville

Metz

Gondreville

Savonnières

Verdun

Tusey

MOSELLE

Valenciennes

Cambrai

Péronne

Laon

Soissons

Reims

Châlons

Ponthion

Meaux

SOMME

Aubigny

Amiens

Compiègne

Beauvais

Senlis

Paris

Melun

OISE

AISNE

MARNE

Rouen

Olsse

SEINE

WEST FRANKS

NEUSTRIA

Ferrières

Sens

Auxerre

Fontenoy

YONNE

BURGUNDY

Rhaetia

RHONE

SAONE

Mâcon

Lyon

LYONNAIS

VIENNOIS

PROVENCE

RHONE

Coulaines

Le Mans

Blois

Orléans

Tours

Angers

LOIRE

Bourges

Poitiers

A q u i t a i n e

Redon

Nantes

Brittany

Gascony

Septimania

Toulouse

Spain

ruler of Italy, and Charles, heir as his firstborn to Frankland—
had died, in 810 and 811. Louis, the youngest, alone remained to
hold the inheritance which should be left by his father.

3

Louis, the third son of Charles and of Hildegard, his second
wife, had been born in 778 in Aquitaine, where the king had
left his queen as he marched on the Spanish expedition which
had ended in the disaster of Roncevaux. At the age of three, when
his brother Pippin had been hallowed as king of Italy by Pope
Hadrian I at Rome, Louis, too, had been blessed at the same
time as king of Aquitaine. Its people were fiercely proud, valiant
lovers of liberty; it had cost Pippin the Short, father of Charles
and king of the Franks from 751 until 768, a long and determined
struggle to conquer their ruling dukes and to bring them into
his dominion. For eight years he had fought their Duke Waifar,
until finally, with Waifar's murder in 768 just before Pippin's
own death, Aquitaine had been absorbed into the realm of the
Franks. But its warriors were always restless, always longing for
their lost freedom. One of the first acts of Charles after, in partnership with his brother Carloman, he had succeeded Pippin in 768
was to march against the rebel Aquitanian Duke Hunald. Carloman would have none of the campaign. But this had made no
difference. Dread of Charles, even though he fought unaided,
had brought Hunald a captive into his hands. Discontent, however, still raised trouble for many years. At last Charles had judged
it expedient to make Aquitaine into a kingdom of its own, administered after Frankish pattern, and to give its people as king
a son of his who should rule them through Frankish ministers,
under the supreme will of himself, the overlord.

In 781, therefore, he had brought Louis, three years old,
to the Aquitanians as their king. At Orléans he had halted the
royal carriage in which they traveled and had sent the little boy,
arrayed as a soldier, with hauberk and spear, riding his horse
across the border to enter into his kingdom, to meet his people
in true kingly style. In Aquitaine Louis had been left by his
father's order, to be brought up according to its custom and
tradition. Four years later, when he was seven, he had come

riding to meet his father in Saxony at the head of his **Aquitanian** warriors, dressed in the Gascon manner common among Aquitanian nobles, his mantle around his shoulders, his tunic fashioned with long, wide sleeves, his hose well lined, his boots armed with spurs, his javelin in his hand.

During his thirty-three years as ruler of Aquitaine under his father's overlordship, from 781 until 814, Louis through the conquests of Charles was to receive those additions to his kingdom which we have already noted, in the annexing of the "Spanish March" and of the land between the Pyrenees and the Ebro. Loyally he had carried out his father's commands. He had presided over assemblies similar to those in Aachen; he had sent out his *missi*, to investigate, to correct, and to aid throughout his realm; he had held his Court here and there with due ceremony. He had marched constantly on campaign: in the field of war against the Saxons with Charles; against Benevento in southern Italy with his brother Pippin; against the Basque raiders of Gascony; into Spain in pursuit of conquest. Here and there he had been successful in subduing rebellion. But, as his expeditions into Saxony were his father's responsibility, so his administration of Aquitaine was largely carried out by his counselors, and his battles for Spanish gain either ended without result or were won by other command than his. In 797 his father's order to him to besiege Huesca brought no success. In 801 a similar command sent him to attack Barcelona. It was, however, not Louis the king but his army, gathered from Gascony, from Burgundy, from Provence, and from Septimania, that brought the siege of the city to a victorious end. He was not even there until the last weeks, when the end seemed in sight. Then his generals sent for him in order that the king's presence might add luster to the taking. In 809 he was unable to capture Tortosa, which, as we saw, two years later offered its keys to King Charles. That great general of Charles, William, Count of Toulouse, who fought the Basques and the Arabs, at the head of a long-enduring force at last brought Barcelona to surrender; the same Count William who in 806 said farewell to the world and lived his last years as a monk in the abbey of Gellone which he himself had built in Aquitaine.

King Louis, indeed, understood this last decision of Count
William better than that driving urge of his father for battle
and conquest. From his early years he had been a lover of spiritual
exercise and monastic discipline; and example had strengthened
his inborn bent. All his life he was deeply attached to those whom
he singled out as his companions for their religious fervor, their
philosophic thought, their charm and appeal. Alcuin, who had
known him from childhood, once wrote to the eldest son of King
Charles and Hildegard: "Your brother Louis has asked me to
write often to give him my counsel. This I have been doing, and,
God willing, I shall continue to do; he reads my letters in great
humility of heart." In 811 the learned priest, Claudius, whom
later Louis was to appoint bishop of Turin in Italy, wrote that
he had been summoned by the king of Aquitaine to come and
work in his palace of Chasseneuil.

Above all, Benedict, abbot of Aniane in Aquitaine itself,
was for Louis his friend, his hero, and his spiritual guide. It was
under the influence of this man that William, Count of Toulouse,
had turned from soldier to monk; his abbey of Gellone was only
a few miles from that of Aniane. Fortified and led by the same
Benedict, Louis as king of Aquitaine set himself with all determination to reform the monasteries in his lands, to bring them
from their slack, tepid working into a strict obedience to the
discipline originally prescribed in the sixth century by St. Benedict
of Nursia.

This, then, was the son who was to succeed Charles the
Great as king and emperor. Charles knew his nature only too
well: humble in his own eyes, distrustful of himself and his acts,
given overmuch to yielding his will to those whom he loved and
admired, prone to introspection and scruple, revering those set
in the seats of authority for their office rather than for their
character as men.

Yet Louis had constantly been at his father's side and had
learned from him the tradition of his house, the meaning of
kingship, the divinely appointed responsibility of a king's consecration and honor. Since the death of both his elder brothers he
had known that in all probability this burden before many years

would descend upon his own soul, for kingly service in the sight of that God Who for this very purpose had brought him into being.

4

There was, however, as we know, another and a very real side to Charles, his father, the king and emperor, a side intimately bound up with his royal power and renown. His, unlike that of Louis, was no life of spiritual austerity. Both the life of absorbing ambition for himself and his people, and the life of a Court, in season gay and worldly, seemed to him entirely natural and good. With equal zest he sat at the head of his Council table, watched over synods of the Church, led out his armies; then turned to relax among his friends. Did not the joyous spirit of his Court spring from the mind, and was not the body the handmaid of both mind and soul? The same vitality which drove him to war and council ran in his veins at home, whether he was holding his Court at Aachen, or at Worms, or Frankfurt, or Ingelheim on the bank of the Rhine, or at Thionville on the Moselle, or at Herstal near the Meuse, or at Nijmegen on the Waal in the Netherlands. Contemporary verse and prose picture the king sitting in the midst of his great hall, presiding serenely over a varied multitude of guests, ordering, as host, for each one his generous portion of the feast. Around him rises the confused noise of debate and argument, of laughter in riddle and quip; courtiers and visitors, ministers and envoys make merry or sit absorbed in serious discussion. Theology, philosophy, politics, jest and verse, all serve his table, and he takes his part in all, with question, with retort, with delight of arguments, while butler and seneschal, servers and pages, stand in readiness at their appointed stations or hurry to and fro to do his bidding.

Charles had married four times; after the death of Liutgard, his fourth wife, he had taken in turn four mistresses. Of the sons born in lawful marriage, as we have seen, only Louis was living at the time of his death in 814; of illegitimate birth he had three: Drogo, Hugh, and Thierry. His eldest legitimate daughter, Rotrud, had died in 810. Four more, also his own in law and right, were still with him: Bertha, Gisela, Theodrad, and Hiltrud. In the lustful, boisterous days of his Court during his latter years, for the greater part spent at Aachen as the strength of his body waned and spent in easy disregard of strictness of morals, these daughters took their own pleasure. He had never allowed them to marry. He loved too much their presence about him, he said; a better reason has argued that he wanted no difficult entanglements with other powers. Two of them bore sons of secret love.

Amid his lively company Charles in his last months saw with content men whom he counted on as statesmen, as supporters and defenders of the Empire when his son Louis should be sitting in his place. Alcuin had died in 804. There was still Theodulf, the Goth driven from his native Spain by trouble of politics and gladly received by Charles for the joy of his wit, the depths of his learning, his skill alike in offering counsel and in writing verse. On all matters he could talk: of state, of the Church, of books old and new. Charles had made him bishop of Orléans; now and again he sent him out as *missus*, as royal envoy, on errands of diplomacy, of law, and of arbitration.

There were the two brothers, Adalard and Wala, grandsons of Charles Martel and therefore cousins of Charles himself. They had been brought up from boyhood in the school of the royal Palace and knew everything and everyone within its halls. Both were loyal to the Empire with all their hearts, honest, honorable, zealous. Both, it was true, preferred their own conscience even before the will of their king. Adalard had so disapproved of the repudiation by Charles of his first wife, another daughter of the Lombard king, Desiderius, that he had left the Court to enter religious life in the monastery of Corbie, near Amiens, and had been elected its abbot. Since that time, however, about 772, a reconciliation had been made, and Adalard had often been chosen for work of high importance in the administration. It was he who had been sent by Charles, with Wala, to rule Italy in the name of its boy king, Pippin. Their sister, Gundrada, was also a favorite with her royal cousin. Alcuin had known Adalard as his "brother" at Court, had loved him well and sent him many letters. Gundrada was his "dearest daughter"; he wrote assiduously to her on the philosophy of the soul.

There was Hildebald, whom Charles had set as archbishop

in Cologne, and as head of the chaplains and secretaries of his Palace, as keeper of its archives and writer of official documents. So greatly had the king desired his presence that he had obtained special permission from the Pope for Hildebald's frequent absences from his see in Cologne. So important, indeed, was Hildebald in Aachen that Frankish record called him "Archbishop of the sacred Palace."

There was Jesse, bishop of Amiens, who together with those named above had already, while Charles still lived, put witness of signature to the last will and testament of his king. There was Hugh, Count of Tours, whom in 811 Charles had sent on a mission of peace to Nicephorus, Emperor in Constantinople.

From near at hand, then, the state of the Empire might seem prosperous. On the horizon, however, clouds were rising which in time might, indeed, hide the sun. From this record of conquest, of the building of realm and rule, Charles turned in his last months, in 813, to face a darker page. Much, he well knew, remained to be done, and he had long in his inner mind feared for the future. Around and underneath his achievement there lay many problems, many troubles, and day by day he saw their increase in his land. There was the difficulty of control of an Empire of many peoples of all sorts and conditions; the unceasing drive to uphold sovereign power against disorder and lawlessness in Church and state, against the ambition of his nobles and the hunger of those whom they oppressed. Again and again he had issued his commands and sent them out in the hands of his legates, had declared them in the assemblies of his people; yet always the need for control, the necessity for drive, arose anew before his face.

It was too late to ponder these things with any hope of satisfaction. His long rule was coming to an end, and the years of his life were pressing him hard. He knew that there was but one thing of importance which was his to do before he should die.

In 812 the Emperor Michael, as we have seen, had acknowledged him as his brother in imperial honor. Now therefore, in 813, Charles summoned his son and heir, Louis of Aquitaine, to the Court of Aachen. Louis duly arrived. From Thegan, who wrote a Life of this one surviving son, we have a detailed description of the events following his arrival: "With all his army, his bishops and abbots, his dukes and counts, Charles, the Emperor, held Council in his Palace. There he bade them all to give assurance of loyalty towards this son of his; there he asked them all, from the greatest to the most humble: Was it their pleasure that he, Charles, should give share in the name and dignity of Emperor to Louis?"

All willingly assented. On the next Sunday, September 11, arrayed in his imperial robes, the crown upon his head, Charles walked in procession of state to the Palace Chapel which he himself had built, and to its high altar of the Lord Christ. On this had been laid by his command a second crown of gold. For a long time father and son knelt in prayer. Then, in the hearing of a great congregation, the Emperor commanded his son to love and fear God, to guide and defend the churches of his realm, to show all kindness to his sisters and brothers, to honor his bishops and priests as fathers, to care for his subjects as sons, to turn the proud and evil into the way of salvation, to comfort the religious, and to protect the poor. When Louis had declared his readiness to obey, his father required him to take that imperial crown of gold from the altar and to place it upon his head. Mass was now chanted as the two crowned Emperors knelt in thanksgiving for this new accession; then all returned to feast with joy.

Another record—which, indeed, seems more probably true— has it that Charles himself crowned his son and thus dedicated him to a sharing in the imperial dignity. At any rate, no Pope, no bishop, was called upon to celebrate this ritual of coronation. Charles, Emperor and King, himself imparted to his heir by, as he firmly believed, the will of divine disposing, that authority and character which God had impressed upon his own soul. To him this kingly character here approached that of the priest.

Louis saw his father no more after this September of 813. During the next few months Charles lived, so far as was possible for him, in his accustomed way at Aachen. He had now arranged the affairs of his realm; Italy was placed in this same year under the royal tenure of his grandson, Bernard, son of Pippin. In October the king and his Court, as usual, went hunting through the forest which lay near at hand. As of old, he appeared in his

Palace to receive envoys and visitors. He wore, as was his custom, the Frankish national dress; he spoke the Frankish native speech; he delighted in the collection of old Frankish heathen poetry which he had ordered assembled and preserved; perhaps he thought of finishing the grammar of the Frankish language which once he had begun. In formal Latin he received ambassadors from without, or dictated his official letters. When his health allowed it, he worked on the text of the Latin Vulgate Bible and compared Alcuin's version with others. Often he turned to prayer; every day, as he had done down the years of his ruling, he heard Mass and Office in his Chapel. He looked with pleasure and with pride upon that chapel of the Palace at Aachen, which in its building recalled Ravenna's church of San Vitale; upon the marble and the pillars brought from Ravenna, brought, too, from Rome by special grace of the Pope; upon the mosaics, which recalled those of the Eastern Empire, Byzantine in their art. As he went in and out of his Palace, he saw in its courtyard the great statue of Theodoric the Goth, conqueror of Rome. Theodoric had been of barbarian descent. So was Charles himself. But his was a splendid ancestry, the line of the Arnulfings. Had not his great-grandfather, Pippin of Herstal, united under his hand the rule of the Franks, east and west? Had not his grandfather, Charles Martel, driven out the heathen and worked with the Papacy and Archbishop Boniface for the unity of Frankland under Arnulfing control? Had not Arnulfing power triumphed when the last Merovingian king was dismissed—needed no longer—and when Boniface, acting by will and command of the Pope, with his own hands had anointed Pippin the Short, father of Charles, as king of the Franks? So had Charles, too, their descendant, conquered and ruled. And was he not himself now not only King of the Franks but Emperor of the Romans, in union with Constantinople, that "second Rome"? Such thoughts kindled light amid those clouds which were settling heavily on his mind.

Then came January 814 when sudden cold and fever fell upon him. For a week he lay in bed. On January 27 he called to his bedside Hildebald, his friend and chief chaplain, and received from him the last sacraments of the Church. On the morrow he died.

Not long afterwards some simple monk—his name is not known—wrote a Lament for Charlemagne:

> *Francia diras perpessa iniurias*
> *Nullum iam talem dolorem sustinuit,*
> *Heu mihi misero;*
> *Quando augustum facundumque Karolum*
> *In Aquisgrani glebis terrae tradidit,*
> *Heu mihi misero:*
> Dire sufferings has France endured,
> Yet never grief like unto this,
> Woe is me for misery;
> Now Charles, voice of majesty and power,
> To Aachen's soil she has given,
> Woe is me for misery.

Nearly eleven centuries later Albert Hauck in his *Kirchengeschichte Deutschlands* was of the same mind:

"Selten ist ein Mann unersetzlich. Karl der Grosse war es."

Chapter II

LOUIS THE PIOUS
KING AND EMPEROR

1

The messenger, Rampo, bearing word of the Emperor's death, reached Louis in his kingdom of Aquitaine, at the royal manor of Doué-la-Fontaine near Saumur and the Loire. Offices and masses for the dead were chanted for four days; and then the king, known to tradition as Louis "the Pious," set out for Aachen and his high destiny.

He was now in his thirty-sixth year, of strong and muscular build and average height; good-looking, with clear, open eyes, well-shaped hands, and deep, resonant voice. Hunting and all outdoor activities were his delight. So, also, were his books: his ancient classics, his writings of the Fathers of the Church. In manner he was grave; sober and restrained alike in his dress and in his conduct at social gatherings, "he never laughed aloud"; a man generous in nature, often overcome by access of anger, but ready to forget offense. With unfailing devotion he assisted at mass and other ritual of the Church's days and years. He was married to one Irmengard; and he had three young sons, Lothar, Pippin, and Louis.

Crowds acclaimed their king as he journeyed, surrounded by his men-at-arms. Yet fear, too, went with him, fear deeper and wider than he himself could clearly describe or define. Not at this time could he understand the problems that lay in his path; but some things he did know from his own observation and experience. He knew well that it had been the strength and the glamour of the character and influence of his father, Charles the Great, which had kept the dissonant elements of his Empire in subjection to his will, at least in outward union. Charles had been confident in his power, sure of his success, intolerant of criticism, utterly determined to stand firm as temporal Lord of his people in matters of both state and Church, to draw into his Empire those who dwelt outside. And therefore fear beset the heart of his son. How could he, so dependent on the opinion of those nearest him, sit in the seat of this father of his? How could he, the solitary, monastic-minded soul, stimulate and hold together his Court as the all-pervading, laughter-and-lust-loving spirit of Charles had done?

There was more, too, of trouble in his thought as he rode onward toward his destiny. Men of genius had risen under Charles to high office and wealth in state and Church, a rising which had made them in their turn lords of those, clergy as well as layfolk, who labored on the estates given to their masters by gift of the Emperor. Now many, both lords and laborers, had begun as years had passed to nurse in their hearts a spirit of unrest, even of rebellion, against those to whom they owed a necessary and ordered obedience and servitude: the nobles against their Emperor, now old and slowly relaxing his tight hold of the reins of government; the laborers against their feudal masters, the nobles, who exacted from them their daily due of toil.

These discontents were partly fathered, partly aggravated, by economic factors. Once the brilliant conquests of Charles had been assured and the glow of victory had faded, reaction had set in. On the heels of war and its weariness had followed depletion of funds, poverty, famine, plague, ever and again sweeping the country. Now in 814 draftees were evading the call to arms; soldiers were deserting; officials were growing slack; administrators were escaping from their duties; conscription of labor was in full force; injustice and corruption pervaded the courts of law; robbers, often slaves running from bondage, infested the roads; taxes bore down heavily, pressed by hands secular and ecclesiastic; already, from without, the Northmen by their menace had been driving Charles the Great to prepare means of defense.

Even more formidable to the thought of this Emperor Louis the Pious, as he drew near his Palace of Aachen, was the face of Christianity as it looked upon him from this long-Christian land which he was to rule in the Name of God. So, too, had his father ruled it in the Name of God. Yet the religion of Charles, and of the Frankish people under Charles, had been concerned primarily with outward discipline and observance, a pattern imposed from without and outwardly obeyed. One attended mass and received the sacraments according to the bidding of the Church; one conscientiously kept feast and fast, even though one rebelled against abstinence; one built houses of religion, even though one yielded them and their revenues to laymen in return for their support; one gave alms generously, firmly brought the heathen to baptism; and all this in its different and various workings was largely true, not only of the king-emperor who ordered, but also of the clergy who administered, and of the peasants who fulfilled their duties. All, nevertheless, was of the letter rather than of the spirit. Neither Charles nor the courtiers who followed him to mass in his royal chapel at Aachen could have understood the unending struggle of this new Emperor, Louis the Pious, to calm the voice of his insistent conscience, could have sympathized with his instinctive impulse to rely upon a decision other than his own. How was he as Emperor to raise his people, monks, clergy, layfolk, noble and simple, to a pattern of public and private life which might be blessed by his most trusted adviser, Benedict of Aniane? In spite of the commands and capitularies issued under his father's name, drawn up repeatedly in synod and council, bishops were still fighting under arms, hunting in sport, feasting in revel; priests were still ignorant and lustful; Irish clergy, true or spurious, were still wandering the Frankish highways, begging alms, deceiving the people, under no control; vowed monks were living in disorder and negligence; peasants were turning from Holy Church to secret practice of heathen customs and rites.

There was fear, too, in this Emperor's mind, of individual leaders among his people, of those who had been nearest at Court to his father; especially of those two men of his own royal line, the grandsons of Charles Martel. Adalard had been frequently at Court, even though he was abbot of Corbie. Wala in the last years of Charles the Great had reached the height of political power in the Frankish Palace, "second only to the Emperor himself," men were saying. It was, therefore, a great relief to Louis when not only Theodulf, bishop of Orléans, but Wala, also, met him on his way, offering homage to him as Emperor. After Wala, too, came riding a great company of the leading nobles of the land.

Together with fear, aversion lay heavily upon him, dislike
of the Court which would now be his. The Palace of Aachen in
the eyes of this Louis would need a thorough purging before he
could call it his own. He had stayed there the year before and
had found things very contrary to his ideas of what was decent
and proper. Now he sent Wala on before him, with others, to
start work on driving out evil influence. As was natural, they
obeyed his order unwillingly, slow to attack their companions
in this life at Court. When they did begin, their work for reform
led indirectly, through tumult of resistance, to battle, mutilation,
and death.

Reports of these happenings moved Louis to anger when at
last he entered Aachen, on February 27. Promptly he dealt out
punishment for this violence in the Court and began a cleansing
more orderly, but scarcely less drastic. To his sisters born of lawful marriage, Bertha, Gisela, Theodrad, and Hiltrud, he gave portions from the great treasure left by their father, Charles, in
accordance with his intention in the years before his death. He
then ruthlessly ordered them to leave Court for the convents to
which, he declared, they properly belonged. With them he drove
out the many women who on one pretext or another were living
in the Palace; only those entirely necessary for its round of work
would he keep. His three illegitimate brothers, Drogo, Hugh, and
Thierry, still only children, he allowed to remain.

Much of the treasure left by his father was given by Louis,
as Charles had wished, to the Church, although in regard both
to the Church and to other beneficiary he had, it would seem, no
scruple in disregarding the exact instructions left by Charles. The
collection of pagan Frankish poetry so prized by the late Emperor was now by order of Louis thrown out and destroyed.

His thought turned next to his counselors. Adalard, a poten-
tial rival for power, was promptly banished, not even allowed to
return to his own abbey of Corbie; he was sent instead to the
monastery of Noirmoutier, on an island at the mouth of the Loire.
Gundrada, sister of Adalard, was dispatched to the nuns of Sainte-
Radegonde at Poitiers. Their brother, Wala, foreseeing banishment, of his own will entered Corbie as novice. Theodulf of
Orléans, who was not of the Frankish royal line and therefore a

lesser source of fear to Louis, remained in favor as envoy of state. Hildebald of Cologne was still for a while archchaplain of the Palace. He died in 818, and about 822 we find his office in the holding of Hilduin, abbot of Saint-Denis.

But above all, in the early years of this new reign, we find as advisers and guides at the Frankish Court two men whom Louis brought from Aquitaine. One was Helisachar, who had been his chancellor there and was now given the same high office at Aachen. It was his duty to attend to matters of law, and also, with the Archchaplain, to rule the clergy of the imperial Palace. The other counselor-in-chief was Benedict of Aniane, for whom Louis now built a monastery, the abbey of Kornelimünster, near Aachen. Here Benedict not only ordered the life of the monastic houses of his Emperor's realms, but was conveniently available at all times for the advising and directing of Louis himself.

Two conceptions of empire—its basis and its function—were at this time working in his Court and in his kingdom of the Franks. On the one hand, there were those—like Adalard, Wala, and Theodulf—who had found their ideal in their King Charles during the high years of his authority: the ideal of a firm, autocratic rule which conquered its aggressors, beat down its enemies, directed its governing, protected its subjects, aided and defended its Church, and presided over all functioning, lay and spiritual alike. To their mind the Frankish Empire must be a unity, as it had been in the days of Charles: knit together in one whole by the force of one person, one source of law, its all-controlling Emperor. Charles, it was true, in 806 had followed Frankish tradition by portioning out the lands of his Empire among his three sons. Providence had intervened; and now there was but one, who had inherited the Empire as one whole.

In the letters written by him as Emperor, Louis was to reveal a quite different spirit; he was to describe himself simply as "Emperor and Majesty by will of Divine Providence." To his mind his function as Emperor was not primarily to rule and organize an Empire of vast extent in which under himself the law of the Church, as of the state, should be obeyed. It was instead for him as Emperor to serve the Church; and all, from himself down to his humblest subjects, were to work toward this end. For this end, then, the Empire, in his own desire at the beginning of his reign, was to be a different unity, a unity standing in its secular might behind the Church which directed and blessed its work. Not the person, not the force of the Emperor, but the Church was to Louis the center and the mainspring of the state.

This conception held within itself its own dangers. It made possible the sacrifice of the independence, the responsibility, and the dignity of the Crown to the will of the bishops administering Frankish dioceses. Through their zeal for the Church and her authority—in the best of them, desire for her holiness and faithful following of discipline, in the less worthy of them, desire for their own power and wealth among Frankish men—these ecclesiastical leaders might demand from a ruler, crowned by God but beset by problems to which he was not equal, the prey of conflicting impulses, in doubt of his own conscience, a surrender by no means in keeping with his high dedication.

2

The reign opened in comparative peace. The Emperor called his nephew, Bernard, king of Italy, to his Court, welcomed him, and confirmed his right to rule. Envoys from Constantinople again acknowledged the imperial title of the king of the Franks. Barbarian risings at first caused little trouble; the tradition imposed by Charles still held its power of control. For the peoples of Saxony and Frisia Louis relaxed the iron Frankish law in force during his father's reign, and was rewarded long afterward by Saxon gratitude in the hour of crisis.

Soon, however, from the North, Viking pirates began to descend in raids upon the monastery of Noirmoutier, so conveniently placed at the river's outlet to the sea, so rich in booty; at last, about 819, its monks began to despair of their home. In 820 some damage was done by these Northmen also on the coasts of Flanders and Aquitaine, and wealth of plunder was carried away. Still it was sixteen years later, in 837, when, in spite of distress in his Court affairs, the menace compelled Louis to take serious action. In Denmark, meanwhile, a long rivalry of rule brought a Danish king, Harald, time after time to ask the aid of Frankland against the sons of that Godfrid who had irritated the peace of

Charles the Great; in 826 Louis rejoiced in receiving this Harald at Mainz from the font of baptism as his godson. The ceremony was celebrated with splendid ritual, and the convert carried away with him gifts and promises in plenty.

In regard to Rome Louis, as we have seen, looked to it for guidance, held himself responsible for its protection, and believed that it was his to serve. In 815, indeed, he commanded Bernard, king of Italy, to hold inquiry into charges made against Pope Leo III that he had put conspirators to death; but the Pope sent envoys to the Frankish Court for the maintaining of his cause, and the matter was promptly dismissed. In 816 the next Pope, Stephen IV, journeyed to Reims to crown the Emperor with his own hands. Louis sent Theodulf, bishop of Orléans, and Hildebald, archchaplain of the Palace at Aachen, to meet him on his way, and welcomed him at Reims with all courtesy and reverence. This Papal action confirmed the bond between the Church Catholic and the Frankish Empire under Louis the Pious.

The year 817 was marked by several events of importance. In July, at a Council assembled in Aachen, rules and regulations for the fostering and upholding of Benedictine discipline in Frankish monasteries were declared and put into action under the leadership of Benedict of Aniane. At Aachen Louis made known also his will for the future ruling of his Empire. "By no means," he now informed his people, "has it seemed good to us, and to our advisers in their discretion, that the unity of the Empire entrusted to us by God should be broken by human dividing, through love or partiality on our part towards our sons. For thus would scandal arise in Holy Church, and we should incur the wrath of Him in Whose power stand the laws and rights of all kingdoms." For three days prior to these events fasting, prayer, and almsgiving had been ordered for general observance throughout the realm.

Finally, the decisions which should govern its rule both before and after the death of Louis, the Emperor, were made known, in a document regarded, not as a "Division," but as an "Ordinance of Empire." Lothar, eldest son of Louis, was to receive at once solemn coronation as Emperor in union with his father, who, however, was to be supreme in rule throughout the Empire as long as he lived. Upon his death succession to the imperial title, and rule over the Empire's territories, were to pass to Lothar, with these exceptions: To the second son, Pippin, was assigned kingship over Aquitaine, Gascony, the region of Toulouse, and part of Burgundy; to the third son, Louis, was given the kingdom of Bavaria, with the outlying lands of Carinthia and Bohemia. These two younger brothers, after their father had departed this life, were to administer their portions under the constant protection, counsel, and aiding of Lothar; in general, they were to be subject to his will, even in the matter of their marriages. Succession to the throne, in the kingdoms of both, was not to fall automatically to their sons, not even to sons born of lawful marriage; it was rather to be decided in each case by the people of the land. The successors thus elected were to reign under the guidance of their uncle, Lothar, as long as he should live.

By thus assuring the complete precedence of Lothar as Emperor down the years Louis hoped to keep a united Empire, standing as a bulwark of the Church. During his lifetime Lothar was to remain and to work with him; Pippin was to rule Aquitaine and to reside in that country; Louis, known to history as Louis the German, was to rule Bavaria and to reside at the Bavarian Court.

Unity in Empire, it was hoped, would thus draw together all its peoples in a Christian bond. In or about this year of 817, Agobard, archbishop of Lyons, a passionate upholder of unity in things both spiritual and temporal, wrote to Louis, his Emperor, of the glory of the brotherhood of all men in Christ and prayed earnestly that, as all ideally should be one in Him by obedience to the Catholic faith, so might all Christians be united in secular usage of Christian law.

3

Thus, at any rate, by this Ordinance of Louis the Pious peace was designed, and Agobard and his friends hoped that it might last. It lasted but briefly; very soon interruption broke from an unexpected quarter. In the autumn, when Louis returned from his sport of hunting in the Vosges to spend the winter at Aachen, word arrived that Bernard, king of Italy, had risen in revolt against the domination of the Emperor, his uncle. He was only eighteen years old, and his advisers in Italy had been encouraging in him a spirit of resentment and alarm on the score that he had been given no assurance of his future. Rashly the young man, pushed by his counselors, consented to blockade the passes over the Alps into France. Soon word came that Louis the Pious had gathered an immense army and already had reached Chalon-sur-Saône on his march toward Italy itself. Bernard saw at once that his position was hopeless. He fled in haste to Chalon and begged mercy from his royal uncle. Sentence of death was passed upon him, commuted by Louis to what seemed, in a strange mercy, to be a more lenient punishment, the sentence of blinding. This was carried out shortly after Easter 818, and two days later Bernard died of the shock. So, too, were blinded, or sent into exile, a number of his friends of high standing. Among them, to the wonder of many men, was Theodulf, the poet, wit, courtier, and prelate of power under Charles the Great. He now lost his bishopric of Orléans and was sent to prison within the monastery of Angers, where he spent nearly all the rest of his life, constantly protesting his innocence. At last, if chronicle be true, he was released; but only to die. The Church still sings his hymn, *Gloria, laus et honor,* once long ago written by him and sung in his hearing by a choir of children on Palm Sunday and answered in chorus of refrain by the people at large.

The severity of these punishments sprang, we may think— as had sprung, four years before, that purging of his Palace of Aachen—from fear in the Emperor's mind. No heir, no rival, must threaten his security. Soon he decided that it would be safer to place behind monastic walls his three brothers of illegitimate birth: Drogo, Hugh, and Thierry.

Further trouble, and harder to bear, now fell upon him. In October 818 his queen and Empress, Irmengard, died. The loss drove him into a melancholy which lasted for many weeks; his friends at Court began to fear that unless some stimulus of comfort were found to arouse him from his passive state, he might even abandon his throne and enter religious life within a cloister. In haste they searched throughout Frankland for young women of rank, beauty, and distinction. Their search was rewarded. In

February 819 Louis married the daughter of a man of noble descent, Count Welf, owner of wide lands in Alemannia and Bavaria. Her name was Judith. She was not only of a rare loveliness, but she delighted all at Court by her charm, her quick mind, her friendly welcome. Her fervor for religion was only second to that of Louis himself. Above all, as wife and Empress she seemed entirely ready to follow the political and religious ideals of her husband. To Louis she seemed perfect; his constant joy from this time onward was to do her pleasure.

As years went on, he needed comfort. In 821 death took from him his beloved counselor and guide, Benedict of Aniane. To this loss was added worry. His conscience for long had been pricking him hard as he thought of that torture which he had ordered for his nephew Bernard, of the banishment which he had brought about for his cousins Adalard and Wala, men who had been so strong to support his father's hands and who were so devoted to their country. Remorse led to action. In this same year, 821, in the midst of the applause which rang through his Palace at Thionville, some twenty miles from Metz, when his son and co-Emperor, Lothar, took as bride the daughter of Hugh, Count of Tours, Louis declared a pardon for those concerned in the rebellion of Bernard of Italy; a recall of Adalard from Noirmoutier to the abbey of Corbie; and an invitation to Wala. Would Wala, Louis now sent word, would Wala attend henceforward once again the Frankish Court as he had done in the days of the Emperor Charles the Great?

Even this penitence was not enough. His bishops, Louis knew, were insisting that in those acts against his nephew and the nobles of his Court he had done dishonor to his sacred dedication as king and Emperor. The imperialist leaders, those who longed for the hand of a man like his father at the helm of state, were also full of wrath at his treatment of Wala. Wala himself and his brother Adalard were waiting for a more open sign of apology for the affront shown to them, kinsmen of the Emperor.

To all this feeling Louis fell an easy victim. Soon a growing consciousness of guilt, fostered by his spiritual counselors, compelled him to yield. In 822, at Attigny on the Aisne, where the conquered Saxon chieftain Widukind had bowed his head for baptism before Charles the Great, Louis, his son, King-Emperor of the Franks, made public profession of penitence for his sins in the presence of a great gathering of his Frankish people. The bishops of his realm at the same time had the grace to admit their own errors and negligences. Wala at once returned to Court and to power; for some weeks he was constantly at Aachen, trying with all his energy to root out evil from Church and state, and supported by Adalard from Corbie.

With Adalard and Wala were working those who were eager, as they were eager, for the continued rule in unity and peace over the Frankish realm: Agobard, since 816 archbishop of Lyons; Jesse, bishop of Amiens; Hilduin, abbot of Saint-Denis, Arch-chaplain of the Imperial Court; Helisachar, who had ceased in 819 to hold office as chancellor of Louis the Pious, but who was still influential as abbot of Saint-Riquier, the great house of religion near Abbeville in northeast France; and the half-brothers of the Emperor, Drogo and Hugh, now once again in favor with him through his change of heart. In 823 Louis appointed Drogo to the see of Metz as its bishop; to Hugh he gave the abbacies of Saint-Quentin in Picardy and of Laubach, near the Rhine. Both men, in spite of the distrust and insult shown them by the Emperor in 818, were loyal to him until his death. Far less single-minded were others who also, if but outwardly, professed the ideals of Wala and his fellow-thinkers. Among those who combined this professing with a fervent ambition for their own interests were Hugh, count of Tours, father-in-law of Lothar, and Matfrid, count of Orléans, both prominent in affairs of state.

Here we come to one, Ebbo, who partly through share in the ideals of Wala, partly through his own yearning for fame, was to be drawn from an early loyalty and gratitude toward Louis the Pious into leadership of bitter revolt against him. Ebbo's story had begun in joy and was to find a tragic end. He had been born in bondage, son of a serf working on the lands of Charles the Great; as a matter of course he himself as boy and lad had labored in the imperial service. So able, however, and so quick in intelligence had he shown himself as he grew up, that the King-Emperor, always interested in all around him, high or low, had given this promising youth not only his freedom, but a training in matters intellectual which at last brought him to ordination as priest in the Church. Finally, he had sent him to Aquitaine, into the household of its king, Louis the Pious, where Ebbo served as librarian and won high favor from his royal patron. Louis called him to Aachen when he succeeded Charles as king and Emperor, and there Ebbo spent two years, in work both administrative and literary.

In 816, when Pope Stephen IV anointed and crowned Louis the Pious at Reims, a shadow was cast upon the ceremony by the grave illness of its Archbishop Wulfar. Before the year had ended Wulfar was dead, and the clergy and people of the archdiocese had elected one Gislemar as his successor. Alas! when the bishops of neighboring sees gathered for the formal investigation of the candidate, customary before such appointment could be confirmed, Gislemar sat dumbfounded, trying in vain to read the Vulgate in its Latin. His learned examiners were horrified and promptly voted his rejection. This easily opened the way for a suggestion from the Emperor Louis the Pious that Ebbo be chosen. All in the diocese of Reims accepted the proposal and thus gained an archbishop of powerful influence and wide learning.

Not only in books and in administration was Ebbo a man of note; he had a passion for art, for the inscribing and adorning of manuscripts. When he left Aachen for Reims in 816, he carried with him the desire to promote in its diocese a working upon texts which in execution should be worthy of those of Aachen itself.

His wish was fulfilled. In the diocese of Reims a "school" was born which—largely, we may think, through his inspiring—became known for the lively vigor and energy of the men, the animals, the landscapes drawn upon the pages of its texts. From this "school" came forth manuscripts that have lived down the ages: those of the Utrecht Psalter, full of dynamic, vital force, and of its relative, a copy of the Gospels known by the name of Archbishop Ebbo himself and wrought in the abbey of Hautvillers, near Reims. Later in this ninth century we shall see both Ebbo and this abbey looking upon scenes of their own individual and private misery.

Ebbo's loyalty to the Emperor Louis who had brought him to

his high rank endured in constancy through many years. Not until after 830 shall we find it turn its course.

Meanwhile, since the death of its king, Bernard, affairs in the Frankish realm of northern Italy had been falling into confusion through neglect. It was therefore decided that Lothar, the eldest son, heir, and co-Emperor with his father, should receive its crown. In 822 imperial command sent him on his way; and Wala, also, was directed to leave for Rome that he might guide Lothar by his counsel in diplomatic matters, especially in regard to the Papal See.

The diplomatic experience of Wala was to be of great service here. At Eastertide of 823 Pope Paschal I crowned Lothar in St. Peter's as king of Italy and emperor of the Romans. Unhappily, not long after this event messengers reported at Aachen that two Papal officials of high standing had been blinded and then beheaded in the Lateran, on the ground that they had shown too much enthusiasm for the young Frankish king. There was rumor, moreover, which declared that the Pope himself had ordered or, at least, had advised this execution. Louis immediately sent off envoys to Rome, bidding Lothar to inquire into the matter. The inquiry came abruptly to an end when Pope Paschal, through ambassadors of his own, made sworn affirmation to Louis that the men put to death had been guilty of high treason and had fully merited their fate.

Paschal died in the following year, 824, and the election of his successor, Eugenius II, gave Wala and his young king in November an excellent occasion for statesmanship. This was embodied in the *Constitutio Romana,* now drawn up by them to regulate the uneasy and at times difficult relations between the Frankish Empire and the Holy See. The Pope expected obedience from the Emperor, his spiritual son; he also needed secular support. The Emperor gave this support, and looked for recognition in return. The detailed provisions of this new *Constitution,* approved by both Papal and imperial consent, ruled that the election of a Pope was to rest solely with the people of Rome; that not only all electors of a Pope, but the Pope himself, after his election by the Roman people, must swear loyalty to the Frankish Emperor of the Romans; that the Roman people were themselves to decide under what law they wished to live; that the administration of Roman law and justice was to be placed in the hands of judges and *missi,* appointed in part by the Pope, in part by the Frankish imperial power.

4

The year 823, both at Aachen and in many parts of Frankland, had been marked by dire portents and calamities. The Palace at Aachen shivered through earthquake; strange sounds were heard in the night; lightning struck men, beasts, and their homes; thunder pealed in a clear sky; hail fell in great stones, ruining the harvests; plague sowed death far and wide. Men's hearts failed them for fear of what all these visitations might foretell; and Louis, seeing here the hand of an angry God, anxiously hurried his chaplains to fast and litany. He himself stood still, hesitant and undecided, awaiting some inspiration from Heaven, voiced directly or by human means on earth.

The omen to be dreaded, however, came not of angels or of men, but of a woman. The woman was Judith, that adored queen of Louis. Hitherto for the four years of their marriage she had remained all sweetness and light, content to serve her husband's desire, to charm his friends by her gracious presence, to inspire writers, young and eager, with her own enthusiasm for books, for art, for poetry, to welcome hungry scholars to the comfort of her Court.

Henceforth, another element was to be felt in her character, and that a compelling one. On a June day of this year, 823, the omen of change to come arrived in Aachen to the sound of joyful shout and cry. A son was born to this second wife of Louis, and his birth aroused in her hitherto tranquil spirit a passion of mother love, of jealous ambition for the future of this little boy lying by her side. Nothing, she determined, should prevent him from gaining his share of rule—and she placed no limit to that share— among his three half brothers, sons of Louis by another woman. In pursuit of this end, according to the words of her contemporary, Paschasius Radbert, "she brought her power to bear upon the rule of all the realm; she stirred up waves and seas; she drove the winds; she turned the hearts of men to all that she willed; she moved all things at her command."

She began by giving her child the name of Charles. He was to be great as his grandfather had been great. She induced her husband "to bid anxiously the aid" of the heir, Lothar, for this half brother of his, until at last Lothar consented to be godfather of Charles and to declare with solemn oath "that his father, the Emperor, might give to Charles whatever portion of realm he desired to give; that, also, he, Lothar, would protect the boy and defend him against all enemies in years to come." The oath was not at all to Lothar's liking; but he did not dare to refuse. He foresaw the trouble to come, for already he recognized his stepmother's intent.

Soon, indeed, the nobles and bishops who stood for unity in the realm as provided by the Ordinance of 817 were sharing his fear. How short a time under Judith's determined working would it be before her husband made assault upon that unity in favor of her son? How soon would discord among its princes begin to disrupt the Frankish empire?

As time went on, this foreboding for the future was increasingly mingled with a very present discontent. Government, abroad and at home, was slipping into weakness and lack of control. The strong arm of Charles the Great was now missed not only by idealist bishops and nobles, but by the multitude throughout the realm. The Frankish peasants were crying their grievances: poverty, agricultural distress, tyranny of landlords. The clergy were lax in discipline; monasteries and convents no longer felt the stern oversight of Benedict of Aniane. On Frankish borders the Bretons were restless, until in 826 the authority of their chieftain, Nominoë, was recognized by Louis the Pious. Bulgars, Sorbs, Slavs, Wiltzi were constantly pressing forward, in complaint, in revolt, in hunger; the Northmen from beyond the Elbe were descending in raids. Above all, there was trouble in Spain. There the Basque people had risen in their wrath and had only been subdued by great effort. The Saracens, too, in Spanish territory were giving grave cause for alarm; in 826 a Gothic chieftain, named Aizo, sought their aid for attack upon land held by the Franks. According to the reliable witness of the royal

Frankish annals in regard to this fear: "The Emperor was truly much upset by the news. But, he decided, nothing must be done without due counsel; he had better wait for the arrival at Court of his advisers. And so he went off in the meantime for his usual autumn season of hunting." In 827 Helisachar, abbot though he was, was sent with an army to restrain Aizo and his Saracen allies; he had but little success. After him the two counts, Hugh of Tours and Matfrid of Orléans, were ordered to this front, but with no result.

They were not, in fact, working for result. They were hoping that by lack of support on their part their rival, Count Bernard of Septimania, would fail to drive back the invaders. Jealousy of Count Bernard was the basis of their hope. It availed them nothing. Early in 828 they were dismissed from service and deprived of the properties they were holding under feudal tenure.

Bernard was a son of that Count William of Toulouse, who had fought for Charles the Great and had aided Louis when Louis was ruling Aquitaine; and he was a son worthy of his father in courage and determination. Now he was carrying on that father's work, as soldier and as administrator in southern France and in the Spanish March. During the months which followed the dismissal of Hugh and Matfrid he held Barcelona with grim defiance from capture by the Saracens, until at last they withdrew. His brilliance and his daring in battle were to win for him his Emperor's confidence; and with this the enduring enmity of the party working for imperial unity, a party led by Wala and his friends.

Among them dissatisfaction was slowly rising day by day. We can still read the angry words of Archbishop Agobard, written to Matfrid before 828, while this Count of Orléans was still holding tenure and power: "In my part of the country," Agobard declared, "disloyalty has reached such a point of carefree recklessness that hardly anyone has any regard for justice. Reverence for kings and laws has died down in the minds of many; indeed, most people have come to think that no one now is to be feared. They say quietly to themselves: 'If any complaint concerning me reaches the Palace, I shall find relatives and friends in number to support me; I shall run into no trouble; a secret gift will turn aside all wrath.' Of a truth it is that faith which under God I owe to the Emperor which is driving me to say these things."

In 828 Wala, abbot of Corbie since his brother Adalard's death two years before, on the evidence of a memorandum full of notes, carefully prepared by his own labor, declared in the presence of Louis himself, now presiding over an assembly at last summoned by him, the duties of the Crown at this time of trouble. Let the Emperor and king, he stormed, serve his own office and the things which pertain to his own authority, and leave the sacred things of God to bishops and ministers of the Church. And let him see to it that he be diligent in his own proper work. For "unless, O King, unless you keep faithfully that which is bidden, the more cruel shall be your crucifying; and all men, if God turn from us, shall meet in you one and the same death. Therefore neglect in no wise that which is your bounden care; for in you alone, as Solomon told, is stablished our whole realm."

In 829, as Paschasius Radbert wrote in his *Life of Wala*, Wala "was forever talking like a second Jeremiah": of the greed and avarice of the chaplains of the royal Court; of laymen placed in rule over monasteries, "a filthy disease within the Church"; of general decadence in Frankish houses of religion. The same year saw four councils of Frankish bishops laying bare the sins which befouled Church and state: sins of the bishops themselves, as they admitted, and sins of the Emperor, Louis the Pious, set forth in a report addressed by these bishops to Louis in the month of August. Here they solemnly called to his remembrance the Gelasian dictum that the authority of the episcopal Order excels even that of the king: "Were not bishops by the charge of God to be required at the Last Judgment to render account for kings as under their pastoral care on earth? Let Louis, then, Emperor though he was, reverence the dignity of their Ordering and listen to their words. Let him follow his father's example and work for reform in things ecclesiastical and secular; let him control the clergy constantly running in and out of his royal Palace; let him strive for the ending of bloodshed, of feuds between his nobles; let him use caution and prudence in appointing his ministers of state and Court, for the avoiding of all quarrel, discord and malice."

5

What, we may ask, had happened to that fervor of Louis the Pious, that passion for the Church which had marked him at the beginning of his reign? To that ideal of a Frankish Empire designed by Heaven under himself as Emperor to be one united power, standing as bulwark for the Church in the Frankish realms?

Two hostile influences had now for years been at work in him, breaking down the striving for that ideal. One was his growing sense that the problems of state and Church were too complicated, too numerous, for him to solve or even to attempt to solve. It had become increasingly hard for him to initiate action, unless some dominant force impelled him to act.

That dominant force, the second hostile influence, had arrived and was hard at work within him. It was embodied in his Empress Judith and her will to gain all she could for the advancement of her son, an end the easier to reach because of the love her husband held both for her and for that youngest of his children, dearer to him than any one of the three whom Irmengard had borne.

It was fear, then, which lay behind the rebukes levied at Louis the Emperor by his statesmen and his bishops, fear of his weakness and of the strength of his wife. After an assembly held at Worms in this same August 829, these fears soon received dour confirmation. Three major decisions now became known, declared by imperial authority:

First, Louis was erasing the name of his heir, Lothar, hitherto his co-worker in matters of state, from imperial edicts and charters, and sending him off to Italy as king and ruler. Second, he was giving his youngest son, Charles, a portion of the Frankish realm: Alemannia, on the borders of Bavaria; also Rhaetia, a land of the upper Rhine, on the borders of Alemannia; Alsace; and part of Burgundy. Third, he was calling Count Bernard from Septimania to take charge as chamberlain of the administration of affairs in the Palace of Aachen.

The inference was all too clear. Lothar from this moment would have no share in his father's imperial policy. It was from Lothar's lands that this portion was being carved out for Charles, and therefore resentment on the part of the eldest son and heir would be keen. And lastly, by this gift to Charles, the Ordinance of 817, if not broken in the letter, was at least covertly attacked in the spirit. A new kingdom, said the angry upholders of unity, was being founded within the Empire.

With all her energy the Empress put to use the power placed in her hands by these measures born of her own devising. We do not know that the story, freely whispered and even told in record, is in fact true: that she made Bernard her lover. Undoubtedly, she influenced him as she did her husband, and always for her own ends.

All the winter there was talk, and with the talk growing wrath among the sons of the Emperor and men high in the state. In their anger they spoke of the arrogance of Count Bernard; of his constant meetings in private with the Empress; of the insolence of Judith's two brothers, Conrad and Rudolf, who, they said, were always appearing at Court; of the menace to other heirs, threatened by her favored son. In the spring of 830 this anger was swollen to high tide by the fury of peasants and farmers when Bernard ordered the Frankish national army into action against the Bretons, once more in revolt. The time could not have been worse. Roads were almost impassable through the mud of the spring thaw; and the start of the march was set for Holy Thursday, a most sacred season of the year.

Men refused to march. They gathered in Paris, sounding the signal for rebellion, a signal heard gladly across the Alps by the Emperor's eldest son. For Lothar, held in Italy, now saw hope of release. The supporters of unity, as he knew, were thinking more and more that in him, rather than in his father, lay their chance of keeping the Frankish Empire in one single harmony.

His hope was strengthened by the sudden movements of his two brothers. Pippin, hearing of the revolt of the Frankish army and anxious to lose no possible profit by his absence at a critical moment, promptly marched with many of his men from Aquitaine to Verberie, near Compiègne. The third brother, Louis the German, came in haste from Bavaria to join him.

Report of these movements reached the Emperor and drove him into action. He told his chamberlain, Bernard, by all means to flee for his life to Barcelona, in the Spanish March. He himself, with a courage worthy of his crown, took his way to Compiègne. At first he directed the Empress to follow and to join him there; then, feeling that this would not be safe for her, he sent word that she was to seek shelter in Saint Mary's abbey at Laon. This she did; but in vain. From Verberie the rebels sent a strong force to Laon, took her from the nuns of Saint Mary's, and carried her with them to their camp. There she received her orders: Under threat of death itself she was to do her utmost to persuade her husband to lay down arms and to retreat into a monastery; she was to tell him that she, also, was about to accept the cloistered life. With these instructions in her ears and armed men surrounding her, she made the brief journey to meet the Emperor, now at Compiègne. In the scant privacy which her guards permitted, she delivered her message. Louis, fearful for her life, consented that she should enter religion. He himself, ordered to yield the reins of government, neither gave nor refused consent, but merely asked for time to think. Shortly afterwards the Empress was taken by order of Pippin and his followers to the convent of Sainte-Radegonde at Poitiers and forced to assume the habit of a nun. Her brothers, Conrad and Rudolf, were also sent into monastic prison.

The uprising now settled its center in Compiègne, around Pippin and Louis the German. Its leaders included Wala of Corbie; the Archchaplain Hilduin; Jesse of Amiens; Helisachar of Saint-Riquier, who of late years had been more and more turning toward revolution; and the counts Hugh and Matfrid, bitter enemies of Louis since their condemnation in 828. Hugh, moreover, as we know, was father-in-law of Lothar.

After Easter Lothar arrived from Italy. He had delayed his coming, uncertain of his policy, until he did not dare to risk his career by a longer absence from the scene. He continued, however, to act with caution. He approved what had been done concerning Judith, and he sentenced Herbert, brother of Count Bernard, to lose his sight in punishment for aid given her. For himself he assumed once again imperial title and privilege; but nothing of open assault was ordered by him against his father. Louis the Pious was still Emperor, in union with this eldest of his sons.

The summer of 830 was spent in parley at Compiègne between the two opposing camps, the father and his rebellious heirs, the Emperor and his angry subjects. As its days went by, Louis gained the reward of his courage, passive though it had been. Little by little, while he constantly declared his desire to serve their interests, men began to long for peace, and feeling slowly veered round to his side. At last he won his aim that a general assembly should be held in October of this year, 830, for discussion, for voting, at the royal Palace of Nijmegen, in the Netherlands.

This was a victory. Louis knew that at Nijmegen the Saxons, always loyal to him, would be at hand in their multitude for his support. He took heart and met the assembly with a bold stand. Hilduin, who, contrary to an agreement that none should appear in armor, entered the assembly hall at the head of a troop of his followers, bristling in mail, their hands on their swords, was ordered by him to leave the Palace. He did, with his knights; all who were present understood at once that power was at last changing hands. The rebels passed a sleepless night in sharply divided debate, which grew more divided when morning brought word from the Emperor to Lothar, bidding him come to a meeting without fear, as a son to his father. Lothar came. He was received with honor, and also with determination; he returned to report to the friends awaiting him, some in scorn, some in deep anxiety, that they had no chance of success. Evidence proved his point, and his adherents scattered, each man to his home. A detail related by a contemporary, the historian Nithard, himself a nephew of Louis the Pious, is of some interest. It tells that the Emperor, under pretext of religious business, had sent a message by a monk to his younger sons, Pippin and Louis the German, promising to enrich their kingdoms if they would aid his cause. They had agreed, it was said, since the prospect of subjection to their elder brother as Emperor had by this time become anything but happy to them.

In 831, therefore, the first rebellion of those who desired unity in the state was over. Order was again established, at least for a while; Louis the Pious was once more in command. The Empress had left her convent in Poitiers; the Pope, now Gregory IV, had released her from monastic discipline brought upon her by force. She had returned to Aachen; before a public assembly held at its Palace in February she had declared herself guiltless of the charges levied against her. With her at Aachen were her two brothers, also freed. Count Bernard of Septimania was again at Court. He, too, made on oath a defense of his actions; but he did not return to his office of chamberlain. Lothar was dispatched back to Italy and commanded to stay there; Pippin and Louis, forgiven and kindly received in the Palace, were again in the countries of their ruling.

Other leaders of the rebellion had been condemned to exile or to imprisonment. Wala had been banished to some distant place, seemingly in the wilds of Switzerland; Helisachar had also been sent from his home and deprived of the rule and revenues of Saint-Riquier and other monasteries of importance. Hilduin, who had been dismissed as archehaplain of the royal Palace after his bold disregard of orders at Nijmegen, had also lost his privilege as abbot of Saint-Denis, the shrine of Frankish kings. Worse still, the Emperor's anger had sent him to endure winter cold in an army hut at Paderborn among the barbarian Saxons; afterwards, it would seem, he was transferred to the Saxon monastery of Corvey.

In each case, however, some form of restoration was soon granted, for the religion of this Louis the Pious turned him constantly to mercy and forgiveness, whether toward his sons or toward his nobles. Wala returned to Corbie, where we shall find him again supporting Lothar in opposition to his father, the Emperor. Helisachar is heard of once more as "abbot" under Louis; but from this time of 831 he ceases to appear in records of high political importance. Hilduin regained his rule at Saint-Denis, where history will see him writing happily to instruct his Emperor, who feared him less than he feared Helisachar or Wala.

6

Nevertheless, in spite of punishment and of reconciliation, the seeds of political trouble lived on and took root. The child Charles was again with his parents at Court; his mother was still dreaming her dreams for his future; the Emperor, after enduring penance, defeat, and humiliation, humiliation for his Empress as for himself, was doubtless eager to assert the independence of his crown and of himself as its wearer. It was in this year of 831 that a new document of state issued from his hand. Significantly, this was no longer an *Ordinatio;* it was a *Divisio Imperii,* and it recalled in its wording the division drawn up by Charles the Great in 806. It made no mention of Italy or of Lothar as co-Emperor. To Pippin, in addition to Aquitaine, now were given the territories between the Loire and the Seine, and, north of the Seine, of Châlons, Meaux, Amiens, and Ponthieu, stretching to the coast. Louis the German now added Thuringia, Saxony, and Frisia, with part of northern France and much of Belgium and the Netherlands, to his original rule of Bavaria. We have seen young Charles in possession of Alemannia, Rhaetia, Alsace, and part of Burgundy; he was now to hold that same Burgundy (except the portion given in 817 to Pippin); lands on the Meuse and the Moselle; Reims and the surrounding country; Provence, Septimania, and the Spanish March.

Some interesting words are found among these provisions: "If any one of our three sons" (Lothar, Pippin, Louis the German) "by signal obedience and goodwill towards Almighty God and, secondly, towards ourselves, shall have earned merit in this desire to please, it will delight us to confer upon him yet greater honour and power, taking such increase from the portion of a brother who shall not have thus essayed to please."

Under these conditions the peace, it may easily be imagined, was brief in lasting. Lothar, the neglected heir, was infuriated; Pippin and Louis the German, in spite of the rewards assigned them, resented the further portion given to the boy Charles, that son of their stepmother. The upholders of one supreme rule saw with keen discontent a revival of the old Frankish custom of dividing. Who, they asked, was to rule and keep harmony throughout the Empire when Louis the Pious was dead?

Soon these fermenting thoughts burst into action, the second rebellion of the sons of Louis the Emperor. News arrived, early in 832, that Louis the German, encouraged by his brothers, had crossed the Bavarian border to invade Alemannia, land of Charles, now some nine years old. Quickly the Empress spurred her husband to resistance. He assembled another formidable army, of Franks and Saxons mingled, marched to the Rhine, crossed it, pitched his camp, and awaited attack. It did not come. Louis the German knew himself outmustered by superior force; he fled home to Bavaria. Pippin was more stubborn. With determined insolence he refused to obey the Emperor's commands, until, before the year had ended, his father ordered that the kingdom of Aquitaine be taken from him and transferred to the holding of Charles.

This added fuel to the smoldering fire. In 833 the men of Aquitaine rose to restore their king to his crown and lands. Once more all three sons of the Emperor joined together in resolute league against him and against the Empress and her son. Wala, who had not only endured the loneliness of Swiss wilds, but also of Noirmoutier on its isle at the mouth of the Loire, now, with his exiled friends, once more at home, once more active in Frankish politics, felt compelled to urge forward a protest against the Emperor's behavior. This was supported by many and was voiced in a letter to Louis the Pious composed by Agobard, archbishop of Lyons:

All men owe loyalty to their king. And how can one be faithful to you if, seeing the danger in which you stand, he does not give you such warning as he may?

We are living in a year of conflict and tumult, of troubles which no man can number. And yet no necessity has compelled this affliction. Had you, Sire, only willed it, well might you be living now with your sons in that same peace and quiet in which your father and your grandfather passed their days.

No! This is the reason of your ills. You yourself, in 817, gave to your son Lothar, with fast and prayer and the consent of all men, and by the inspiring of God Himself, a fellowship in your Imperial name and title. Your two younger sons, Pippin and Louis, received from you portions of your Empire; but with this provision. To make sure that there should be one realm of Empire and not three, you preferred in power above his brothers that son, Lothar, to whom you gave it to share with you during your life-time the Imperial and sovereign dignity.

This Ordinance you signed and sealed, and bade all men swear to keep it with loyalty; this you sent to Rome for assent and confirmation from the Holy Father himself.

And now this Ordinance is overthrown, and the name of your fellow Emperor has disappeared from your Imperial charters and cartularies. Without any reason, unbidden of God, you have repudiated him whom you chose under God's guiding hand.

God knows that we who live in the light of truth love you with sincerity and faithfully desire for you eternal happiness. For this very reason we grieve over the crimes which during this year have followed upon your action; we greatly fear lest the anger of God be raised against you. We have known the fervor of your religious zeal in days past. There is danger now, it may be, lest this be waning, growing cold.

Lastly, it were not wise to hide from your Excellence how widely men are murmuring among themselves through these diverse and contrary acts of yours. Yes, and not only murmuring. We see their sullen mien. We hear the words in which they assault you openly.

In April Agobard wrote again. Lothar had now left Italy to join his brothers, who had moved into camp near Colmar and the Rhine. With him traveled the Pope, Gregory IV, induced to do so by Lothar as being, so Lothar declared, "the only power who could, and therefore should, reconcile the father with his sons."

"If, Most Gracious Sire," Agobard now wrote to his king and Emperor, Louis, "if Pope Gregory is coming merely to fight, without due cause, he will retreat, conquered in his effort. But if he comes to labor for peace and quiet for you and your people, striving well and with reason, it is not for you to resist him."

There were, it is true, besides his half-brother Drogo, other bishops to uphold the cause of the Emperor. The Pope had invited the bishops of Frankland to come in a body to meet him when he arrived. Some of these dared to write back to him that they would have been glad to do so, had not an order from the

Emperor prevented them. This daring brought upon them a fiery answer in rebuke. "These words of yours are reprehensible," retorted Gregory. "Do you not know that the rule over souls, committed to us as Pontiff, is higher than the rule of an Emperor, which belongs but to time? If I did not declare the Emperor's sins against the unity of his realm, I should be committing perjury. You say that the Division made by him in 817 has now been changed by him because of timely need, brought about by changed circumstances. This assertion, I tell you, is utterly untrue and false. Not in season is this change, but out of season; seeing that it is the cause and origin of tumult and discord, of turbulence and robbery and of more evils than may here be told."

The Pope, escorted by Lothar, duly arrived at the camp of Pippin and Louis the German. Their father was at Worms, gathering his army. For some weeks of May and June letters, protestations, suggestions, passed to and fro between Colmar and Worms. When all seemed futile and productive of no result, the Emperor marched out to meet the rebels and pitched his camp opposite theirs, on the same plain, near Colmar. The plain is known in geography as "the Rothfeld"; but in tradition it is "the Lügenfeld," "the Field of Lies." Here Louis remained for some days, making no attempt to force issue by battle.

On June 24, 833, the Feast of St. John the Baptist, this Field saw the opening of tragedy. Pope Gregory, fearing alike for Louis and for the Empire which he ruled, crossed the space between the two camps to meet him in his tent. "You come strangely," said Louis to his visitor, "and therefore strangely must you be received." Gregory protested that he came but to try to bring peace out of this "inexorable discord." They talked long, but to no purpose, although the Pope remained for some days. At last he went back to his own quarters. That night deserters in multitude began to move from the Emperor's army across the field to the camp of his sons, "flowing like a torrent; partly won away by bribes, partly induced by promises, partly terrified by threats." Only the Empress, the boy Charles, and a few bishops and nobles, among them the faithful half-brothers, Drogo of Metz and Hugh, remained with Louis. Soon, seeing that all was lost, he bade them, also, cross over to his sons; nothing more, he said, could they do for him. It was folly to remain, a useless loyalty; the multitude on the other side already could only by force be held back from rushing across to destroy and to kill.

As the danger grew more and more real, Louis in his terror for his wife and child called upon Lothar for rescue. Answer came that he himself must cross the field. He went, taking with him Judith and Charles. All three were at once arrested. Judith was sent under guard to Tortona, north of Genoa in Italy, Charles to the abbey of Prüm, near Trier. The Pope in great distress made his way back to Rome. Lothar brought his father, now a prisoner, through Metz to Soissons, where he held him within the monastery of Saint-Médard. The sending of his youngest son, not yet ten years old, away to that cloister prison in Germany caused Louis far more distress than his own captivity.

At Compiègne, on October 1, 833, Lothar appeared, wearing the imperial robes and crown, held a general assembly, and received as Emperor the homage of all who were present, the great and the simple. He then gave reward to his brothers Pippin and Louis for their support; Louis, in particular, received German territory of the Eastern Franks which his father had given as portion to Charles. Content with their gifts, the two returned to their own lands.

7

Meanwhile, Agobard, archbishop of Lyons, had again broken silence. He had already, in the summer of this year, sent out to all who would share his indignation a venomous attack upon the Empress Judith and her iniquities, with an equally powerful defense of the sons of Louis, at the time when Louis the Pious was moving forward to meet them near Colmar. Now in October he poured forth further denunciation of Judith and admonition to her husband, caught, as he declared, in her toils:

We say not these things that we may compare our Lord Emperor to impious and faithless kings. But, because he has allowed himself to be deceived by a wicked woman, that has befallen him which is written: "He that troubleth his own house shall inherit the winds." Through this troubling and inheritance of winds countless treacheries and unmeas- ured ruin have been brought to pass: manslaughter, adultery, and incest. For all these sins it is needful that our Emperor, once so faithful to religion, shall now return to his own heart and do penance, humbled beneath the mighty hand of God. God is able to exalt him in the life eternal which is to come. But majesty in this world of time is not for him who has brought his own house and heart into distraction, who by Divine justice and judgment has lost his place on earth. That place has now been given, not to an enemy or a stranger, but to his beloved son.

In the Name of God and of Our Lord Jesus Christ, in the year of his Incarnation eight hundred and thirty-three, by my hand, Agobard.

Now the voice of Ebbo, archbishop of Reims, joined that of Agobard. For a long time his loyalty had been wavering, and he had felt more and more in sympathy with the promoters of rebellion. Now, as accusations against the Emperor broke out from one after another, it was Ebbo who exhorted the prisoner at Saint-Médard "to repent him of his crimes lest he lose his own soul," and his words were re-echoed by a delegation of his fellow bishops. Louis asked for a few days in which to consider what he should do. Then, after a second visitation which brought to his cell all the bishops present at Compiègne, Ebbo among them, to declare to him his offenses against God and man, then the Emperor gave way. Once more, as at Attigny in 822, he made public profession of penitence. But this time it was not shared by his bishops.

A careful description of its proceeding was drawn up in October 833 by all the bishops concerned; each of these bishops, also, wrote out his own detailed testimony, signed it with his name, and gave it into Lothar's keeping. We have the one from the pen of Agobard. In the united record all declared that as vicars of Christ, as keepers of the keys of Heaven, and as those who watched over the souls of men, bishops of the Frankish Empire, they had deemed it their duty to gather at Compiègne and to listen humbly to the words of Lothar, now their Lord and Emperor. They had clearly declared in that assembly, before all who were there present, the power of their sacred ministry, and of the requirement, under pain of damnation, of obedience to its mandates.

Much, they continued, had happened under Louis for the scandal of the Church. The peace of unity which had prevailed under Charles and his predecessors on the throne had by his negligence turned to shame and sorrow for his people and to derision for their enemies. Therefore, by Divine judgment the imperial power had been taken from him. He was no longer Emperor. All he could do now was to offer penance for the saving of his guilty soul.

The bishops then came to the heart of their report. In Our Lady's church of the abbey of Saint-Médard at Soissons, so they declared, in the presence of Lothar, his son, sitting to preside as Emperor, and of a congregation of bishops, nobles, monks, clergy, and simpler people, Louis had bowed himself to the earth upon a carpet of haircloth before the high altar, had confessed himself guilty of grievous sins against God, against the Church, against the people of the Franks. Holding in his hand a paper delivered to him by his bishops, he had declared himself truly and rightly accused of the crimes which it told: of cruelty to his brothers and sisters and to his nephew Bernard, in 814 and 818; of breaking the unity of the Empire by the Act of Division of 831; of ordering the Frankish army to march against the Bretons on Holy Thursday, 830; of rising against his sons in 833, contrary to the common peace. For these, and for other acts of ill-considered, of impious and of cruel sort, he had prayed forgiveness.

The accusing paper he had then placed upon the altar; he had laid aside his sword and all marks of imperial and military honor; he had received from the bishops surrounding him the mournful habit of a penitent. "After penance of so great degree," these bishops added as they brought their record to its end, "no man could dream of returning to hold office in this world." For long they had been trying to wring from him a promise to enter a monastery; yet without success.

8

Such was the proceeding as Agobard and his colleagues described it. A friend and defender of Louis the Pious would doubtless have seen it differently. He would have reported that Louis had merely read from that paper thrust upon him by his bishops the accusations and record of guilt which they had commanded him to admit, that it would be difficult to tell how far his own conscience acknowledged their justice. Long afterward his son Charles was to declare in writing to the Pope himself that Louis the Pious on this occasion "neither made confession nor was convicted of sin," and that there were present in the abbey of Saint-Médard "bishops who looked with keen reluctance upon this scene."

It was too much even for the ambitious sons of Louis, for Pippin and Louis the German. Again they realized that life under Lothar as Emperor would please them no more than under their father, if, indeed, as much. In a conference at Mainz his brother Louis pleaded with Lothar to change his harshness for milder measures. It was to no effect. Lothar remained firm; and from this time Louis the German began to work for his father's rescue.

The captive Emperor, now declared deposed, was hurried from Compiègne to Aachen, where Lothar had determined to hold him under close guard. There he remained during the winter of 833–34. He was still firmly resisting all attempts to drive him into monastic retreat. Whatever errors, sins, or negligences he had to his account, he was still, he held, king and Emperor, in duty bound by the will of Heaven. Louis the German, having failed to move Lothar, next made his appeal to Pippin in Aquitaine, and was joined in his petitioning by his uncles, Hugh of Saint-Quentin and Drogo of Metz. The appeal was answered. An army of Austrasians, Saxons, and Alemannians, led by himself and by Pippin, made ready to march upon Aachen.

Upon these tidings, early in February 834, Lothar fled to Paris, and from there to the abbey of Saint-Denis, carrying his father with him. Fresh surprise and alarm awaited him there. Not only the sons of the royal prisoner, but the Frankish people now were turning from resentment to sympathy with the fate of this man, so lately the king and Emperor in the land. Was he not, after all, born of a glorious line of Frankish tradition? Threats were hurled at Lothar. He retorted that not he himself, but the bishops of the Church had bidden penance from Louis.

Finally, at the end of February he fled from Paris, leaving his father behind, at liberty once again. Promptly the supporters of Louis the Pious, and their number and power were increasing day by day, begged him to assume anew the imperial title and crown. "Not so," he replied. "Bishops of the Church have taken these from me under their authority. By that same authority will I be reconciled with the Church and restored to my sacred office."

On the first day of March 834, in the abbey of Saint-Denis, Louis the Pious received the satisfaction he desired: solemn reconciliation with the Church, followed by an equally solemn ceremony which again gave to him the outer and inner character of imperial honor. Outside were heard the cheers of a great multitude crowding around the doors. Even Nature—thus we read in the *Life* of Louis—had risen in wrath at the things done in this land. So fierce a storm of wind and rain had been raging for days that no one could cross the Seine because of its flooding; yet at the very hour of the King-Emperor's restoration to Church and throne the heavens ceased to hurl their anger upon guilty men.

From Paris Louis journeyed to the royal manor of Quierzy, on the Oise near Laon, to celebrate Laetare Sunday with joyful anthem on March 15. There, without rancor or remembrance of the past, thinking only of recent aid, he embraced his son, Louis the German. Lothar and his partisans were still in flight. Many urged the Emperor to pursue him for punishment; but he refused, at the bidding of one whom he reverenced deeply. Hraban Maur, abbot of the famous monastery of Fulda in Germany, throughout his life stood aloof from politics that he might devote his leisure hours to books; but he remained loyal to his Emperor during all the days of crisis. Now in 834 he wrote for him a long defense: on the respectful obedience due from sons to their fathers; on the evils of avarice and greed; on the folly of accusing as guilty those whom evidence holds innocent; on the justice of the Emperor's action in regard to Bernard of Italy. At its end he begged Louis the Pious to forgive his son, Lothar, once Lothar should have admitted his fault.

Easter found the Emperor in his Court at Aachen, the Aachen where he had spent those winter months as the prisoner of Lothar. Now he welcomed Pippin, coming to him from Aquitaine; the Empress Judith, coming home from Italy; and from Germany the boy Charles whom he held so dear. Lothar, trying to keep his fighting men together, had fled to Vienne on the Rhône. He was next heard of at Chalon-sur-Saône. For five days he assaulted the city walls and then captured it, seized much plunder and killed or took prisoner its chief men. And not only men. He threw into the Saône, bound within a cask, the sister of Bernard of Septimania. Her name was Gerberga, and, like her father, Count William of Toulouse, she had left the world for a cloister. But Lothar declared her skilled in black magic.

All these happenings at last induced Louis to leave Aachen in pursuit. From place to place he followed Lothar; and Pippin gave him aid in men from his own army. Finally, once again, as on the "Field of Lies," the forces of father and son faced one another, at Blois. It was now the autumn of 834. Again there was no battle, and this time there was no arrest. The Emperor was in command. As he had done in 830, now again he sent word to Lothar that he come to him in peace. Lothar came, bowed before his father as he sat within his tent, and acknowledged that he had done him great wrong. At once Louis again forgave all; the only conditions exacted were that Lothar should at once return to his kingdom of Italy, that he should remain there, and should promise on oath never again to raise revolt against his father's rule. He obeyed and departed into virtual exile. Those who had consistently supported him against his father—Wala, Agobard, Counts Hugh and Matfrid, and Jesse of Amiens—followed him to Italy.

The last acts of reparation and reprisal were carried out in the early spring of 835, at Thionville and at Metz. At an assembly held at Thionville, some twenty miles north of Metz, on the Feast of the Purification, February 2, Frankish bishops, gathered from many cathedral cities, both those who had condemned and those who had defended the Emperor, now declared his deposing to be unmerited and struck it off the record as null and void. They signed and sealed the assurance that Louis was now restored to his crown and his proper majesty.

Nearly a month later, on Quinquagesima Sunday, February 28, in the presence of a congregation which crowded the Cathedral of Saint Stephen at Metz, and under the presidency of Drogo, its bishop, mass was celebrated with solemn ritual. Witness of reconciliation was chanted over the Emperor as he knelt before

the high altar; the imperial crown, lying there as it had lain on
the altar at Aachen in 813, was lifted by the officiating ministers
and given to Louis as mark and symbol of his restoration. Whereupon all gave thanks to God.

There followed a less joyful scene, at least for its chief
figure. Ebbo, archbishop of Reims, that leader in the recent
revolution, had fled from his see upon the revival of power for
Louis, to hide in a hermit's cell in Paris. There he had been discovered and had been carried to captivity in the monastery of
Fulda. Now, conducted by his guards into this cathedral of
Metz, he mounted its pulpit and openly declared the iniquity of
all that had been done against the Emperor and the justice of his
return to his rightful dignity and honor.

A few days afterward, in the presence of another synod of
bishops assembled at Thionville, the Emperor made formal accusation against Ebbo as author of the lying charges which had
caused his own humiliation. On March 4 before his fellow prelates
Ebbo confessed himself convicted of guilt by the judgment of
his peers and in his own eyes unworthy of episcopal office. After
this, Agobard, archbishop of Lyons, was commanded to appear
for a like admission. Three times his name was called. When no
answer was heard, he was held in judgment as one banished from
his diocese. Ebbo seems to have hoped that the Empress Judith
would gain leniency for him. It was in vain, and he, too, went
into exile.

For the moment there was joy at Court, and Louis wrote
to Hilduin, whose abbey of Saint-Denis had seen in 834 the Emperor's reconciliation with Church and state, those well-known
words of gratitude to God and His saint:

"From many, oft-repeated gifts we have received blessings in
the changing course of this life on earth. By the just judgment of
God—for this must always be confessed—we were visited by the
rod of His chastening. And then by the staff of His sweet mercy
and through the merits and before the altar of our most reverend
Father, holy Denis, we were raised up to stand once more upon
our feet. By the judgment and authority of our bishops we once
again buckled on the sword."

9

Yet not even all these ceremonies, these rituals and assurances, were to keep peace in permanence within the kingdom of the Franks under Louis the Pious. Soon thanksgivings yielded to prayers for relief from the troubles which now rose in new vigor from without and from within. From 834 until the end of the reign of Louis, Viking raids descended in force on Frankish coasts: upon Frisia, upon Noirmoutier, upon the region of the Rhine. The Emperor did what he could against the threatening storm. His mind, however, was full of other things, as he anxiously wrestled once more with the problems of his own Court and rule.

The Empress Judith, safely restored from exile, had again with new energy set her ambition to work for her son Charles. The Emperor was growing old and frail in health, she protested. What would happen if she and her boy were left unprotected at his death? They needed badly the support of someone in power; and who could give them this support better than Lothar, the Emperor's eldest son?

In 836 Louis, helpless as ever before her pleading, sent envoys to Lothar in Italy. Would he come to Aachen, the Emperor requested. In answer Wala arrived from Lothar's Court, and there was a long conference. Wala was forgiven his opposition and his flight; he was allowed to return to Italy for the persuading of Lothar. But in Italy during this and the following year an epidemic of plague was raging. Many died, including some among the exiles from Aachen: Wala himself in 836, and the counts Hugh and Matfrid, with Jesse of Amiens, probably in 837. Lothar, according to his own story, was attacked by plague and could not travel across the Alps. Nevertheless, news reached his father that he was stirring up much trouble for the Holy See in Rome. Louis not only sent a strong rebuke for this unseemly conduct, but planned to travel in person to Italy. The raiding of the Northmen kept him, to his great vexation, from carrying out his resolve. At home the tide of affairs during the next three years flowed persistently, as might be expected, in favor of Judith and her nefarious schemes.

As in 831, the Emperor, after his severe humiliation, was keen to assert his independence, to exercise the power now once again his. Wala was dead; the archbishops Agobard and Ebbo were in disgrace and exile. He himself had not many years in which to act. He would gladly do what he could, before he died, for his youngest son and for his Empress. Accordingly, in October 837, at an assembly in Aachen, he gave to young Charles by imperial assignment the rule over Frisia; over the greater part of Belgium; over the territory extending between the Meuse and the Seine; over Paris, and onward to Troyes, Sens, and Auxerre. These gifts aroused bitter fear in the heart of Louis the German.

The natural result was that all the feeling of loyalty born anew in this Louis through the shame done to his father in 833 now turned sour in a fresh burst of anger. As soon as the spring made movement possible, in March 838, he sent messengers across the Alps to his brother Lothar with a strong complaint and a call for help against this robbery. The action in its turn aroused the wrath of his father, the Emperor, and aroused it so effectually that he again ordered his army to assemble. However, before matters actually flared anew into the conflict which he dreaded, he summoned Louis the German to meet him at Nijmegen in the Netherlands. The place of conference was made necessary because of the raids of Viking pirates; the Emperor was doing all that was in his power at the moment to defend the Netherlands from their attack. Louis arrived; but the interview led only from bad to worse. It ended in stormy quarrel, and in his indignation the Emperor hastened to drastic measures. He issued an imperial decree that his son Louis be deprived of all his holdings and lands, with the exception of his kingdom of Bavaria.

In September, at Quierzy-sur-Oise, the Emperor conferred knighthood upon Charles, now fifteen years of age, and marked the event by presenting the young prince with yet another portion of territory of land, between the Seine and the Loire. In December his second son, Pippin, died. He left, indeed, a son of his own; but that was of minor importance at this time. Louis the German, seething with anger and ready for battle, was stationed with his army at Frankfurt; and therefore the Emperor held it his best policy also to winter near the Rhine. He marched to Mainz, spent the winter months there in camp, and in the spring of 839 started his campaign for the subduing of this angry rebel. He crossed the river, received gladly many who flocked to join him from Saxon lands, advanced upon Louis, already crippled in force by frequent desertion from his ranks, and sent him back in hurried flight to Bavaria, with humiliation added to his sense of loss.

Once more in his Palace at Aachen, increasing anxiety for his health turned the Emperor's thoughts more and more toward the future. Both his elder sons, born of his first wife, were now openly hostile to him, Louis in Bavaria, Lothar in Italy. How would Charles fare in competition with them? He would probably still be under twenty years of age when his father died.

At last this Louis the Pious decided to settle his worry by a move fundamental and stern. He would bring about another reconciliation between himself and his firstborn, Lothar. He would extract from Lothar a sworn promise to assist and to protect his youngest brother, Charles, with all his power. And, finally, he would divide the whole of the Frankish Empire, with the exception of Bavaria, between the two.

Messengers were dispatched to Italy. In answer Lothar met his father at Worms in the end of May 839, and in the presence of a state assembly made humble confession of error and prayer for pardon. Louis once more forgave all. Promptly in favor of Lothar and of Charles a division of the Empire was made into east and west, by a line that followed the course of the Meuse, then ran southwards to Burgundy, the Alps, and the Mediterranean, past the Saône and the Rhône. As the elder, Lothar was given his choice of eastern or western portion, and he chose the eastern; Charles received the western, including the counties of Langres, Chalon-sur-Saône, Lyons, and Geneva. Bavaria, as before, was left as sole portion to Louis the German; and nothing at all was left to the son of that Pippin who had been king of Aquitaine. Lothar now returned to Italy, and his father, the Emperor, made a progress through Aquitaine, charging its people to render homage to their ruler, his son Charles. Doubtless this homage gave peculiar joy to one who himself had ruled there as boy and young man.

The inevitable result once more happened. Within Louis, king of Bavaria, revolt flared up in overwhelming force. In the next year, 840, this broke into action. Mustering an army of Thuringian and Saxon fighters, he marched from Bavaria into Alemannia, now under the rule of Lothar. The spring was only just beginning; the roads were bad; it was impossible for Louis the Emperor to start out on campaign then and there. He was nearly sixty-two, and he was ill with bronchial trouble. Lent was about to set in. At Poitiers, where he had spent the winter, he kept the fast and his usual devotion, then went to celebrate Easter at Aachen. This duty fulfilled, and the roads now dry and hard, he hurried on his way to crush this last revolt of his reign.

His sickness steadily grew worse. Nevertheless, he crossed the Rhine, entered Thuringia, where he had heard that Louis the German was by this time encamped, and once more drove him back to Bavaria. On the way homeward he decided to call an Assembly at Worms for the first of July and to ask Lothar to come there from Italy for conference in regard to Louis. His messengers started on their errand; but the Emperor did not live to see July. He knew suddenly that he could do no more; and he ordered his men to bear him to a little island in the Rhine, near Mainz and within sight of his Palace of Ingelheim. There he died on June 20, 840, tended with care by Drogo, who gave him the last rites of the Church and laid his body with a mass of requiem in the basilica of Saint-Arnulf at Metz. In his last hours the Emperor sent forgiveness to Louis the German. He ordered the imperial crown and insignia to be forwarded to Lothar, and he again commended the seventeen-year-old Charles to Lothar's care.

10

The years of Louis the Pious had ended in failure, born of his own frailty. As man, he had been unequal to the struggle demanded of him; as king, he had left drifting, except in times of utter necessity, the helm of government so firmly grasped in his active years by his father, Charles the Great. Yet, weak though he was as king and Emperor, he had never forgotten that he was a Christian monarch, enduring in trial, merciful in victory. As a youth he had seen under his father the rising into name and title of the lands of the Frankish empire to which fate had made him an unwilling heir; his purpose, springing from his passionate devotion to the Church Catholic, had been to hold together this empire in peace and strength as one united realm. Conflicting desire had carried both him and his people into discord and division. And now, perhaps he thought as he looked upon Ingelheim, adorned by scenes from the history of his royal house, how long would this empire of the Carolingians hold its state?

Chapter III

EINHARD OF SELIGENSTADT

1

We have thus briefly looked at the days of Charles the Great and Louis the Pious in order to place against their scenes of turbulent history the character of writers who lived under their rule. The ninth century, even in the midst of its tumult and travail, was to bring forth many men of letters. Some of them still stand out clearly from the darkness and disaster of their time: thinkers, poets, men of Court, men of religion, busy in the active life of state and Church or far from the world in quiet retreat.

One of the earliest in point of time was Einhard. All students of medieval literature know him in his relation to Charles the Great; comparatively few have followed him into the days of Louis the Pious. Yet it was only in those days that he reached his highest renown at Court. In his latter years he turned from that Court and from the political troubles of his country to find his own ideal of peace and content.

He was born in Germany of the East Franks about 770, in the valley of the Main, the Maingau; and as a child he spoke the East Frankish tongue, which we know as Old High German. His parents appear to have been people of substance; tradition has seen their names in a deed of gift made by "Einhart and his wife Engelfrit," bestowing "fields, meadows, woods, houses and their tenants" upon the monastery of Fulda.

To Fulda they had already sent their son as a boy of ten or eleven for his early training, and there he stayed some twelve years. Just about the time of his entrance, perhaps a little before, the abbey lost its first ruler, Sturm the Bavarian; the date of his death is given as 779. It was Sturm who had founded the monastery. Thirty-six years before, in 743, he had been sent by his bishop, Boniface, the great missionary to German lands, to search in the dense forest along the Fulda River for a clearing in which might be built a center for work among the heathen dwelling thereabouts. In 744 the search had ended, and on the bank of that same river in Hesse, where the heights of the Rhön Gebirge look down on the one side and the Vogels Berg on the other, the abbey had slowly risen, and the building in stone of its church of the Holy Savior had begun. In 780 Baugulf, a monk of Fulda, succeeded to the rule of its community, which by this time held more than four hundred men.

It was to this Abbot Baugulf that Charles the Great sent, as we have seen, probably between 794 and 800, and therefore probably a short while after Einhard ended his study in Fulda, his letter on the Pursuit of Learning. Knowledge of language and letters, the king declared, was indispensable to monks for the true worship of God in the chanting of holy office. Errors in writing, too, shamefully common among men dedicated under religious rule, pointed to a dangerous lack of understanding; and understanding was most certainly necessary for the study of sacred truths.

The fact that this letter was sent in the first place to Fulda's abbot shows that Fulda already held rank of distinction among Frankish monasteries. In its library Einhard toiled at Latin words and grammar until he could read from the Latin Bible; in the course of years he followed not only the study of Fathers of the Church, but also of Latin pagan classics: Virgil, Livy, Tacitus, Suetonius. At Fulda, too, he learned to write his Latin in clear and orderly sequence after the Roman classical manner. There, also, he learned the art of fair and formal penmanship. We can still read the words of six legal deeds, carefully written out by him during the years 788 to 791 and signed by his name as scribe for the abbey under Baugulf.

At Fulda he began also to take a keen interest in other work of art: crafts of building, of modeling in metal, of design and decoration. He often watched the brethren at their manual labors and looked curiously at structures already in place. To the first rude church of Fulda, Sturm in course of time had added pillars, strong beams, and new roofing. Inside, he had placed on the Boniface altar a tabernacle overlaid with design in wrought gold. He had thought at the same time of his monks' bodily welfare.

He had set them hard at work in digging an aqueduct which eventually brought the water of the Fulda river within the monastery's walls. Abbot Baugulf continued the progress. In 791 his community began to raise a new church, to be dedicated in honor of their Founder; its building was inspired and directed by one of their own house, a monk named Ratgar, who was greatly skilled in art and architecture. Einhard followed eagerly its planning and its form.

Above all, at Fulda he received that training in religion which was to remain with him all his years. He was never to be monk or priest or missionary. But a sense of the reality of prayer grew within him as day by day he heard Fulda's monks chant their mass and office in the Benedictine round; as he climbed the hill—in his time still called "The Bishop's Mount"—to the retreat upon its summit, looking down upon the abbey, where Boniface, bishop of Mainz, had loved to spend hours of contemplation in silence and solitude.

Lastly, to this abbey Einhard was in great measure to owe his life-long devotion to the saints of his Catholic heritage. In its church their feasts were kept year by year. In it he saw pilgrims from his own and many other countries, near and distant, kneeling before the shrine of the founder, or before the grave of Leoba, the beloved disciple, friend, and fellow worker of Boniface in Germany. Perhaps he had been present as a boy at Fulda when in 780 she had been laid to rest on the north side of its high altar.

2

Thus the years passed, and Einhard was in his early twenties. For some time Abbot Baugulf had been feeling that the young man's zeal for things written and wrought needed a guidance and a surrounding which Fulda could not give him. The monks of Fulda were missionaries in its earlier years rather than scholars. Near them, on the east and northeast, stretched the wild forests of Thuringia and the lands of the warrior Saxons, desperately fighting against Fulda's own Frankish king, Charles the Great, for their Saxon independence and liberty. Fear for their abbey again and again distracted the monks at their prayers. We read that in 778, shortly before Einhard's entrance as pupil, "through menace of the Saxons they fled fourteen miles from the monastery, bearing with them the relics of holy Boniface." The tradition of Fulda even holds that Baugulf once welcomed Charles himself there; if this is true, the visit must have been made while the king was on one of his Saxon campaigns. Perhaps Einhard at that time looked with awe upon the great conqueror himself.

From about 793 onward he was to see the king daily. For now Baugulf sent him to Aachen, to learn from the scholars whom Charles had gathered there for the quickening of intellectual life at his Court and "Palace School." This change in Einhard's days must have been difficult, to say the least. From the ordered quiet of prayer and study he now was to take his part in the restless, crowded activity of the Palace: the constant comings and goings of messengers and envoys; the unending errands; the preparations for the march into war; the discussions, serious and light-hearted, in the great hall during meals, in the baths, in the forest around Aachen as the hunters rested a moment from their sport, in the society of girls and women—discussions turning from philosophy, from theology, from science and mathematics, to witty or sharp-edged criticism of men and books, according to the mood of Charles, his family, and his friends.

And the lively crowd, always ready to find fresh ground for jest and satire, was soon poking fun at this little pigmy of a youth—for Einhard was abnormally small—who hurried so earnestly from place to place as his duties called him. In 796 Theodulf of Orléans was writing of "Little Nard, who runs back and forth with ceaseless pace like some tiny ant; laden, like the ant, with his burden, books or heavy packages."

Yet in spite of their teasing all liked and respected this serious worker. Alcuin, head of the Palace School, wrote a poem in his honor:

> There is a house; it has a little door,
> And little is the one who dwells therein.
> But, reader, scorn not littleness in "Nard,"
> For "Nard" means balsam, fragrant in the field.
> Small is the bee, yet bears its honey's store;
> Small, is it not? the pupil of man's eye,
> But master of his body's life and will.

Master of all his house is little "Nard";
So, reader, greeting give to little "Nard" today!

All men knew, also, that Einhard had a quick temper. He could turn round and hurl his own shaft of derision, as he did once against an Irishman, whose name history has not told.

He was respected not only by the company around the king. The poet Walafrid Strabo was to write of him after Charles the Great was dead: "The little fellow—so small that he seemed of no account—won in the Court of Charles, that lover of knowledge, so great a reputation by his intelligence and his honest character that among all the servants of his royal Majesty there was scarcely one to whom the king confided more secrets of his inner mind."

Einhard held no purely political office under Charles, at least so far as we know. Twice his name appears in the records of the king's reign. The Royal Annals tell that it was he who carried the act of 806 to Rome for confirmation by signature of Pope Leo III; and Ermoldus Nigellus, in his books of verse, "In Honour of the Emperor Louis"—verse written in the hope of winning his return from disgrace of exile imposed by this Louis the Pious —describes Einhard, "so dear to Charles," as coming forward in a council of 813 to act as spokesman for his fellow courtiers in imploring Charles, king and Emperor, to grant to his son Louis the sharing of the imperial title with himself.

It was Einhard's enthusiastic love of books and of art which brought him to the notice of Charles. In a letter of Alcuin, written to the king after Alcuin's retirement from Aachen to Tours, we find these words: "If my letter does not give you enough illustration of style in verse, Beseleel, always at hand to help both you and me, will be able to supply more. And he is well able, also, to think out problems in arithmetic."

Alcuin had often given names of his own imagining in play and in affection to his pupils in the Palace, according to some special quality which he saw in each. Einhard had been marked by the name of "Beseleel," in memory of that maker of the tabernacle of the covenant of whom the Lord spoke to Moses in the thirty-first chapter of Exodus:

Behold, I have called by name Bezaleel, the son of Uri, the son of Hur, of the tribe of Judah;

And I have filled him with the spirit of God, in wisdom and in understanding, and in knowledge, and in all manner of workmanship,

To devise cunning works, to work in gold, and in silver, and in brass,

And in cutting of stones, to set them, and in carving of timber, to work in all manner of workmanship.

The interest of the king in "Beseleel" grew rapidly, then finally took a practical form, and Einhard was appointed director of Royal Works for the Frankish Court. He succeeded so well that before long he was given an assistant, one Ansegis, abbot of Saint-Germer-de-Flay in the diocese of Beauvais, France. Now he kept his eyes and mind upon the new Palace of Aachen as its design came slowly to fulfillment.

For long Aachen had held attraction for the king because of the hot springs which made bathing a pleasure; and after the royal residence at Worms caught fire one night in 790 and burned to the ground, there was greater need for Aachen to become a new central focus of his activities. From about 796 onward for many years Einhard was busy at work: upon the great hall of this Palace at Aachen, a hall dominated by its high throne; upon the courtyards, fair with flowers and trees, among which stood buildings filled with archives, books, jewels; upon the swimming pool; on the homes to be seen here and there in the Palace enclosure, built for those in attendance on the king. At last all was done. As Einhard looked up, he could see on the roof of the Palace the great bronze eagle with its wings outstretched; below, he could follow the covered way, adorned with columns and nearly four hundred feet long, which led down the slope from the Palace on its height to the chapel of Our Lady at its base, that chapel to which Charles had given of his wealth and his energy without end.

The chapel, as Einhard saw it, was "most beautiful, glowing with gold and silver and the light of lamps, enriched with grilles and doors of solid bronze." Its material was stone, and its shape octagonal. On the ground floor, at each point of the octagon, stood a massive pillar, and from pillar to pillar rose and fell arch after arch. Behind each pillar and its arch lay a deep recess, its walls covered with mosaic work. A gallery ran round the first floor of the building, above which rose narrower arches, supported by columns. Between the great arches of the ground floor and the smaller ones above, on the wall immediately below the gallery, an inscription in red letters told that the Lord Charles had made this house of God. As one looked higher, there were still further arches with slender columns, and then the chapel walls, here also painted with mosaic art, met in its dome. Outside the chapel this dome was crowned by a great golden ball, a mark in the sunlight to travelers far and wide. Mass and the Hours were said or chanted before altars, standing one on the ground floor, the other on the floor above. This higher altar was reached by a little stairway near the entrance to the chapel.

Einhard, deep as was his concern for it, did not design or build this chapel; its architect was Odo, probably of Metz. Einhard, indeed, was not an architect at all, in the professional sense. That he studied the science of building may be inferred from a letter which he wrote, we do not know when, to a pupil of his named Vussin. This letter shows his knowledge of Vitruvius, author under the Roman Emperor Augustus of a treatise on architecture which won lasting fame.

His special joy and delight lay largely, it would seem, in what we know as the fine arts. The work of illuminating, of carving in wood and ivory, of tooling in bronze, silver, and gold, by which men of Carolingian days honored their altars and their churches, may owe more to Einhard than we are now able to prove. Tradition of Fulda was to describe him as "a man highly skilled in various arts." From Fulda itself came young Bruun, already showing much promise in painting, sent by Ratgar, then Fulda's abbot, to study under Einhard at Aachen. Walafrid Strabo described Einhard as "Father Beseleel, who with vigilant care directed all the work of his craftsmen"; and Alcuin, once his master, seems to have marveled at Tours that Einhard was not chosen to follow him as head of the Palace School.

3

In 814 Charles the Great died. Splendid funeral rites were celebrated around the tomb in the church which he himself had built. Above the tomb was to rise an arch rich in gold, bearing his portrait and an inscription in Latin:

Under this stone rests the body of Charles, Great and Orthodox Emperor, who nobly enlarged the kingdom of the Franks and for forty-seven years governed it happily.

No one then could visit Aachen without thinking of Charles the Great. But, as years went on and no memorial of the king appeared in writing, Einhard decided that this duty, this debt, was his to discharge and to pay.

Much has been written on his *Life of Charles,* the outstanding biography of these early medieval times. Often has the question been discussed: When did Einhard write it? This question should rightly be dealt with here, although it will compel us for a moment to look forward to Einhard's later years. Internal evidence—mention in chapter 12 of a rising against the Franks by their former allies, the Abodrites, and another notice in chapter 17 of a raid by the Northmen—has told us that it was composed after 817. The inclusion of the *Life* in a Catalogue of books in the monastery of Reichenau, a list compiled in 821 or 821–22, has pointed out to many students its latest date of composition. This would mean that it was written at Aachen, at the Court of Louis the Pious; for Einhard was there, at least part of each year, until 830. A strong possibility has been ably argued that the names of books, including that of this *Life of Charles* by Einhard, might easily have been inserted in this Catalogue after the date of 821, without alteration of the original recording of that year. Further argument has been put forward, leading to the thought that the work was actually written, as Martin Lintzel put it, "in the years after 830, still better, after 833." Einhard would then have been in his abbey at Seligenstadt, that retreat of his later years. The book, it is argued, is devoted to praise of the days of old, of Charles the Great and his reign; in contrast, Louis the Pious is neglected, perhaps indirectly censured in comparison with his father; Einhard's effort to move him—and his effort was doubtless little enough—had seemingly failed of effect. There is evidence in Einhard's letters of his admiration, or assumed admiration, of the Emperor Lothar; there is evidence of homage paid to Louis the German, in whose realm Seligenstadt lay. It would seem that, as in the case of Ebbo, a warm friendship had cooled off here also; in any case, Einhard showed himself no bold and courageous friend of his Emperor and benefactor in the crisis of 833. A later date for the *Life of Charles* would also account for the errors found in its pages, errors of which no one living and writing at Aachen could have been guilty. Finally, the *Life*, as we shall see, was mentioned, with great enthusiasm for its style of writing, by Lupus of Ferrières in a letter to Einhard during his own years as a student at Fulda, from about 829 until 836. Lupus had discovered the *Life* in Fulda's library. We do not know when it arrived there, or when Lupus wrote this letter. But the letter could well have been written as late as 834, and Lupus, that eager student of books, would probably have discovered the *Life* in Fulda's collection as soon as this was possible.

From the question of its date we turn to the book itself. It is set in high relief among the *Lives* of saints which were already being composed in monasteries; for, unlike these saints, its hero is not swathed in an unending narrative of his virtues in the sight of God and man, and eulogy does not sweep through it in a sticky, swollen flood.

It has, indeed, as critics have noted, many faults. It presents the king in a recital of his wars and conquests, taken, at times with borrowing, not only factual but verbal, from the historical sources of the day: the royal annals, the continuators of Fredegarius, and the royal archives. This, of course, in itself is understandable. But it uses them carelessly, with errors of place, of date, of deed. Now and then in its enthusiasm it omits detail unfavorable to its hero, or exaggerates his merit. There is not a word concerning the unspeakable beheading of forty-five hundred rebel Saxons by order of Charles at Verden on the Aller in 782, although Frankish record had declared it; and the territory conquered by the king is here larger than it actually was.

There is fault, also, in Einhard's usage of his chief literary model, his ideal pattern for treatment and style: Suetonius, who wrote in the second century A.D. his Latin *Lives* of the Roman Emperors. Many details describing the Frankish king's appearance and manner of life are given in the very words in which Suetonius drew his picture of the Roman Emperor Augustus; so many, in fact, that often without our wider knowledge from other sources it would be difficult to know whether we have here in Einhard the reality of truth.

And yet from this faulty portrait there looks out at us a man whom we can see and accept. As Einhard protests in his Preface: "I knew that no one could write of King Charles more truthfully than I, for I was witness of the things which I was to tell." The story is told as briefly as may be: "I was anxious to tell all I know," he declares, "and yet not to offend critics by running into too great length." He himself had learned Latin as a foreign language in his native Germany, and he had worked hard to understand how to choose and to arrange Latin words. Yet he was still diffident of his power. "You may ask," he pleads before his readers, "why I, a barbarian Frank, little exercised in Roman style of writing, should think that I could write decent and fitting Latin? You may say that I have shut my eyes to those words of Cicero: 'The man who puts his thoughts into writing when he cannot place them in the order, in the light which is their need, when he cannot capture his readers by any gift of charm, is both wasting his own time and sinning grievously against the art of letters.' "

From a simple, concise, and clear narrative, then, Charles the Great here looks out at us: his figure tall and rather full, his head rounded at the top, his hair white but still abundant, his nose rather long, his eyes keen and bright, his smile twinkling and gay in hours of peace and leisure. His step is firm; his bearing shows one accustomed to authority. Only when he speaks are those who bow before him conscious of unseemliness, since his voice comes forth from that strong, virile face both small and thin. In all other respects he is a man of vigor and vitality. Hunting has been his joy from his boyhood. He has built his Palace at Aachen because of his delight in swimming; not one of his courtiers can conquer him in the pool.

One sees him in the Frankish dress: linen shirt and drawers; tunic bordered with silk; leggings and shoes of thongs intertwined; vest of otter skin for cold weather. The blue cloak is thrown, as usual, over his shoulders; the sword is buckled at his side, its hilt shining with silver or gold. On high days his mantle is woven of gold thread, fastened by a golden brooch; from his shoes to the crown upon his head jewels flash back the light.

One sees him at dinner with his nobles in the great hall, hungrily awaiting the entry of the servers who bear the roast venison which he loves, waving away in disgust the boiled meat ordered by his physicians; turning an earnest ear to the words of the *City of God* by Saint Augustine, his favorite book, often read aloud at his command. Was he himself not·working to bring into being a City of God upon earth? One finds him in Einhard's picture enjoying his moments of relaxation: resting after his midday meal; bent over calculations of astronomy, his great interest; asking questions of his teacher, Alcuin, and disputing Alcuin's replies; receiving visitors in his throne room; entertaining so many guests, from so many lands, that Einhard pauses in his story to sigh as he remembers: "Their multitude was so vast that really they seemed a burden not only to the Palace but even to the whole Frankish realm." One catches sight of him as he travels in his coach, putting his hand beneath his pillows to draw out the leaves of parchment on which he practiced, whenever he had time to spare, that craft of writing which his hands found so difficult. Above all, day and night one finds him in his chapel of Our Lady; always, even while he listens to the prayers, alert to notice anything dirty, faded, or worn; any lack of care in reading, in song, or in chant; anything unseemly in sacred vessel or vestment. Not even the doorkeepers escape his eye; they are always at their posts, arrayed as he holds right and proper for their duties.

From the outer surroundings of his king Einhard brings us to his inner character. Charles was one of utterly determined will. Whatever he set his hand to do, he did it to the end, never counting the cost. *Constantia, perseverantia, patientia,* Stoic constancy, perseverance, endurance, are the words which describe him, whether fighting the men of Aquitaine or pursuing the stubborn Saxons. "Nothing of that which had to be undertaken, nothing which was to be followed through, did he refuse for its labor or for dread of its danger; he had learned to undergo and to bear whatever happened, of whatever nature; neither in time of crisis would he yield to disaster nor in success would he bow to fortune's false, flattering smile." Fortune, Einhard admits, did smile constantly upon the king; yet in front of Fortune walked always *prudentia,* his sense of what at the moment it was wise and politic to do.

So in peace and in war to Einhard Charles was ever the Great King; *magnanimitas* was his high quality. Great of mind he was. He lived splendidly. He built royally: in the work upon his palaces, not only at Aachen but at Ingelheim and at Nijmegen; in his restoration of old and ruined churches throughout the realm; in his engineering of the great bridge which spanned the Rhine at Mainz. He was known, feared, and respected by his fellow monarchs, by princes and by chieftains, West and East; he sent his gifts, his alms for the poor, not only to Rome and to Constantinople, but to Syria, to Egypt, to Jerusalem, to Alexandria, and to Carthage.

And to individual men he gave his friendship. Einhard, who could write that Charles grieved even to tears at the death of Pope Hadrian I, now and again writes words which reflect his own close association with the king. It was Charles, he tells us, who taught and trained him, to whom he owed and was always in gratitude to owe, the life and the affection, which had been his at the Palace among the royal family. With Charles, he, too, as a born Frank, knew bitterness against the Saxons, the treacherous enemy that had terrified the monks of Fulda. He thought with growing fear in the last years of the king's life upon those omens of tragedy which Charles would not allow himself to heed: that stroke of lightning which hurled the golden ball from the chapel's cupola; that burning of the great bridge over the Rhine, the king's special pride and joy; that falling of the king himself from his horse.

In the light of this friendship it seems rash to conclude that Einhard was unconsciously or even deliberately asserting what was not true when in regard to the king's coronation by Pope Leo at Rome on Christmas Day 800 he wrote: "At first the king was so averse to this that he declared he would not have set foot within Saint Peter's, even on so high a Feast day, had he known what the Pope had in mind." As we have noted, Einhard sometimes did, through carelessness or forgetfulness, record what was false in regard to date or place; he even acknowledged his lack of memory. But these words sound like an angry outburst made spontaneously, perhaps privately, by the king to a trusted member of his Palace. The irritation caused by the premature conferring of imperial title did not stay Charles, in his deep reverence for Rome, from offering magnificent gifts to St. Peter's, or induce him to forbid the consecration on that same day of his eldest son Charles. He vented his annoyance in private and bided his time.

4

This, then, was Charles the Great as Einhard thought of him, perhaps long after his son, Louis the Pious, had succeeded him on the royal and imperial throne. Even in the first days of the reign of this successor, from 814 onward, the change in rule was hard for one so devoted to King Charles as Einhard had been, although a bond of religious fervor and practice united him with Louis and although the two had known one another more or less at Court during some twenty years. In 814 Einhard was in his mid-forties. Under the new reign we find him not only continuing his duties as commissioner of royal works, but acting as secretary and counselor to this new king and Emperor. Furthermore, in 817 he was entrusted with the education of Lothar, the eldest son of Louis; and he held this trust until 822, when Lothar, with Wala as his adviser, left Frankland to assume the crown of Italy.

The years passed quietly for him, busy in writing, in working at the Palace. He had now a home in Aachen, for at some time, either under Charles or in the first months of the reign of Louis, he had made a happy marriage with Imma, a woman of noble rank, as serious and as faithful in devotion to the Church and to the Court as he himself. Soon their service to the king was rewarded. On January 11, 815, Louis made a gift to Einhard and Imma of two villages lying in Einhard's own Eastern Frankland: Michelstadt, in the Mümling valley amid the woods and mountains of the Odenwald, and Mülinheim, nearly thirty miles to the north, on the bank of the Main. This gift was to be of far greater importance than Einhard then knew.

Other honors followed in quick succession. In spite of his longing to fulfill that strictness of Benedictine monasticism required during these very years by his chief counselor, Benedict of Aniane, Louis could not find it in him to forego the usual practice of Carolingian kings: the offering to laymen of prominence, as vassals of the sovereign under feudal tenure, of the rule of abbeys rich in revenue, a reward for service done or service expected. As "abbots" these laymen held the revenue from abbey lands, from stock growing and grazing, at their own disposal. Such gifts were not only a source of comfort to the unscrupulous, but, in fewer cases, a burden to the conscientious. Many of these houses of religion held men sadly in want of their daily bread, for body as well as for soul.

Nor did Einhard on his side refuse such offers from the king. In 815 we find him lay abbot of Saint-Pierre at Ghent in Belgium; at the same time, perhaps, and certainly by 819, he was ruling another abbey in Ghent, of Saint-Bavon; in 816 Louis gave him control of the famous monastery of Fontenelle, near Rouen, dedicated to Saint Wandrille; in 819 or 821 he became abbot of Saint-Servais at Maastricht in the Netherlands. And more. By gift of the same King Louis he held in Italy, at Pavia, a cloister of Saint-Jean-Baptiste; and elsewhere, it would seem, two others of uncertain site: one of Saint-Cloud, possibly the well-known one of that name near Paris; and one of Fritzlar, perhaps the abbey in Hesse founded by Boniface.

Many of the letters which we have from Einhard's pen show his constant activity as ruler of these abbeys. He improved immensely their standard of living; he examined and ordered their sources and supplies of food, their buildings and furniture, their round of prayer and work, the security of their future. In him his communities found one who cared not only for the brethren of the choir, but for all who served them in humbler ways. In the minds of those churchmen who still believed in true Benedictine discipline the horrid fact that Einhard was a layman and that he filled his monasteries with secular clergy was somewhat offset by this care of his for his multiple charge.

He did not reside in any one of these abbeys, nor, so far as we know, did he even visit all of them in person. Instead he ruled them by his *vicedominus,* his representative, often in priest's ordering. From time to time he went for quiet retreat to one of the two houses at Ghent: that of Saint-Pierre on the height of the Mont Blandin, or that of Saint-Bavon, which stood at the meeting of the river Lys with the Escaut. For both houses he had a deep affection, and tradition has left us some detailed story of his work for Saint-Pierre. Both abbeys had been founded in the seventh century, and both had suffered terribly under Charles Martel, that grandfather of Charles the Great who had robbed the monasteries of Frankland for the rewarding of his men of war and council. Saint-Pierre was reduced to such want that many of its monks forsook it for the world outside. Charles the Great gave it no support, and its life remained stagnant and desolate, "brought almost to nothing," until Louis the Pious, in hope of better things, gave it to Einhard. In a charter granted to its community by Einhard as abbot we read: "It is well known that under those who preceded me in rule your resources were meager and insufficient, that very often of your necessity you have suffered want. Therefore for love of God and blessed Peter and for the brotherly affection which has come about between us, I have decided to bestow upon you from the properties of this abbey—hitherto held in common by you, the community, and me, the abbot—your own inalienable portion, for your own use in permanence." There follows a list, drawn up with scrupulous detail, of lands to be marked off and used by the brethren for the pasturing of cows, sheep, and pigs, for the cultivating of vines, with adequate funds for their maintenance.

In return for his care Einhard expected from his abbeys the secular service which he held due to himself. To his deputy in charge at Saint-Servais he writes, probably in 828, after a prolonged absence from the Court: "I hope, please God, to return to Aachen about Martinmas" (November 11). "Will you send men to my house there to carry out needed cleaning and repairs; and will you send, also, from the harvests of Saint-Servais the supplies which I shall need in Aachen: flour, grain for the brewing of beer and wine, and also what is needed for the making of cheese? And send to Lanaken"—a place near Maastricht—"the oxen which must be slaughtered."

A sterner note is seen in a letter sent about the same time to his representative at Fritzlar: "I am extremely surprised to find that you have not touched any of the things I told you to do. From what I hear, you have sent to Mülinheim from your yearly produce of grain for the making of flour and beer, absolutely nothing; and nothing else, except thirty pigs, and these not really good, only average, with three bushels of vegetables. That is all, not one thing besides. And what is more, all the winter past we have not caught sight of you, or of your messenger, to tell us how matters are going at Fritzlar. Now, then, if you care at all for my good opinion, please with all energy begin to make up for this neglect."

Several letters deal with the paying over of their quotas of revenue by abbeys belonging to Einhard under royal benefit. Once or twice he seems, perhaps, to make an unduly free use of this benefit. In 823 he yielded rule of the abbey of Fontenelle to Ansegis, who had worked under him in the care of buildings raised by Charles and by Louis the Pious. Afterward, although no longer abbot, he had no scruple in using his influence with this successor: "Will you kindly allow N., once a vassal of mine," he writes to Ansegis, "to continue his tenure of a benefice which I granted him, until I shall be able to obtain by royal favour another one for his holding?"

5

In the meantime his power at Court was steadily increasing. He was corresponding with men of distinction and rank in the realm, both asking their help for his friends and dependents and receiving their petitions for his own kind offices in time of need. A notable instance of his repute was given in 828 or 829 when the chapter of the cathedral of Sens wrote to beg him to aid them in electing the bishop of their own choice, a business in which they had already twice been defeated by royal authority. Bernard, bishop of Worms, now at the point of death, implored him to use his influence for the wise election of his successor in that see.

No less than in matters constitutional, Einhard's authority in the problems of learning—literary, theological, and philosophical—was now accepted by the world of his time. A cleric—his name is unknown—wrote to Louis the Pious on the triple nature of man's soul, created in the image of God; Three in One. At the end of his letter he added: "If you read this, Einhard, do not be surprised should you find me at fault. Indeed, I would rather have you surprised to see something rightly declared by me."

There was ample encouragement for both religious and literary discussion at the Court of this Louis. Fridugis, the Anglo-Saxon pupil of Alcuin, who had so interested Charles the Great and his courtiers in a discussion of the real existence of "Nothing" and the material substance of "Darkness," in 819 was chancellor under Louis; Agobard of Lyons shortly after 816 sent to Louis his denunciation of the heresy of Felix of Urgel; Hilduin, archchaplain of the Palace, was the friend of Hraban Maur, who from his abbey of Fulda was coming to Court from time to time to talk not only of politics, but of the commentaries on books of the Bible which he was steadily writing; Dungal, the hermit of Saint-Denis, in 827 dedicated to Louis and his eldest son, Lothar, an energetic attack upon the "ravings and blasphemies" of Claudius, bishop of Turin, poured out by Claudius against veneration of the Holy Cross. Modoin, since 815 bishop of Autun, a constant friend of Louis, was occupying his leisure hours in writing verse, as he had already done for Charles the Great with high flattery of Einhard. The minor poets clustered around the Empress Judith sang her praise. Einhard listened and gave his own share to the round of criticism, applause, argument, and dispute.

6

It was all very pleasant. But, as time went on, Einhard was forced to admit that things were changing for the worse in the Frankish land, in the Palace, even in himself. The resentment of those younger sons against the Ordinance of 817; the rebellion of Bernard of Italy and his death; the shock of the Penitence of Louis at Attigny in 822; the grave dissatisfaction of Wala, of Agobard, of other men of high importance in the kingdom; the growing discontent of Frankish people at large—all these troubles weighed upon his mind. Far more heavily pressed his sense, sharpened year by year, of the apathy, the lack of wisdom and of power shown by the Emperor. Not that the Empire as such mattered vitally to Einhard. He was a true Frank among the men of many nationalities who crowded the Palace, and the royal

kingship of the Frankish house to him was all in all. The thought
of its decline and fall from the height it had reached in Charles
was intolerable. Then had come the year 823 when the Empress
was adding much to his mind's anxiety. Like Wala and Wala's
friends he, too, could not face the breaking up into divided independent shares of the one united Frankish realm. Could it be
that possibly the future of his country lay with Lothar, the young
heir, whom he himself had taught? Could Lothar follow good
counsel and keep Frankland as one power in peace?

With the year 827 things were growing steadily worse. What,
thought Einhard in his depression, what could he himself do?
In 827 he was approaching his sixtieth year. His health and
strength were no more what they once had been; day by day he
was feeling less eager, less able to meet the responsibilities of
life at Court. Would it not be better to leave these responsibilities
to younger men? Long since he had begun to free himself from
some part of his labor. In 818 he had given up his office of director
of Royal Works to Gerward, librarian in the Palace; in 823, as
we saw, he had handed over the charge of Fontenelle's abbey to
Ansegis.

These thoughts, tempting as they were, were but negative
in nature. Behind them was rising a positive, a more convincing
reason to his mind for his retiring from public life. It was born
of his religion and also of that gift to him by Louis the Pious in
815 of those East Frankish villages, Michelstadt and Mülinheim.
Much had already been done by him for their benefit and his
own happiness. By 827 he had raised for each village the bare
walls and the temporary roof of a new church to replace the
small, poor building he had found when he arrived. Many plans
were on foot for a good and true roofing of lead, for interior fur-
nishing and decoration. He cherished hopes also for a house in
which he and his wife might stay from time to time, and for the
well-being of the peasants who looked up to him as lord of the
domain. From 827 onward it became his custom to spend spring
and summer in one or the other of these villages in his own East
Frankish country and to return to the Court at Aachen for the
winter alone.

In 827 then, his villages and his rising churches were already speaking to him of the joy of retreat. As he thought of them in January of that year, one thing only seemed lacking to his plans. To be complete, for the content of his own soul and for the comfort of natives and strangers alike, one of his churches, if not both, must be hallowed by the presence within it of some sacred relic, some portion of the mortal remains of one of God's saints. This was the desire of all founders of churches in this early medieval age; and Einhard's longing had become even greater since he had heard that Hilduin, the archchaplain of the Court and the abbot of Saint-Denis, whom he saw daily when he was at Aachen, had obtained relics of St. Sebastian for the monastery of Saint-Médard at Soissons, which was also under his rule.

Hope was nearer fulfillment than he dreamed. In January 827 he was at Aachen, busy in his duties at Court. To Aachen had come a deacon of the Church of Rome, named Deusdona, to ask the aid of Louis the Pious in some trouble which was worrying him. He had gained what he wanted and was on the point of leaving, when Einhard with hospitable courtesy invited him to lunch. Over their wine they talked of many things. Presently, the subject of relics came up, perhaps in connection with Hilduin; and Einhard confessed his ambition for his own smaller churches. Surely, he said, there are relics in abundance in Rome? Deusdona saw what his host had in mind, hesitated, and said that he would think about the matter. The two men met again the next day; and now it was agreed that if Einhard would give him a mule for his journey and a companion for his travel, Deusdona would return to Rome and procure there for him relics of some holy man of God. Einhard was delighted. He gave Deusdona one of his own mules and ordered his clerk Ratleic, who was eager to go to Rome on pilgrimage, to set out with him. In addition, Einhard gave them money for their expenses on the way.

They started and came first to Soissons, where its abbot, Hilduin, promptly seized upon the same chance. He already had the bones of St. Sebastian. Would Deusdona in kindness try to get him more treasure of this sort? Deusdona readily promised, and Hilduin sent with him to Rome a priest to bring the treasure safely to Soissons.

Again the travelers took the road; but soon Ratleic sensed

trouble in the air. Before he ever entered Rome, he had become convinced that Deusdona was a liar, that he had never had the least intention of carrying out his promises. In Rome the suspicion proved true. Nothing was to be gained from him, and Ratleic almost started back for Aachen. Then, after thinking things over, he decided to set to work by methods of his own.

Having made inquiries, he learned that along the Via Lavicana were lying buried many relics of well-known saints. Accompanied by a guide and by Hilduin's priest, but not by Deusdona, to whom he said nothing of his plan, he found his way to this Via Lavicana, three miles from the city, and to a church which held in its crypt, his guide assured him, a tomb containing the relics of two saints, Marcellinus and Peter, martyrs for their Christian faith under the early Roman Empire; their names are still today called to mind in the canon of the mass. After examining the tomb on the outside, Ratleic went back to his lodging and meditated on the next thing to do.

Then somehow Deusdona discovered what was happening. If Ratleic after all was going to find relics, it would be better, Deusdona decided, to get credit for helping him. Ratleic at length consented to work again with this unreliable deacon, who at least did know Rome and its churches. He fasted and prayed for three days, and then, this time with both Hilduin's priest and Deusdona, he returned secretly by night along those three miles to the same church and crept in silence down to the crypt. There he called upon the Name of the Lord Christ, begged aid in great reverence from the holy martyrs, and with Deusdona's help easily lifted the lid of their tomb. In its upper part lay dust and fragments of bone. Near these a marble tablet had been fastened, a tablet which declared they were indeed the relics of holy Marcellinus. Ratleic lifted them out, wrapped them carefully in fine muslin and departed home to bed.

Once safely in the house where he was staying, however, he began again to think. He was still not wholly satisfied. Would Einhard, he asked himself, think it right to carry off the dust of Marcellinus alone, separated and divided from that of Peter, his companion and fellow-martyr, when their relics had lain together in that tomb for over five hundred years? Surely not! He could neither eat nor sleep in his worry. Again, therefore, by night he walked the three miles to the tomb, and Hilduin's priest went with him. From it he gathered more dust, sure that here were the relics of Peter which he had come to find. For a few days he stayed, first in Rome, afterward at Einhard's abbey in Pavia, and then, his precious burden, as he hoped, safely secured, he started on his journey back to his own Frankish land.

All this business of travel and search had taken the greater part of the year 827. In November, when Einhard was staying at his abbey of Saint-Bavon in Ghent, he received word that the sacred relics of Marcellinus and Peter—a wonderful find— were on their way. Quickly he gave orders that a convoy of priests, minor clergy, and laymen should set out to meet and to escort them home. With great joy and pride of their bearers and acclaimed by crowds of people as they passed, they were carried to Strasbourg, then by boat along the Rhine, and finally for a short distance overland to Michelstadt. In its church, amid hymns and shouts of praise to Heaven from the peasants of the village, they were solemnly placed in a shrine visible to all. Thither Einhard hastened to do them all reverence.

Alas! They did not remain there very long. A vision soon declared that Michelstadt's church was not the place in which Marcellinus and Peter wished their dust to repose. Einhard, to whom the watcher in the church who received this vision of the night hurried with his news, was terribly distressed. Since the saints had given him no hint of the destination which they did desire, after anxious thought he decided to wait awhile in the hope of further enlightenment. He used this time in making new silken bags for his treasure's safety; and, as he filled the bags, he noticed that the dust of holy Marcellinus was distinctly less in quantity than that of Saint Peter. Of course, he concluded, Marcellinus must have been a smaller man. But here he was wrong.

Vision and warning, more and more grim, still continued to haunt the nights of those who prayed in the church of Michelstadt; and still Einhard debated "with seething anxiety" what he was to do. What servant of Christ in that wild region of the Odenwald could advise him? There were, it was true, monasteries nearby; but not a monk within them would be held holy or wise enough, Einhard knew well, for a problem such as this. For several nights he and his household watched in prayer; and each night some one, and sometimes two or three of the watchers, heard in the silence the order from Heaven that the relics must depart elsewhere.

At last Einhard could wait no longer. He set out to walk with the bearers of his treasure whither the Lord and His saints should direct. It was daybreak on January 16, 828. All night long rain had poured down, and the sky was dark with clouds. Once again those who were early abroad bowed in reverence as the holy burden passed, preceded by the Cross, and stayed awhile to join in psalms and hymns.

The Lord directed them, as Einhard tells—and it is his story —to his other village of Mülinheim, and on the morrow they reached it. By this time the multitude, of those escorting and of those awaiting the arrival, was so great that the bearers could not get near the church. An altar was set up, and mass was offered on the slope of a meadow close at hand. The next day, January 18, the relics were safely lying at rest in the apse of the church which was their destiny. As soon as could be, a shrine was made for them, veiled in curtains of linen and silk. Above it, as was the Frankish custom, rose an arch of wood. Nearby stood an altar, and two crosses, one on either side of the altar, symbols of the Lord's Passion.

Here, then, was a little chapel of honor, and here Mass and the Hours were regularly said by priests and clerics set apart for this purpose. In time this little band grew into a religious community, with Einhard once again in charge as lay abbot.

(Those who are not content, with him, to ascribe the cause of this removal of relics from Michelstadt to visions and warnings from Heaven, may find more natural reason in an act of Einhard and his wife. In 819 they had given Michelstadt in Odenwald for permanent holding to the abbey of Lorsch, near Worms, under condition that they themselves should retain right of residence and occupation as long as they should live.)

Now Einhard's church of Mülinheim could in truth be called a home of prayer; yet to his mind it was anything but complete, either in material or in spiritual readiness; and much time was to pass before he could feel satisfied with his labors in its behalf. At the moment, however, duty was urgently calling him to Aachen, since his usual winter stay there was overdue.

He had been there only a week or so when early one morning, as he came into the Palace for his daily conference with the king, he found Hilduin, the archchaplain, present for the same purpose. Naturally they fell into talk, and naturally Einhard spoke of the finding of his relics. Hilduin seemed strangely moved by the story. "Why so excited?" asked Einhard. In answer the archchaplain, after a short silence, said: "You will hear, anyway, from others, so I had better tell you myself." Then he told, half-reluctantly, half-triumphantly, that his priest, worried because he had not been able to obtain the relics which he wanted for Hilduin, had stolen at Pavia part of Einhard's treasure and had proudly brought it home for the delight of his superior. Hilduin, as now he frankly declared to Einhard, had allowed the theft; and at that very moment the sacred dust, twice stolen though it was, was being venerated by a multitude of pilgrims in the church of Saint-Médard at Soissons!

This most unexpected revelation was more than Einhard could bear, and he at once demanded the immediate return of his prize. It took long argument, accusation, pleading, and even threat to induce Hilduin to yield. But yield he did, and gave his promise to return all. The version of the matter which he had offered to Einhard was not entirely correct. The priest had not stolen Einhard's treasure by any daring act of his own, but had obtained part of the relics of St. Marcellinus at Rome by bribing the man appointed to guard them there, a brother of Deusdona. This brother, summoned to Aachen by Einhard, readily confessed his guilt; and Einhard, in his joy over this recovered portion of his treasure, allowed him to go freely on his way.

The relics were now brought from Soissons to Aachen and laid for a while in its Palace church of Our Lady, where the king, Louis the Pious, knelt long before them and where mass was celebrated. In honor of Marcellinus Louis presented to Einhard a small tract of land and a vineyard near the river Ahr; and his wife, Judith, gave the girdle which clasped her dress, a girdle rich with gold and jewels.

For more than forty days the treasure remained in a chapel at Einhard's house at Aachen, and then it was taken with all solemnity to Mülinheim. The month of June 828 had nearly gone by when the missing dust from the body of Marcellinus was placed in Mülinheim's church; and November had come before, in obedience to yet another vision of warning, it was united with the relics which were already there.

7

This story, perhaps more than a little incredible to twentieth-century minds, is of interest since it comes from a narrative written by Einhard himself: his *Translation and Miracles of Saints Marcellinus and Peter*. In it he shows us much of his own character in later life, from the year 827 onward. The visions and miracles of which he tells with faith and gratitude were seen by him himself, he declares, or by witnesses whom he could trust. In the course of years the name of Einhard's dedicated village was changed from Mülinheim to Seligenstadt, "City of the Blessed," the name by which the present little town is known.

And, secondly, Einhard's story, in its long, full detail, is worth reading for the light it throws upon the passion for gaining and owning relics which possessed Christian souls in this ninth century. Here Einhard, without hesitation, scruple, or apology, but with faith and delight, tells that he received and enshrined in his church relics stolen from a church in Rome by his clerk. His only distress rises from the seizure, also through theft, of part of his stolen joy by the archchaplain of the royal Palace for his own happiness and pride!

There is, moreover, a third reason for interest in this narrative of Einhard; for here he also describes his endeavors, through visions occurring at Mülinheim, to save his king, Louis the Pious, from the evil now increasing in his land.

In November 828 Einhard unwillingly left his village for Aachen, since Louis desired his presence at an assembly to be held in December. Wala and Agobard of Lyons were stirring up men's minds against the Emperor. The Court was full of discord, while Einhard's own mind was full of thoughts of his church and its marvels.

He had been on duty in the Palace for some weeks when he received an unexpected visit from his clerk, Ratleic, whose work had kept him at Mülinheim. In Ratleic's hands was a small book, and he had an exciting tale to tell.

"The other night," he said, "when I was in the church for prayer, the blind man, Albric, came up to me and asked to speak with me in private." This Albric had come to Mülinheim two years before, seeking relief from acute sickness of palsy. He had been miraculously cured, as Einhard and many others declared, in the sight of the clergy of its church; and ever since that time he had devoted his life to its service.

"In a little cell of the church," Ratleic continued, "Albric told me that only the night before, as he was waiting for the signal for Office, suddenly a vision had appeared before him of an old, venerable man, whom in his awe he felt must be St. Marcellinus himself. 'No,' the vision had said; 'I am the Archangel Gabriel, to whom the Lord has given charge of all things pertaining to holy Marcellinus and Peter. Now listen with great care to what I have to say. Let Ratleic write it all out and carry the writing to your lord Einhard at the Palace and bid him give it to the Emperor Louis to read. It contains things not only for the Emperor's knowledge, but for action by him. By command from Heaven did those holy Martyrs come expressly to his kingdom.'"

Einhard did as he was ordered. Louis the Pious read the writing. "But," in Einhard's words, "few were the things ordered or advised in it which he cared to carry out."

Forty-six years later, against the year 874, the *Annals of Fulda* recorded: "In January Louis the German, son of the Emperor Louis the Pious, visited the church of Saints Marcellinus and Peter to hold secret conference with certain friends of his father. About February the first he went to Frankfurt and there took counsel with his trusted advisers on problems of his kingdom, especially in regard to prevailing discord. When Lent set in and he turned from secular business to prayer, he had one night a terrible dream. Before him stood the Emperor Louis the Pious, his face wrung by anguish of pain. Then from this vision came words; Louis the German clearly remembered afterwards that they were Latin words. 'I beseech thee, my son,' said his father, dead since 840, 'by Our Lord Jesus Christ and by the Majesty of the Trinity, that thou rescue me from the torture which now holds me fast, that after long endurance I may win the life everlasting.' "

Louis the German, the record of Fulda goes on, was so upset by this vision that he sent letters to all the monasteries of his kingdom of Bavaria, requesting with all his energy that their communities intercede with the Lord for souls in torment. But the comment made here by the annalist of Fulda is rather drastic. "This gives us to understand," he writes, "that although the Emperor Louis the Pious did many things worthy of praise and pleasing to God, yet many things contrary to the law of God did he allow to come to pass in his realm. If, indeed, to omit other matters, he had vigorously resisted the heresy of the Nicolaites, and had paid due heed to the admonitions of Gabriel the Archangel as conveyed to him by Abbot Einhard, perchance he would not have suffered thus."

Einhard does not tell us what these admonitions were; but we can guess from another attempt to warn the Emperor by means of a second document which arrived at Aachen. This was also addressed to Einhard and also written by Ratleic, now back in Mülinheim. From the country district of Höchst in the Odenwald, Ratleic now told, a young peasant girl some sixteen years of age had been brought to the church of Sts. Marcellinus and Peter by her parents. She was possessed by an evil spirit, they said, and in their despair they had come to seek aid. At once one of the priests serving the church began to recite the appointed formula of exorcism. He was interrupted by a flood of Latin from the girl's lips. The priest knew, of course, that the evil spirit was speaking, for the girl had learned no Latin. "Who art thou?" he said. "I," replied the demon, "am named Wiggo; and servant and disciple of Satan I am. For long I was doorkeeper in Hell; but now for some years past with eleven of my comrades I have been laying waste this kingdom of the Franks. Corn and wine and all other fruits born of earth for the use of men have we destroyed, in obedience to orders given us; cattle we have slain by plague; disease and pestilence we have sent forth against men."

"Wherefore was this power given thee?" demanded the priest. "For the wickedness of this people," came the answer, "and the manifold iniquities of those set over them, those who love possessions more than justice. Almost without number are the crimes committed daily by the Frankish people and their rulers: perjury, drunkenness, adultery, manslaughter, theft, pillage. Friend puts no trust in friend; brother hates brother; father has no thought for son. Rarely do men give tithes, more rarely alms. They keep no longer the holy days of the Church; they follow but their own will. Therefore we have been ordered to make them suffer for their faithlessness."

This writing, also, Einhard handed to the Emperor, Louis the Pious.

Such is Einhard's tale. What is the truth concerning these stories of Archangel and devil? That is impossible to say, but in any case they bear witness that, while he was still at Aachen, Einhard was doing all in his power to arouse his Emperor and king to action and by whatever means he could find.

8

Early in 829 Einhard, still at Court, fell seriously ill, and at one time feared that his last hours had come. The Emperor came to visit him, and from his sickbed Einhard did his best to urge him forward. Louis remained friendly, promised assistance for the church at Mülinheim, and continued to be uncertain of what he ought to do.

As we have seen, the spring of 830 brought revolt among the Frankish people. Then in despair Einhard decided to try his influence upon his former pupil Lothar, who was still in Italy. "Word has come to my humble self," he wrote, "that certain men, seeking their own advantage rather than yours, are trying hard to persuade your Highness to forsake the instructions of your father and the obedience which you owe him, by abandoning the post in Italy which he entrusted to you. I hear that you are thinking of coming to Frankland, and for permanent stay. What could be more displeasing to your father, more wrong, more unseemly, than such an act? God knows, I love you, and I send this letter in all faith."

No word came from Lothar, and at last Einhard begged leave from the Emperor to retire from the scene of discord. "I beg and beseech you," his petition ran, "that you have regard for my unhappy state. I am now old and very frail in health. Will you set me free from worldly cares and suffer me to dwell in peace and tranquillity near the tombs of the blessed Martyrs of Christ, your own Patrons at Mülinheim, so that my last hour may find me, not busy in passing and needless cares, but freely given to reading, to prayer, and to meditation on the law of Heaven?"

Fate intervened. The revolt of 830 drove Louis to that meeting with his rebel sons in Compiègne, and the Empress Judith, fearful for her husband's safety, appealed to Einhard by messenger to go at once to the Emperor's support. Sick in mind and in body, he set out for Compiègne, struggled as far as Valenciennes, and from there wrote to Judith:

Most gracious Lady, indeed as your servant I left Aachen to fulfil your desire; but I was so ill upon the road that it took me ten days to travel from Maastricht here to Valenciennes. Such severe pain in kidney and spleen has seized me that now I cannot even ride my horse one mile in a whole day.

I beseech you therefore that you permit me of your grace to go by river to Saint Bavo's abbey at Ghent and to stay there until Almighty God shall give me strength for the journey. As soon as I am able to sit my horse, I will hasten either to you or to my Lord, the Emperor Louis, whichever shall be your will. God is my witness that I have written no falsehood concerning my infirmity. My troubles are such that of the worst of them I cannot speak to you.

But this you must know, that you could not gain greater reward from God in this present need than by permitting me to hasten to the service of the holy Martyrs of Mülinheim as soon as I have the power. I can get there in fifteen days by boat from Ghent.

To a friend, one of the counselors of Louis the Pious, Einhard wrote in greater detail of his troubles, and added: "All the things now coming to pass in the realm were foretold two years ago by those holy Martyrs of Mülinheim." Pleading went also from him at Ghent to the Emperor himself: "I believe that those holy Martyrs will surely intercede for you with God if you are willing to place my service to them before my service to you. For truly in no other part of your realm can I be of greater use to you than at Mülinheim with my Saints, if only you will help me to get there."

9

The month of May 830 found Lothar, with his brothers Pippin and Louis the German, stationed at Compiègne opposite the army of the Emperor. It found Einhard safely in retreat at Mülinheim and in a different mood from that of March and April. He had now returned to the thought of Lothar as the kingdom's best hope. No longer did he deplore the departure from Italy of this son of the Emperor. In May we find him writing to a bishop known to him as one of Lothar's counselors: "I have not ceased to give thanks to God with all my power since I learned that my Lord Lothar has arrived here with you from Italy, safe and sound; and I hope and pray that God will allow me speedily to travel to enjoy the presence of you both. Please, I beg, let nothing lead you to suspect aught of ill in me. I call holy Marcellinus and Peter to witness that I cannot even put into words my love and devotion."

Later he wrote to ask another friend when the General Assembly was to be held—by which we may suppose that he meant that of Nijmegen which took place in October 830—and whether Lothar was to return to Italy or to remain with his father in Frankland? On these two matters, he declared, "depends what I ought to do, if Heaven grant it me to be of some avail." He was watching, it would seem, to see which way the political wind would blow, for Louis or for Lothar, and trying to keep in good grace with both. In a letter to a certain count, sent about the same time, he prayed for his kind offices with Louis the Pious and his sons, "especially my young Lord Lothar, in whose loyalty I have great trust."

In 831 Louis the Pious was once more in power, and he held his stand precariously until the second rebellion of 833–34. The tragedies of these years—of the "Field of Lies," of the capture of the Emperor by his eldest son, of the humiliation of Soissons, of the long imprisonment in Aachen—found Einhard still in the quiet of Mülinheim. From the evidence of letters written by him we may believe that he had no desire to move. The letters, it is true, bear no date; but they seem to point to the events of these or the following years. To a summons from his friend Gerward, librarian of the Palace, he replied: "You urge me, nay, you *advise* me, that I leave my watch over my Martyrs, my constant and bounden duty, to come to the Palace. I would have you know that I have been warned by Heaven not to be absent from them for one week, under pain of punishment; and it takes me in my frail state of health a week just to get to Aachen, to say nothing of any stay there." In sending to Hetti, archbishop of Trier, relics of Marcellinus and Peter—a generous impulse—to grace the dedication of a church by him, Einhard added: "I am quite unable to tell you what you want to know from me, because hardly anything from that source reaches me. Nor am I very keen to hear; for such news does me no good and gives me little pleasure." Once more, to another friend: "I do not ask you to write to me about the state of things in the Palace; for it gives me no joy to hear what is going on there."

Once, it would seem, Einhard did leave his retreat for a little while, when he went to pay homage to Lothar, probably at Aachen in 833. Evidence for this is given in a letter of his to Louis the German, a letter which has come down to us in unsatisfactory manuscript condition, but which has been well edited. After the "Field of Lies" the royal and rebel sons had made new division between themselves of Frankish lands, and Mülinheim had passed to Louis the German. Now, therefore, Einhard was apologizing to Louis for having done homage to Lothar instead of to Louis himself, his feudal lord according to the recent new dividing.

All these events make a sad story. Critics, indeed, have looked with scorn upon this man, himself a Frank, educated at the Court of Charles the Great, brilliant writer of his life, director of his Works, secretary, counselor, and intimate friend of Louis the Pious, recipient of his many gifts, who turned his back upon his Frankish king in the hour of his country's greatest need; who, it would appear, offered his homage to the rebel and victorious sons of his king; who hid himself during Frankland's years of crisis in his own Frankish sanctuary. The only apologies for him are those which we have noted, and they are powerful: his age, sixty years and more; his illness, if this really was genuine; his conviction that he could do his best service for king and country by offering his prayers where he wanted to offer them and where he felt called upon to offer them, before the shrine of his saints at Mülinheim; his thought, it may be, that his land and its people might fare better under Lothar and his supporters than under the weaker rule of Louis the Pious.

Six years of life in Mülinheim—or Seligenstadt, as Einhard called it—were left him after Louis in 834 had been restored by his Frankish prelates to imperial dignity and honor. At first much of his thought was given to completion of the material structure of his church, a task involving heavy cost. Two letters of his are of interest here, both written about 834. One went to his feudal lord, Louis the German, king in Eastern Frankland, praying him for his support. Would he order the bishops of his realm to give their aid to the work which must be carried out for the shrine of the blessed martyrs? The second went to an abbot, probably, as Dümmler has suggested, to that Fulk, who in the same year succeeded Einhard's friend Ansegis in the rule of the monastery of Fontenelle, near Rouen.

"You remember," Einhard wrote, "that talk of ours, when we were both at the Palace, about the permanent roof of the church of Saints Marcellinus and Peter, and our agreement that I should buy lead for its covering at a price of fifty pounds? So many things have happened since that day, and the matter may easily have slipped your mind. But I really am worried. It is entirely necessary now to get this roofing done, and I do not know how much time on this earth is left to me. Please, will you write to me what, if anything, has been done about it?"

Some two years later, in 836, all his work was stayed for a considerable while by the shock of his wife's death. Imma had been his constant and faithful partner in all the undertaking at Seligenstadt. We have two letters written by her, of no particular interest except as those of a woman in this early medieval age. The Emperor came to visit him, to offer words of comfort and sympathy. Louis bore Einhard no lasting resentment for his lack of support during those years of trial, 830 to 833; perhaps he was too painfully aware of weakness in his own soul.

At last, however, time brought recovery, and once again the hours free from prayer were given to study and to writing. Many are the letters still in our possession which show Einhard's eagerness to aid his friends or his feudal vassals on his estates and abbey lands. Many letters came also from these, asking his help, and they were always answered. In the latter part of 837 he wrote a last warning to Louis the Pious in regard to the menace of omen and portent. Some time before, a comet had appeared in the sky; all who saw it had been alarmed at its ugly, threatening look. What had it meant? Most certainly, Einhard reasoned, it had told of some evil, past or to come, and men must straightway call to God in penitence. If only, he went on, the disaster which it declared might already have passed into record; if only this omen of ill were recalling the descent already made in June of this year by Viking pirates upon the Frisian coast! "I fear, however," Einhard concluded, "that something even more drastic is in store for us."

We think of him, especially, at work in 836 in his home at Mülinheim upon the short but carefully considered writing which gave him relief from sorrow. Here he told his thoughts concerning that subject of fierce contention in the eighth and ninth centuries, the attitude properly due from men to images and pictures of sacred things and persons.

In this treatise, still to be read under the title of *An Inquiry Concerning Adoration of the Cross*, Einhard made clear distinction between that "adoration" which is often called "veneration," a bowing or prostration of the body in reverence before the thing or the person that tells of God and belongs to Him, and "adoration" in its higher and more proper sense, the prostration of mind and spirit before God Himself. To God, indeed, he declared, belong both "veneration" and "adoration," the full homage of both body and spirit. "We venerate with bowed body the Cross, and with the eyes of our spirit we adore Him Who hung thereon. Thus shall the Cross hold its own proper honour; and God, in Whom and from Whom and through Whom, as said blessed Augustine, cometh their holiness to all things which are holy, with due veneration is adored."

As Einhard was writing on this distinction between the reverence due to God and to the creatures of God, another problem occurred to him, more difficult to determine in his view of matters divine. Adoration of God is offered in prayer; and prayer, of whatever kind, to be acceptable to God must be rightly offered. As said Saint James: "Ye ask and receive not, because ye ask amiss"; and Saint Paul, in his Epistle to the Romans: "We know not what we should pray for as we ought." Now the Catholic faith holds firmly that the Father, the Son, and the Holy Spirit are of one substance and power in the unity of the Godhead. But the Lord Christ taught men on earth to pray to the Father. Can we therefore pray aright when we depart from this manner of supplication taught us in the Lord's Prayer? Did not the Third Council of Carthage in 397 place on record its belief that prayer at the altar should always be directed to God the Father? Is it, therefore, right to direct our private and secret prayers to God the Son, Our Lord Christ? Or to His apostles and martyrs? May we invoke those whose souls, we know well, are ever in the Presence of God? "For I remember," Einhard writes, "that certain men have said that the prayers of saints who have left this earth may avail for the good of those who are still here in the body." He continues: "While I was working on the matter of Adoration of the Cross, I fell upon this problem. If it were not one which touches God, I should call it one proper for Hercules. And with that I must leave it."

10

We end on a happier note. It is good to think of Einhard in his last years continuing instant in prayer, wrestling in mind with problems of theology. He died on March 14, 840, some three months before his King-Emperor, Louis the Pious, when he was about seventy years old. He was buried in his church at Mülinheim, and Hraban Maur, abbot of Fulda, once his home, wrote his epitaph:

> Enter this church nor scorn to know
> What it both holds, and, holding, tells.
> Here lies enshrined a noble man,
> Einhard the name his father gave.
> Skilled, honest, eloquent in word
> Was he, and much for art he did.

Nourished in Charles the king's own hall,
Through him he wrought abundantly.
He honoured, too, these saints of his,
Bringing their bodies here from Rome,
To help men's prayers and heal their souls
And win him, too, with Christ a crown.
O Christ, man's Saviour, Maker, Lord,
Grant him in love eternal rest!

The lines, undistinguished in merit of verse, show at least that Hraban Maur, that consistent supporter of Louis the Pious, bore Einhard no enmity at his death. And the brethren of Mülinheim's community must now and again have remembered with pious affection the words which their lay abbot, absent through some brief necessity from his beloved home, had written them not long before he died:

"Be mindful, dear ones, I beseech you in fatherly love, of your promise to honour our holy Martyrs with service constantly, that Our Lord in His goodness through their intercession may give it me to find you in sound health. Guard yourselves ever against the ancient Enemy, lest by some wile he take you unawares. In zeal and in obedience attend upon the Divine Praises; carry your burdens with the help of Christ and His Saints; and may your souls go forward day by day."

Chapter IV

AMALAR OF METZ

1

Under the Roman Empire and under the Merovingian kings of France, Metz was a city of high importance. In the sixth and seventh centuries it was the royal seat of the rulers of Austrasia, land of the eastern Franks. From Arnulf, bishop of Metz, and Pippin of Landen, controller, or, as the title went, mayor, of the royal Palace, the Carolingian reigning house of France in the eighth and ninth centuries drew its direct descent. Metz, then, held its own place in secular interest to Charles the Great and to his son, Louis the Pious. In matters of the Church, also, its tradition was always present in their minds.

It was always present, also, in the mind of Amalar, to whom we now turn. From Metz he drew in part that passion for liturgical research which was to give the ninth century in him one of its most original thinkers. It had been Chrodegang, bishop of Metz, who had brought from Rome to Frankland in 754 a copy of Roman liturgical texts. The Frankish texts, partly Gallican, partly Roman-Italian-Gregorian, in the course of time had grown sadly out of accord with texts used in Rome. Chrodegang, together with King Pippin, worked hard to bring Frankish usage into conformity with the Roman. Schools of liturgical chant, trained and inspired by Roman teaching and example, were set up at Metz by Chrodegang and at Rouen by its bishop Remedius, schools which in the same eighth century became renowned for their importance and for their influence.

This work for the Frankish liturgy under King Pippin at Metz, at Rouen, and at other Frankish cathedral cities was to hand down his first inspiration to young Amalar. A second lay for him in the carrying on of this work by Pippin's son and successor, King Charles the Great. As Chrodegang and Remedius had aided Pippin, so Alcuin, head of the Palace School in the royal city of

Aachen, aided Charles. Once again a copy of Roman texts was sought from Rome. With its aid Alcuin compiled a new liturgy for Frankland, primarily Roman-Gregorian in character, but containing additions from current Frankish national and local usage which should satisfy the needs and desires of Frankish folk. Once again, then, schools teaching Roman chant were set up at Aachen and in other Frankish centers.

2

Amalar was born about 775. Tradition, though not documented proof, has held that he was brought up and ordained deacon and priest in the diocese of Metz. In any case, he was brought up in the memory of the work by Chrodegang; and as a young man he was studying Alcuin's revised Gregorian Book of the Mass.

We meet him first, aptly enough, as a student under Alcuin, possibly at Aachen, more probably at St. Martin's abbey in Tours, after Alcuin had retired from Aachen to become its ruler. With joy Amalar listened to the chanting of Mass and Office on Easter eve and on the days running from the octave of Pentecost to July 1. "I seemed to be but a boy," he writes, "in the presence of Alcuin, the most learned master in all our land."

After this brief glimpse of him in his early twenties, he is again lost to our sight for some thirteen years. Possibly he spent part of this time at Lyons, that city so well known to history, where the river Saône flows into the Rhône. Its cathedral was ruled from 798 until 816 by an archbishop named Leidrad, appointed by Charles the Great. Shortly before Charles died in 814, Leidrad sent to the king a report on his work. In one text of this report we read:

"After I received by your order the charge of this Church of Lyons I did all in my power to gather here a responsible body of clergy, and I think that in great part I have succeeded. At my request you allowed me to call here a cleric from the Church of Metz, through whom, by God's help and your generosity, Sire, the manner of chanting in our ritual here at Lyons has been so changed that, so far as has been possible for us, it seems now to approach the Order of Liturgy followed in your own Palace

Chapel. I have now, indeed, a School of Chant for my Cathedral, and many of its members are so well trained that they can even teach other men."

There is no proof that this "cleric" from Metz was Amalar himself; in later years Amalar with good cause found little joy in the thought of Lyons. But the suggestion has its interest. The word "cleric" need not deter us. No evidence proves that Amalar was ever a monk, although, as he is occasionally addressed as "Abbot Amalar," like many others who made no profession of religious vows, like his master, Alcuin, indeed, he may have been for a while in charge of a monastery.

Much has happened when we see him again. He is now a bishop, indeed archbishop, of Trier, some sixty-five miles from Metz. His appointment by Charles the Great and his consecration took place in or shortly after 809, for his predecessor, one Wizo, died at that time. One of his earliest acts as bishop, if, as may well be believed, he was the "Amalar, a certain bishop of Gaul" mentioned in Rimbert's *Life of St. Anskar*, was the consecration by order of King Charles of the first church built for the people who lived north of the Elbe, on a site where the city of Hamburg was afterward to stand. Tradition has placed this consecration in 811.

Not long after his return to Frankland Amalar received a letter from the king, requesting him, as Charles requested other prelates of his realm, to give to him an account of the method of instruction used by him and his "suffragans" in their preparation of candidates for baptism. The king wanted, also, a clear explanation of the meaning of the various parts of the baptismal rite itself.

Amalar dutifully complied. In regard to "suffragans," he wrote, he was not sure of the king's meaning. Was he referring to priests, deacons, or others of the lesser clergy? If, however, Charles was referring to bishops who in their respective sees had been under the authority of Trier before he himself had arrived there, he hoped that as bishop he would not be blamed if he admitted the truth: that so far he had not ventured to wield an authority over them which he had not considered officially to be his.

Behind these words lay a lack of harmony of which Amalar was doubtless uneasily conscious. Charles himself held him as metropolitan of an archdiocese centered in Trier, as one in authority over his colleagues, the bishops of Verdun, of Toul, of Metz. They, for their part, had never consented to such jurisdiction in his hands, had never held him as their metropolitan.

The king, whatever he thought of Amalar's honest admission, showed further confidence in him. In 813 he sent him as envoy to Constantinople, with a companion named Peter, abbot of a monastery of St. Silvester at Nonántola, near Bologna. The two ambassadors bore a letter from the Frankish ruler to the Emperor Michael Rangabé. It told of Frankish gratitude to heaven for peace concluded between the Empires of East and of West, and stated that Charles was sending Amalar of Trier and Abbot Peter to bring back word to him of its confirmation by the imperial power in the East.

3

The time was spring, and as the boat carrying the two men and their secretaries made its way along the coast, it fell upon stormy weather. Peril, terror, lack of sleep, and seasickness roused rebellion among its crew and passengers alike. Twice it put into harbor, once at Dyrrachium (Durazzo) on the Adriatic in Albania, and again upon the ancient isle of Aegina, now Aiyina, in the Saronic Gulf off Greece. In the end the captain ordered speed, since he was in a hurry to reach Constantinople before the cold of autumn.

There further trouble was in store for Amalar and Peter. In June 813, while they were in mid-journey, the Emperor Michael had been defeated in battle near Adrianople by the dreaded Krum, khan of the Bulgarians, who had already killed Michael's predecessor, Nicephorus. The Emperor's life was saved; but he was unpopular in Constantinople, and this defeat had encouraged a strong force of his subjects to rise against him in favor of one of their army's generals, an Armenian. In July they had proclaimed this soldier as Emperor, as Leo V. Boldly he had then entered Constantinople and had seized its throne, only to face a long siege of the city by the undaunted Bulgar hordes under Krum.

Leo had been Emperor only six days when Krum marched to his attack with a multitude of barbarian fighters on horse and on foot. Around the walls of Constantinople he paraded. He offered pagan sacrifice before the Golden Gate and sent to Leo his messengers to announce his insolent purpose: he would fasten his spear as victor upon the Gate itself. When they returned, bearing from Leo an equally spirited refusal, he retired to his camp; within his heart he knew that he could not take the city by force. Instead of assault, therefore, he sought conference with the Emperor. He came to this conference without fear and was met by treachery, for Leo almost contrived his death. In his fury Krum ravaged lands, churches, and palaces near the city and along the shores of the Bosporus.

In the midst of these doings of terror Amalar and Peter managed to gain entrance to Constantinople. Once within, however, they found its walls bristling with soldiers. For two months they wandered about its streets, looking into church after church as their chief points of interest. Amalar had at least one reward, for in St. Sophia he listened with fervent absorption to the Eastern liturgy of the Mass. Everywhere, however, they were met by suspicious stares from sentinels and guards and by hostile words. It was not the business of stranger monks and clergy to walk abroad through the city, the sentinels told them; they should attend to their own duties in their own quarters.

At last Leo bethought him of these envoys who had arrived in this time of crisis. Since he had no wish to vex the power in Frankland, he now received them graciously and assured them of his will for peace. Promptly they took their leave and made for the harbor. But by this time it was 814, and the storms of early spring were raging. Added to all the dangers and discomforts of their former voyage was terror now of attack by Moorish and Slavic pirates; however, they lived to tell the tale.

Amalar might indeed lack courage to rule his suffragans at Trier; but he had plenty for his own adventures. On the way to Constantinople the travelers had stayed briefly at Zadar (Zara), now a town under Italian rule in a small region carved out from Yugoslavia. Amalar knew it as Iadera, a Byzantine city in Dalmatia. There he had hurried to find its bishop. Soon, as they talked, he discovered a difference between the Greek and the Frankish Church in regard to the dates prescribed for the conferring of holy orders, and he roused up all the bishop's clergy to discuss this during dinner. The argument waxed fierce; and only by firm and repeated refusal did the orthodox Frankish Amalar escape the invitation, hideous to him in its irregularity, of raising a deacon to the priesthood on a day outside the Frankish Ember seasons, on St. Peter's Vigil, June 28. Not even the storms of the Adriatic had been able to keep him from debate and argument. During both the voyages, outward and return, as the boat heaved and tossed and everyone but him felt sick unto death, he had considered with all energy and discussed with anyone able to listen the proper meaning of some of the ritual of the Mass!

This expedition, then, of 813–14 bore fruit other than political. Once back in Italy, we may think that Amalar seized the chance of making a first visit to St. Peter's. If he did, he kept his eyes alert. He tells us how surprised he was to see the Holy Father, Leo III, enter to celebrate mass at daybreak instead of waiting until the third hour. Did not the Church's law prescribe the third hour, the hour of the Lord's crucifying, for celebration of mass by the Pope? Had Leo made an exception to this rule because of some necessity?

The richer through his study of liturgical usage in East and in West, Amalar now returned to Frankland for report at Aachen; not, indeed, to Charles the Great, who had died during his absence, but to Louis the Pious. In this same year of 814 he sent to his fellow-traveler, Peter, the abbot of Nonántola, some verses— *Versus Marini*—describing the adventures of that journey to Constantinople. His hexameters here are as rough as the waves which tossed him; but they give us interesting details. In the last lines he tells Peter of his sorrow in the loss of his king and friend:

> Be mindful, Peter, of your comrade of the sea,
> In charity, my Father. Exiled, sad I am;
> Sad is the sky, weary am I for death of Charles.
> God join us side by side in all eternity
> With him, once king to us.

4

Amalar did not return, it seems, to his bishop's seat at Trier, for in 816 we find Hetti established in it. Perhaps his leaving was due to trouble with those suffragan bishops, or to his intense longing for leisure for research. This longing, we do know, he was able henceforth to satisfy. In 814, together with the *Verses on the Sea*, he sent to Peter three other gifts: a brief *Interpretation of the Canon of the Mass;* also, a gift for which Peter was eagerly waiting, the argument of that storm-beset discussion on the liturgy; and, thirdly, a longer *Interpretation,* made in the peace of free hours at home. These two last writings are to be found in the latest, the best edition of Amalar, by Hanssens, as Codex I and Codex II, or, together, as *Missae expositionis geminus Codex.*

Amalar was sensitive all his life to the opinions of his fellow-men; in years to come he was to suffer greatly from these. He loved his work and feared to see it condemned. Now in the first paragraph of Codex I he wrote: "If any reader of this work of mine suffers nausea as he gets to the end, he is not to blame me, but himself. Before he ever began to read it, he knew quite well how little renown I have for scholarship, and it is only his own fault if he has stuck to it until the last page." And in a letter to Peter: "I beg you, Father, not to publish my work openly, lest I be gnawed by the teeth of carping critics or mocked for my scant learning by the loud laughter of the proud."

In his own heart he knew well what he wanted to do. As he tells Peter here: "In my belief there is no ordinance of the Church, either of ancient or of modern days, which does not have its own reason. Everything which is done in the ritual of the liturgy has its own proper meaning, distinct and designed. If in heathen days men sought to find reasonable interpretation of material things and acts, if in the Bible the unjust steward used material things for his own support and won thereby commendation from the Lord, how much more should the Christian seek to gain from the human acts and provision of this earth the profit of his eternal soul?"

These words might serve as a keynote for our understanding of Amalar. For nearly twenty years, from 814 until 831, his absorption in the study of liturgical words and their meaning is the only thing which we can definitely state as known concerning his life. We do not even know where he worked, although now and again signs seem to point toward Aachen and the Palace of

Louis the Pious. From time to time he carried on correspondence with men of high standing in the Frankish realm. He wrote to Jeremiah, archbishop of Sens, and to Jonas, bishop of Orléans, anxious to learn how in their opinion the Name Jesus really ought to be abbreviated—in the Greek or in the Latin way? He wrote to Rantgar, bishop of Noyon, sending him at his request a discourse on the meaning of the Old and the New Testament.

Twice, indeed, evidence has suggested action of importance on his part during these years. Perhaps he did play a significant part at the time of the Synod of Aachen in 816, when rules were laid down for the discipline of clergy who followed the canonical, the secular life in community, as distinct from the Benedictine life of monks. A chronicler of the eleventh century, Adémar de Chabannes, gives this evidence: "The Synod, held in 816, ordered that a Rule should be made for canonical clergy in the form of a book composed of excerpts from the writings of the Fathers of the Church.... This book Amalar, a deacon, by order of the Emperor has compiled from various teachings of these Doctors, using a copious supply of their works, which were obtained by him through a free access to the Palace Library." Since, however, in the same third book of his *Chronicle*, Adémar writes of "the bishop Amalar" who was sent as envoy to Constantinople, his statement concerning "Amalar the deacon" should be read with caution.

More probably Amalar was one of the two envoys sent by the bishops gathered at the Synod of Paris in 825 to deliver the official report of their deliberations to the Emperor Louis the Pious. These deliberations had dealt with that vexed problem of the proper attitude of mind of the faithful concerning pictures and images in their churches. A preface to the report told that the bishops were sending it by the hands of "the venerable persons, Halitgar and Amalar." Halitgar was bishop of Cambrai; he was afterward sent, in 828, to Constantinople by Louis as ambassador in regard to this same matter of images. By 828 Leo V had long been dead, murdered on Christmas Day 820 in St. Sophia, and Michael II was now Emperor. Amalar, perhaps, had expected again to accompany Halitgar; and it is possible that one of the letters of Einhard was concerned with this plan. Einhard, indeed, as secretary of Louis the Pious, did at one time write instructions to Amalar in regard to a journey he was to make in the Emperor's service. But he did not go again to Constantinople in 828; Halitgar traveled with another companion.

Did Amalar feel strongly concerning the tragic events in his Frankish realm, the strife of parties, the imperial penitence of these years? If he did, there is no evidence of action on his part. There are, it is true, a few words of some interest in a letter written by him in 822 or some following year to Hilduin, abbot of Saint-Denis and archchaplain in the royal Court. With deep respect for Hilduin's high office Amalar here is again seeking assurance on matters of Church ritual and practice. He apologizes for a lack of clarity in his letter: "Often a cloud of temporal anxieties overshadows one's mind," he writes, "so that it cannot see clearly the serene light which is above. Just now I myself am in many ways shaken upon the wheel of my own life."

About 823 he offered to Louis the Pious the first edition of the longest work he took in hand. With his other works it still stands in its Latin, known as his *Liber Officialis,* or *Liber de officiis ecclesiasticis,* his book on the interpretation of the ritual of mass and offices of the Church. His preface to this first edition, in the form of a letter to the Emperor Louis, told that he had long been troubled in mind:

Last summer it seemed to me that, if I may put it thus, I was sitting in some cell deep underground, when suddenly there shone aslant upon me as from a window rays of light in my darkness. So hungry have I been for knowledge that I have not allowed the fear of expert authority to curb me. Instead I have written down here what I myself have seemed to see. And now I send this to you, as the one to whom I would above all entrust it.

Indeed I have been truly anxious to learn what was in the minds of those who in times past composed our ritual. Yet I fear that I have not always been able to adhere to recognized tradition. And so I am trusting for my defence against criticism to St. Augustine's words in his *On Christian Doctrine:* "Whoever shall declare his reasoned belief in such a manner as shall work for charity, and yet cannot definitely prove that his belief is here exactly that of the authority whom he is following— that man is not to be judged guilty of a wilful lie."

Will you, Sire, mark that whenever I insert among my own words sayings borrowed from the Fathers, I place a mark between theirs and mine? I would not be thought guilty of stealing from them.

Some five years later a second edition was ready and was sent to the Palace. With it Amalar made public two letters he had written recently. One was addressed to a certain Hetto, whom Hanssens believes to have been a monk, also known as Haito, of Reichenau, the famous abbey on Lake Constance. He wanted Hetto to decide for him whether the words "cherubim" and "seraphim" should be written as masculine or as neuter in gender. He had searched the work of Jerome and of Bede, but they had not settled the question for him.

The other letter was sent to a pupil of his, a rude and arrogant young man named Guntard, who had rebuked his master Amalar for his habit of spitting, even after mass and communion. In answer Amalar told his "beloved son in Christ" that at first he had been disgusted by the words of Guntard, but that, as he was now on a journey and had had plenty of time to think the matter over, he had decided to instruct Guntard's mind and free it from "vain suspicion."

All things, Guntard must know, are pure to the pure in heart. Among the evils which the Lord listed in His teaching as coming forth from the heart, He did not include spitting, which does not proceed from the heart nor does it defile a man. It is a natural habit, occasions no sin, and makes for health. Did not the Lord Himself make clay from spittle and thus heal the blind? Did He not spit and touch the tongue of the man who had an impediment in his speech, and did not that man straightway speak plain?

"My son," he writes, "I trust the Lord that if my mind is loyal and humble in His sight, He will give me His Body for the quickening of my soul; and that what must be cast forth from my body for its health's sake, He will not allow to be cast out for my soul's undoing. Flee, my son, from the waves of Pelagianism to the sure harbor of Augustine, the Augustine who taught us that each man shall do that which, according to the faith within him, he honestly believes is to be done. Let each follow his conscience. Zacchaeus and the centurion sprang no quarrel in the Gospel when Zacchaeus with joy received the Lord into his home, and the centurion said: 'Lord, I am not worthy that Thou shouldest come under my roof.' "

5

Another journey was in store for Amalar. This was made in 831, when Louis the Pious sent him to Rome on a private mission to Pope Gregory IV. By this time the first rebellion of his sons against the Emperor had passed into quiet, and Louis may well have wished to strengthen his cause in the eyes of the Holy See. Amalar fulfilled his duty; but he was far more eager to talk with the Pope on matters liturgical than political. Perhaps Gregory IV was glad of this, since two years afterward, in 833, he was to journey across the Alps to Frankland as a supporter of Lothar, the Emperor's rebel heir. In any case he seems to have had little time for Amalar. He gave him into the charge of the priests of St. Peter's and especially bade Theodore, archdeacon of Rome, to answer his endless questions.

Chief, however, among Amalar's enquiries was one which he did manage to put before the Pope. Where, he asked, could he find a copy of the text of the liturgical offices as chanted in Rome? The answer came brief and direct. The Pope had not a single copy to give to any one. He regretted this deeply; but, he said, all the spare texts of the offices as used in Rome had been carried off by Wala, abbot of Corbie, near Amiens, when he had been in Italy as adviser to young King Lothar in 823–24. There was nothing for Amalar to do, he decided, but to visit Corbie on his way home.

To his delight he found in its library all he wanted: the Offices of the Night, in three books, and those of the Day, in one, all in the current Roman use, with all the changes and additions which had been introduced, as Amalar knew, in the last quarter of the eighth century. "From an ocean of desire for knowledge," he declared, "I have set my sails for the harbor of peace." Permission was given him to borrow them, provided he stayed at Corbie. There he now settled down. He had worked for long on the form and meaning of the liturgy of the mass. Now he would work on the offices, the Hours of the Day and of the Night, chanted in community in monastery and cathedral; he would now build a new *corpus* of chants in a fusion of Roman and Frankish texts.

This *corpus*, under the name of his *Antiphonary*, was duly compiled by him between 831 and 835, doubtless in great part at Corbie. Only its *Prologue* now remains to us. In it he describes his method of work: "In some places I found that our Frankish books were in need of correction from the Roman, and I made the changes required, writing against the passages I borrowed from the Roman text the letter R, for Rome. In other places I found that our own books were drawn up in a better and more reasonable manner, and I left these better readings just as they were, writing against them the letter M, for Metz. I also put in some additions of my own, prompted by my own thought, where I felt that I could improve upon the books of both Rome and Metz. These alterations of mine I marked with the letters I and C, signifying my prayers for the *indulgence* and *charity* of those who should read them."

In allowing and introducing changes in his new compilation Amalar summoned to his support the words of St. Gregory the Great, written from Rome to the perplexed Augustine, missionary bishop of Canterbury in England during the late sixth and the early seventh century: "My brother, choose from individual and divers churches such things as are religious and right in each. Bind them as it were into one book, and make them familiar in custom to the English mind."

In the same *Prologue* to his *Antiphonary* for the Frankish Church Amalar told of the debt which his book owed to Helisachar, chancellor of the Frankish realm under Louis the Pious from 814 to 819. The story of his work for chanted texts in Frankland is worth recalling here.

As chancellor, Helisachar was of course resident for long periods at Aachen, where he made it his practice to attend with King Louis the Offices of the Day and of the Night in the royal chapel. He was both observant and keen of intellect, and, as time went on, he became more and more impatient of what he held a complete lack of sense in the chanting of matins. He had reason for his annoyance. The Frankish use had made here an unwise departure from the Roman. At the end of each lesson of matins the Roman custom prescribed the chanting of a brief text drawn from the Bible, called the "Responsory." This was followed by another text called the "Versicle," and then this "Versicle" in turn was followed by the chanting in full of the "Responsory" a second time. Here is an example:

R. *Tu es Petrus, ait Dominus ad Simonem*

V. *Ecce Sacerdos magnus qui in diebus suis placuit Deo*

R. *Tu es Petrus, ait Dominus ad Simonem.*

The Frankish use, however, only repeated the second half of the "Responsory," in this case, *ait Dominus ad Simonem*. This gave entirely the wrong intention; for it would be concluded by ignorant listeners that the Lord said to Simon: "Lo, a great Priest who in his days found favour with God," instead of saying: "Thou art Peter." Other examples caused even greater confusion of thought.

For a short while after the accession of Louis the Pious in February 814 and his own arrival in the Palace, Helisachar grumbled alone in his mind. Then to his delight Nidibrius, archbishop of Narbonne, arrived at Court and gave him sympathy. "We have the same stupid practice at Narbonne," he said. "Why, with all your knowledge, Helisachar, why don't you get to work and produce something better for all Frankish choirs to sing?"

Helisachar decided that he would. For years he toiled; and at last, between 819 and 822, when he was no longer chancellor, he wrote from his abbey of Angers to Nidibrius at Narbonne that he had finished what Nidibrius had asked him to do. He had searched throughout the Bible; he had consulted the writings of all the learned authorities within his reach, and finally he had compiled a new book of Responsories and Versicles for the Night Office in Frankland, throwing out the repetition of those half-lines which gave the wrong sense, if, indeed, any sense, and inserting in their place those which fitted well the Versicles preceding them. It would have been easier merely to return to the Roman custom of repeating the whole text of the Responsory; but both Helisachar and Nidibrius were keen on Frankish tradition, and they liked half-lines, provided only that they made sense!

6

During the years 831 to 833 Amalar was also hard at work in preparing the third edition of his *Liber Officialis,* made public about 833. In this he now embodied the wider knowledge he had gained from the answers to those many questions in Rome. The answers were the more valuable because sometimes he had found that the current customs at Rome differed even from the liturgical texts in use there.

He begins this *Liber Officialis,* his symbolic interpretation of the liturgy, with the round of the Church's seasons from Septuagesima until Pentecost. At Septuagesima the people of God, gathered in hope of their souls' renewing, are as though strangers in exile, far away from Jerusalem, in the time of the Captivity; with Nature, also, they mourn their winter, in body as in soul. No *Alleluia* is heard, no *Gloria in Excelsis;* for they are in Babylon, and how shall they sing the Lord's song in a strange land? They stand, as it were, idle, uncertain of their future, hearing but hardly understanding the invitation to toil onward. Sexagesima finds them awakened to consciousness of their distance from God. They have now entered the field of labor and have begun to plant the seed of life. At Quinquagesima they have passed from their first awakening; the seed has taken root and is springing up on its way toward harvest. The first Sunday in Lent finds them hard at work, building in their fields the temple of Jerusalem. For forty-six years that temple was in building; for forty-six days, from Ash Wednesday to Holy Saturday, God's people still strive to set in order the house of their souls.

We are now in Holy Week. In the symbolism of Amalar the altar, stripped and bare from Holy Thursday until Easter eve, brings to mind the flight of the disciples, the stripping from the Lord of their presence, their love and loyalty. As each man of the congregation of Israel took for his household a lamb of the flock on the tenth day and killed it for the Passover on the fourteenth, so Christ entered Jerusalem on Palm Sunday and offered Himself on Good Friday in sacrifice for men. No kiss of peace is given on that day, Amalar declares, through remembrance of the Judas kiss of treachery; yet the Cross is venerated and the Lord of Redemption is adored. No Host, he continues, is consecrated on that day, no wine of the chalice. Did not the disciples of the Lord on that day remain joyless and inactive, in hiding for fear of the Jews? Did not the Lord say to them on Holy Thursday: "I shall not drink again of this fruit of the vine until that day when I drink it anew with you in my Father's kingdom?"

On Easter eve the Paschal candle is blessed, to cast upon the night of this world the light of Resurrection, the more especially for those who are baptized this day into the Church. For them especially the words of the Epistle of the mass on Easter night have their meaning: "If ye then be risen with Christ, seek those things which are above. . . . For ye are dead, and your life is hid with Christ in God."

The year passes on to the Rogation Days which come before the Feast of the Ascension. Amalar tells the story of their origin, which he found in Gregory of Tours: how in the later fifth century great terror fell upon Vienne, the city on the Rhône in France, through shock of earthquake; how its bishop, Mamertus, ordered fast and prayer of three days; and how from that time the custom continued of imploring God's blessing upon the fertility of the earth.

At Pentecost, again in Amalar's symbolism, the rushing, mighty wind drove from the disciples gathered in the upper room all earthly greed and desire just as it drives the dust from the face of the earth. The tongues of fire betokened for him that preaching which was to kindle a flame in the hearts of men; the Holy Spirit under the symbol of a dove spoke of that simplicity of compassion which bears ill-will to none.

The Ember Days bring Amalar's meditation on the Church's seasons to a close. Placed in spring, summer, autumn, and winter, by prescription of fast they restrain the faithful from overindulgence in the joys peculiar to these times of the year: from delighting overlong in the beauty of spring; from yielding to the hot desire of summer; from weariness and failure to gather the harvest of the soul in autumn; from the repletion of the fleshly joys of winter which turn the heart from God. Wednesday brings remembrance of the Jews, taking counsel to slay Christ; on the Friday they slew Him; on the Saturday the disciples mourned

His death. The Lessons of these Days in Amalar's thought speak especially to those soon to be ordained.

We come now in Amalar's *Liber* to the liturgy and ritual of the Mass. As he watches the gathering around the altar, he thinks of the clergy: *clerici*, from *klerus*, lot or heritage; their lot or portion is of the Lord. The Roman tonsure speaks to him of the shearing away of foolish, idle thoughts from the head, the seat of man's knowledge of God; its rounded form recalls the circle of virtue guided by reason. The lower orders of the ministry remind him of ancient tradition. The janitors are the gate-keepers of the Old Testament, standing east, west, north, and south; each lector is an Ezra, opening the book in the sight of all the people to read to them of the Law; the acolytes are the sons of Aaron who tended the lamp in the "tent of meeting" from evening to morning before the Lord; the deacons and subdeacons are the Levites and their assistants. When he saw the bishop with his priests at Pontifical Mass, Amalar thought back to the first chapter of the Epistle to Titus, quoted, he remembered, by Saint Ambrose and Saint Jerome, and to the very early days of the Church. Then, so he believed from this evidence, the "presbyter" or "elder" was identical with the "episcopus" or "overseer." Both words were used of one and the same minister, until a distinction grew up between the two, and the threefold ordering of subdeacon, deacon, and priest became the rule.

The Introit is chanted. From the entry of the ministers of the Mass until the offertory, this *Liber Officialis* of Amalar sees represented here before the altar a symbol of the life and teaching on earth of the Lord and His disciples. The entry of the celebrant recalls the advent of the Lord to this world of men. The celebrant stands before the altar, not alone in body, but alone in soul; he alone, for himself and his people, is to make oblation to God alone. And so the *Kyrie eleison* is in a sense especially his prayer: that he may keep his mind on what he will say with his lips; that he may be worthy of his words to God, so far as human nature allows. On Sundays and feast days the bishop chants the song of the angels in the *Gloria in Excelsis;* the deacon goes to the altar to receive the Book of the Gospels, as, in the vision of Isaiah, the word of the Lord was to go forth from Jerusalem. In the thought of Amalar the altar represents Jerusalem, and to him the Gospel is the teaching of Christ in the Temple.

The Gospel read, Amalar looks with new vision at the celebrant, clothed in the holy garments of his ministry: in the amice, which encircles his throat and guards his voice and his words; in the alb which envelops him with its white folds and tells of his protection from evil; in the chasuble, which brings to mind the discipline of his calling, its hunger and thirst, its watchings, its lessons and psalms of Office, its study, active work, and silence. "In such things," he writes, "no leader of sacred ministry should be negligent."

The second part of the Mass begins. To Amalar it symbolizes the events of Holy Week, in Jerusalem, in Gethsemane, upon Calvary. It opens with the offering by the people of themselves, as signified by their gifts of bread and wine before the altar. The celebrant receives their offering, and then passes to prepare himself for the supreme Oblation, the offering of that Sacrifice of the Lord made once for all upon the Cross. He washes his hands that they may be clean and his heart pure; he calls aloud to the people to unite with him in thanksgiving, in the *Sanctus* and the *Hosanna in Excelsis,* which remind Amalar of Isaiah's song of the seraphim and of the cry of the multitudes that went before and followed the Lord as He entered Jerusalem on the Day of Palms.

The priest is now entering upon the canon of the Mass, and, as the Lord prayed thrice in Gethsemane before His betrayal, so here to Amalar there is threefold petition: first, for the Holy Catholic Church throughout the world; secondly, for the faithful now present and for those for whom the celebrant and his people in duty bound desire to intercede; thirdly, for all priests, "that we in all things be safeguarded by the protection of the Lord." After the words *in electorum tuorum iubeas grege numerari*—"bid us to be numbered in the flock of Thine elect"—in Amalar's view the liturgy passes from the Sacrifice offered for the elect, the pure in heart and faithful, to the Oblation of the Lord upon the Cross for all sinners.

The Consecration takes place. Then we come in this *Liber Officialis* to the third part of Amalar's thought of the Mass, its symbolizing of the Lord's Resurrection and Ascension. Whenever

Amalar himself as celebrant after the Consecration placed a particle of the Host in the chalice, he thought back from this *commixtio* to the symbolic remembrance of body and spirit united once again in the Risen Christ. As he turned to bless the people at the end of the Mass, he thought to see in himself as its priest a reflection of the Lord, leading out His disciples to Bethany and lifting up His hands to bless them before they went their various ways.

These are but a few fragments from the immense abundance of symbolic interpretation poured out by Amalar in this *Liber Officialis*. Much more could be plucked from his eager Latin. He had read his Cyprian, his Ambrose, his Jerome and Augustine, his Gregory the Great and Isidore of Seville, his Venerable Bede, and he filled his work with quotations. To modern students his pages at times become wearisome, his interpretations seem foolish, farfetched, not untouched by danger to himself and his readers. On readers of his ninth century and of the centuries which followed in medieval Europe his work produced two opposite effects: one of approval and pleasure, the other of horror and condemnation. We will look first at the dark side, which was brought into being by an unexpected turn of fortune.

7

In March 835, as we have seen, an august synod of Frankish bishops assembled at Thionville, near Metz. Amalar, full of the joy of his completed work, appeared before them to ask their approval of his *Antiphonary* and of his *Liber Officialis* in its latest edition. The bishops were busy in many matters; they had little time for prolonged and critical reading. They listened to Amalar as he told them of his study, of his work in Rome and at Corbie, of his reverence for Roman authority. They looked at his books. All seemed well, and unanimously they gave their consent.

They then turned to three matters of immediate concern: (1) the acknowledgment by Ebbo, archbishop of Reims, of his wickedness in condemning God's anointed Emperor, Louis the Pious; (2) his removal from his see; (3) the summoning of Agobard, archbishop of Lyons, to answer the same charge of disloyalty to the Frankish throne. Three times Agobard's name was called, and he did not answer. Probably he was already in flight from Frankland to Italy, where Lothar, the rebel heir, was to gather around him the men who had supported his action against his father and king. The Council therefore sentenced Agobard, also, to banishment from his seat, and proceeded to elect a ruler for the church of Lyons. The name of Amalar was proposed and promptly won election. He was a friend of the Emperor, lately reinstated in all honor and dignity of rule; he had shown himself to this very Council as a devoted and able student of the Church's liturgy.

With great delight Amalar entered his cathedral in this same year of 835. He remembered Leidrad, once archbishop here, and his work for its School of Chant, a school now respected far and wide. Here was a wonderful opportunity, given by kindness of fortune, to put into practice his own *corpus* of chanted texts, his *Antiphonary*, and also to spread the teaching, the original thought, of his own *Liber Officialis*, so lately endorsed by episcopal voice.

He lost no time. Hardly had he appeared before his clergy at Lyons as their father in God, when he summoned them to meet in assembly—assistant bishops, archdeacons, priests, and minor ministers. Before them he held up both his works, and then he proceeded to lecture to them for three entire days upon the interpretation of the Mass and upon the system of chant which they would find declared therein. Finally, he arranged for the making of copies of his books and left his cathedral community to study them in detail.

How many of his captive audience had listened with attention during those three long days we do not know; but one listener was already alert for attack. His name was Florus; he was a deacon of Lyons, and he was recognized throughout its diocese as a "master" of learning. In his friendship his late archbishop had held high place of esteem, and he was very angry at Agobard's deprivation. Had not Agobard as archbishop of Lyons revealed the hypocrisy of Felix, that heretic, once bishop of Urgel in the Pyrenees, convicted of the vile error of adoptianism by Alcuin at Aachen in 800 and falsely professing himself a penitent? Had not Agobard denounced the crime of the Jews in refusing Christian baptism to their heathen slaves? Had he not urgently pointed out the evil done by them, appealing to associates of the Imperial Court: Adalard, Wala, Helisachar, Hilduin the Archchaplain, even, in letter after letter, to the Emperor himself? Had he not stood forward boldly to declare the evils of Frankland rampant under this same Louis the Pious? Had he not joined Florus himself in anger and scorn at the folly of superstition still cherished among Frankish folk?

Now Agobard was in exile, and Florus was no friend of his successor. Perhaps he had known Amalar long before in Lyons, if Amalar had indeed stayed there; perhaps he had been bitterly jealous of him in matters liturgical. At any rate, he now hurried to get hold of Amalar's liturgical writings, and he read them diligently from cover to cover. Especially he examined the *Liber Officialis;* and as he read, horror, perhaps not altogether unwelcome, rose within him. Here, he said to himself, here for all to read, is very snare and delusion for the deceiving of the faithful. Amalar alas! in his zeal had not always been cautious to guard against misunderstanding of his words. Now Florus seized upon every statement, every passage which, literally interpreted, might bring upon its author condemnation as one who was denying, or audaciously discussing in unseemly manner, the faith of the Church he served.

One passage, especially, to the mind of Florus carried with it clear taint of heresy. He found it in Amalar's interpretation of the ritual of the Mass customary in his time: The celebrant after the Consecration placed a particle of the Host in the chalice, received a particle in his Communion, gave Communion to his people, and left a particle upon the altar until the ending of the Mass. The interpretation of this ritual in Amalar's symbolic thought runs thus: in its original Latin:

> *Triforme est corpus Christi, eorum scilicet qui gustaverunt mortem et morituri sunt. Primum videlicet sanctum et immaculatum, quod assumptum est ex Maria virgine; alterum, quod ambulat in terra; tertium, quod iacet in sepulchris.*
>
> *Per particulam oblatae immissae in calicem ostenditur Christi corpus quod iam resurrexit a mortuis; per comestam a sacerdote vel a populo, ambulans adhuc super terram; per relictam in altari, iacens in sepulchris. Idem corpus oblatam ducit secum ad sepulchrum et vocat illam*

sancta ecclesia viaticum morientis, ut ostendatur non eos debere, qui in Christo moriuntur, deputari mortuos, sed dormientes. Unde et Paulus ad Corinthios: "Mulier alligata est legi quanto tempore vir eius vivit; quod si dormierit vir eius, liberata est." Remanetque in altari ipsa particula usque ad finem missae, quia usque in finem saeculi corpora sanctorum quiescent in sepulchris.

In English translation:

Threefold is the Body of Christ, of those who have tasted of death and those who have yet to die. The first is that holy and immaculate Body which He took of the Virgin Mary; the second, that which walks on earth; the third, that which lies in graves.

By the particle of the Oblation placed in the chalice is shown the Body of Christ which now is risen from the dead; by that part consumed by the priest and by the people is shown the Body which still walks on earth; by that left upon the altar is shown the Body lying in graves. That Body takes with it to the grave the Oblation which the holy Church calls the *viaticum* of the dying; hence it may be shown that those who die in Christ ought not to be thought of as dead, but as sleeping. Thus Paul wrote to the Corinthians: *A woman is bound to the Law, as long as her husband lives; but if her husband fall asleep, she is free.* The particle remains upon the altar until the end of the Mass because until the end of the world the bodies of the saints shall lie in their graves.

In the symbolic thought of Amalar, then, the particle of the Host placed in the chalice represented the Body of the Risen Lord; the part consumed by the priest signified to him the Church Militant, still living on earth; the part left upon the altar until the end of the Mass recalled for him the souls of the faithful departed, the Church Expectant, whose relics were lying in their graves, whose souls were awaiting the joy of the Beatific Vision in Heaven. For him, both the Church Militant and the Church Expectant were members of the One Mystical Body of Christ.

But to Florus the words *Triforme est corpus Christi* meant only "Three bodies hath Christ"; and that was rank heresy, entirely opposed to the teaching of the Bible and of the Church. The Council of Thionville was still in session. He hastened there with all speed, demanded leave to appear before it, and passionately besought its bishops to reconsider and to annul their approval of Amalar's work.

"Most Reverend Fathers," he implored, "in the hearing of God listen to my words. I speak of the Faith, of Catholic heritage, which the head of the Church of Lyons is now persistently debasing and perverting by tongue and by pen. And, you, the very eyes of the Church of Christ, he declares as his supporters and accomplices in this. He has even made this his boast in a public meeting of our diocese, declaring that you all have willingly and deliberately subscribed to his most vain and foolish books. I could not believe it of men of so great dignity! Even though I myself, compared with you, Fathers, am but as a dead dog or a tiny flea, I would rather cut off the thumb and two fingers with which I write than confirm errors of Amalar's sort with the signature of my own hand! The very bishops and archdeacons to whom he read from these books of his at Lyons laughed at them in scorn and contempt. I speak, as God hears me, not through hurt of anger, but through hatred of error and through love of truth."

8

The appeal failed; the bishops were not moved to study these books at length and admit that they had made a wrong decision. Florus, nevertheless, persevered in his campaign. He returned to Lyons and busied himself in speaking and writing the same accusations. In the years between 835 and 838, perhaps in 837, there came from his pen, it would seem, a pamphlet bearing the strange title, *Invectio canonica Martini papae in Amalarium officiographum:* "A Canonical Charge of Pope Martin against Amalar, writer on the liturgy." Martin had ruled as Pope from 649 until 653. Exactly why his name appeared here as author we do not know; perhaps by mistake of later time, perhaps by desire of Florus to conceal the true source. That Florus himself wrote it seems a reasonable conclusion on the ground of the violence of its language; it is especially directed against the passage telling of the "threefold Body of Christ."

"Here," Florus declares, "is wisdom of this earth, wisdom of the brute and the Devil, rising up in pride against the knowledge of God, working for the destruction of weak and ignorant men." That he was still studying Amalar's pages with fierce concentration is shown in a long list of jottings which have come down to us, apparently made by him on the margin of his copy of the *Liber Officialis*. "Madness," we read; "ravings"; "mere superstition"; "nonsense"; "no good, not a bit of it"; "heresy"; "devil's talk"; "if tonsure of the head means shearing away idle thoughts, *you* had better shave off your mind!"; "sheer blasphemy and accursed lie!"

From Italy came writing of Agobard to swell the assault. A work entitled *Against the Four Books of Abbot Amalar* is included in Agobard's works and may, therefore, reasonably be assigned to him; its tone, though severe, is not marked by savage invective. More interesting is a mention by Florus of a complaint addressed, it would appear, to Louis the Pious by a "shepherd anxious for the salvation of his flock." This shepherd presumably was Agobard. If Florus is to be trusted here, the Emperor was so disturbed by this appeal that he brought the matter up for consideration by another council of bishops, called by him to meet in his royal residence of Quierzy-sur-Oise, near Laon, for the debating of "many problems of the Church."

At this Council, which gathered in 838, Amalar promptly appeared, to answer, if he could, the accusations of Florus and of Agobard. He seems to have arrived with a sanguine hope of acquittal; for he brought with him a "Supplement" to his other writing—*Embolis*, he called it—which he had had sumptuously adorned with silk ribbons as a gift for the president of the assembly.

On the other side, Florus had prepared *his* way by a strong letter, composed by him and sent, just as the Council was gathering, to five men prominent in the Frankish Church: Drogo, archbishop of Metz; Hetti, archbishop of Trier; Aldric, bishop of Le Mans; Alberic, bishop of Langres; and Hraban Maur, abbot of Fulda. In this document Florus remarked: "There is no need for me to go into great detail about the writings of Amalar. His books are to be found almost everywhere, are known to almost everyone."

Chief among the charges levied against Amalar, either at Quierzy or in the various writings which attacked his teaching, are these:

1. He wrote of "three bodies of Christ."
2. He taught that, as the Host in the Mass was the Body of Christ, so the chalice held the Blood of Christ which was His Soul, forming together One Whole Christ.
3. He declared that oblation was made in the Mass, first for the elect, those without sin, and, secondly, for sinners. This—to hold that there exist men, not only potentially but actually sinless—must be condemned as worse than Pelagian error.
4. He discussed in irreverent and unseemly manner the question: What happens to the Host after reception in the mouth of a faithful Christian? Does the supernatural or the natural come into action here?
5. In foolish and wild allegory he wrote of the altar as that Jerusalem whence the Gospel was brought to men; of the chalice of the Mass as the tomb of the Lord, and the celebrant as Joseph of Arimathea; of the deacons, bowing their heads in the rite, as the disciples, bent in fear during the Passion of the Lord; of the subdeacons, erect before the altar, as the women standing steadfast before the Cross.
6. He wrote childishly in symbolic imagination of the vessels and vestments which arrayed the altar of the Lord and His ministers, using words stupid, fatuous, and worthy of all ridicule.

Amalar was condemned. In an account of the proceedings of the Council of Quierzy, written by Florus, who, although seething with enmity towards the accused, may be trusted to describe literally the outline of the Council's action, if not the feeling of all its members, we read: "When in the ears of the Fathers assembled his absurd and profane devisings of new inventions were read aloud, in the presence of the man who had brought them forth from the arrogant vanity of his heart, these Godfearing bishops shuddered to hear such blasphemies. They put to him the question: 'Is this teaching really yours?' He could not deny it, seeing that it was to be found almost everywhere in the many books he had published. 'Where, then,' they asked, 'did you come upon these things?' This question caught and held him fast. Not from Scripture had he taken them, nor from the teachings of the Catholic Fathers, not even from the words of heretics themselves. He gave the only answer possible: 'I read them in my own soul.' Without delay the reverend Council, in scorn of words so insolent, so inane, declared: 'Truly it was the soul of error.'"

His pastoral charge now lost to him by these scathing words of his judges, there was nothing for Amalar but to retire into obscurity; and we may believe that he settled with his books not far from the cathedral of Metz. In triumph Florus now saw Agobard recalled from exile to rule again in his archbishop's seat at Lyons.

9

Once there, Agobard set to work to correct what he held to be the wrong done by Amalar, so far as he could correct it. About 839 he delivered to the clergy and cantors of his Cathedral an Antiphonary of revised edition. In a letter written to them as preface he declared that this revised Book of Chants had been drawn up in accordance with the authority of the Fathers and with rejection of recent invented imaginings; for good measure he described a few of the "ineptitudes" of Amalar's version.

It may be that in his years of retirement Amalar, too, wrote on chant and its music, and that to these years belongs the work from his pen, still extant, which he called *De Ordine Antiphonarii*, an explanation and interpretation of that Antiphonary of his now unhappily lost to us. At any rate, another attack was launched against him from Lyons, entitled *On the Divine Psalmody*. This, it is true, is also printed among the writings of Agobard; but its words are surely the words of Florus. It begins: "Of recent days that fool and knave, known to all men by his silliness and dishonesty, has broken out in attack upon our holy Church of Lyons and does not cease to wound us by his shafts of written words, which declare that in our chant we do not follow due tradition of ancient Patristic rule. It has therefore been necessary to publish a definitive edition of an Antiphonary, with a preface by Agobard, our pious and orthodox Father in God."

Florus, it seems probable, was writing here in fervent support of the Antiphonary put forward by Agobard. He ended this onslaught with the words: "If any one"—meaning, of course, Amalar—"in his quarrelsome obstinacy wills to drink from a muddy river rather than from the pure fountain head, he runs great risk of falling dangerously ill."

Here doubtless he had in mind the words spoken by Charles the Great in his concern over the discrepancy between his Frankish use and that of the Roman Church. To Romans and Franks, quarreling in his presence over the merits of their respective liturgies, the king—so we are told by John the Deacon in his *Life of Gregory the Great*—had turned to put a question: "Which keeps its water more pure, the river or the fountain head?" And when, of course, the answer had come: "The fountain head," he had remarked: "Then we in Frankland, who hitherto have drunk the polluted water of the river, of necessity must now return to that fountain head."

This, despite Florus, was exactly what Amalar had done. His imagination may at times have lacked dignity; but neither in his thought nor in his intention was he ever heretic, fool, or knave.

10

Shortly before his death Amalar came into public notice once more, and once again, too, in connection with controversy. This time the controversy had to do with the long strife among theologians which was born of the views held by the young Gottschalk on the problem of predestination of the souls of men. Its story will meet us when we come to Walafrid Strabo and to Hincmar of Reims. Here we may note briefly that Amalar, again inspired to action, wrote a letter, now lost, in aid of the cause of Hincmar, of Hraban Maur, and of Pardulus, bishop of Laon, against Gottschalk. About 852 one of the members or friends of the Church of Lyons, in a writing called *Liber de tribus epistulis*—"On the Three Letters" (of Hincmar, Hraban Maur, and Pardulus)—again dipped a pen in venom: "That on so deep a problem as predestination Amalar was called to write, with John the Scot, we have heard with much vexation and distress."

By this time, however, Amalar was beyond the reach of human attack. Death ended his toil about 850, in Metz, and pilgrims came to pray around his tomb in its church of Saint Arnulf. There his relics lay not far from those of his Emperor, Louis the Pious, to whom he had offered his labor and his love. We may well wish that we had some witness in writing of his intervention in the troubles of his country during his life. That he did care deeply for Louis is shown in his letter to Archchaplain Hilduin:

"May God so guide him that the citizens of Heaven with joy shall welcome him when he goeth hence." That he cared even more deeply for his labor for the liturgy serves but to show what manner of man he was.

11

Lastly, we turn to the brighter side, to see what Amalar in his dedicated work meant to men both simple and learned in the Middle Ages, from his own ninth to the thirteenth century. We have seen that Florus himself acknowledged the widely spread circulation of Amalar's writings. After Amalar's death the anonymous author of the *Liber de tribus epistulis* angrily admitted the same: "To think that men of prudence in the Church should have done their cause so great harm as to ask the aid of Amalar, that man who by his errors, his phantasies and heretical words, has poisoned and corrupted nearly all the churches in Frankland, and some, too, of other countries! Truly, instead of asking him to give his views on the Faith, directly he was dead they should have burned all he had written!"

Nevertheless, for thousands of the faithful Amalar quickened their sense of the living action, the inner meaning of the liturgy: for priests and monks who chanted its ritual; for the layfolk who watched and listened, day by day, night by night, feast, feria, and fast, all the round of the year. Every act, at the altar or about the altar, of the bishop at Pontifical High Mass, of priest, deacon, subdeacon, cantor, thurifer, acolyte, had for him a meaning—artificial, it may be, and hard for us nowadays to conceive—but a meaning which was real to medieval men who loved to see truth represented by symbol and religious teaching made clear by dramatic act.

Liturgists of France, of Germany, of Switzerland, of Italy, and of England read and pondered this man's work. The author of the *Liber de divinis officiis*, once attributed to Alcuin, but really written in the late ninth or the tenth century, wrote under Amalar's influence; in the tenth century we find a priest named Gerhard quoting him in a letter sent to an archbishop of Mainz. Berno, abbot of Reichenau, who died in 1048, borrowed from him and praised him highly as "a most skilful researcher into Divine Office, whose words are buttressed by Catholic authorities." In the late eleventh century the *Micrologus de ecclesiasticis observationibus*, ascribed to Bernold of Constance, took note of Amalar's following of Roman usage, as well as of his probing into symbol. Rupert, the learned abbot of Deutz, on the Rhine opposite Cologne, who died in 1135, showed in his *De divinis officiis per anni circulum* his respect for Amalar's knowledge. His contemporary, Honorius, the scholastic theologian, whether of Autun or of southern Germany—authorities differ on this point—followed Amalar closely in his *Gemma animae de divinis officiis*, even repeating those words so vehemently condemned in 838: *corpus Domini est triforme*. The same earlier twelfth century found interest in his thought still clearly alive in England, where William of Malmesbury was making an abridgment of the *Liber Officialis*. In a letter to the man for whom he did this work William wrote: "Your wish, friend Robert, turned me from my writing of history, when, not long ago, as we were sitting in our library [at Malmesbury Abbey], each busy in his own research, you fell upon Amalar, *De ecclesiasticis officiis*. Keen as you were to study this, on account of your recent profession, the abundance of quotation and the difficulty of its style worried you so much that you asked me to make a précis of its content." This William had done, and at the close of his letter he gave the names of other liturgical authorities to his friend, with these final words: "Another perchance has written more eloquently than Amalar; but no man, surely, from a deeper experience."

The importance, in fact, of Amalar for England was alive as late as the seventeenth century, through the medium of that Honorius who knew his words so well. In 1633 William Prynne of England, a Protestant of fiery zeal, wrote in his *Histrio-Mastix, The Player's Scourge:*

The historie of Christ's death and the celebration of his blessed Sacraments are ofttimes prophaned in theatricall enterludes, especially by Popist Priests and Jesuites in foraigne parts; who, as they have turned the Sacrament of Christ's body and blood into a Masse-play, so have likewise transformed their Mass it-selfe, together with the whole story of Christ's birth, his life, his Passion, and all other parts of their Ecclesiastical service, into Stage-playes. . . .

Honorius Augustodunensis, an Author of some credit among the Romanists, in his Booke, *De Antiquo Ritu Missarum*, lib. I, cap. 83. the title of which chapter is, *De Tragediis*, to signifie to the world, that the Popish *Masse* is now no other but a *Tragicke Play*, writes thus . . . "When the Presbyter saith, (Pray ye,) he acteth or expresseth Christ, who was cast into an agony for us, when he admonished his Apostles to pray. By his secret silence, he signifieth Christ led to the slaughter as a Lambe, without a voyce. By the stretching out of his hands, he denotes the extension of Christ upon the Crosse. By the Song of the Preface, he expresseth the cry of Christ, hanging upon the Crosse, etc." Loe! here a Roman Masse-priest becomes a *Player*, and in stead of preaching, of reading, acts Christ's Passion in the Masse, which this Author stiles a Tragedy.

To modern students Amalar is still of interest. From his writings they can learn much concerning the liturgy of the ninth century, its practice and its problems. His chief importance, indeed, he shares with his master, Alcuin, for in their working, in their fusing of texts Roman, Gallican, Frankish, lies the origin of that liturgy which the Church follows in these, our own days.

Chapter V

WALAFRID STRABO OF REICHENAU

1

The scholars of the ninth century, as is well known, lightened their labor of research among tomes Biblical and patristic by the recreation of writing verses for their benefactors and their friends. So had the Anglo-Saxons done: Aldhelm, Bede, and Boniface; so had Alcuin, at first in England, and afterward among the Franks; so had Theodulf and his fellows in letters and learning at the Court of Charles the Great. The custom continued under Louis the Pious and his sons. True, much of this verse was dull: perhaps a compilation, perhaps a monotonous pattern woven from fragments of pagan classical and early Christian poets. Meter was part of the science of the liberal arts, and to understand meter properly one must try one's hand in its practice. We still possess many pages filled with this travail of creation stillborn and dead. It is, therefore, refreshing to come upon work written during these times which may justly be honored as poetry.

In the early ninth century, perhaps about 816, a boy of some eight years came from that region of Alemannia which bordered on the Boden See, the Lake of Constance, to a monastery standing upon an island in the Unter See, a western arm of the lake, formed by the Rhine as it flows on its way from Constance toward Schaffhausen. Travelers know the island now as Reichenau, and they reach it by a causeway from the mainland. This boy, Walafrid Strabo, "the lad with a squint," arrived by boat at the isle, then surrounded on all sides by water and bearing the name of Augia.

To him the island was always to be "Augia felix," "the happy isle." Alemannia was a land of barbarians, uncouth and ignorant; Walafrid's parents were poor and of humble station and had given him no dower of learning save the rudiments of the Christian faith. These things did not matter to him, for he took to monastic life and study as a wild duck to the stream. His mind was quick and hungry for knowledge; he drank in all that was offered him: Latin, Scripture, the Fathers, the principles of the liberal arts. Above all, he loved his fellowman. All his life he saw the best and praised the best, in his teachers, his pupils, his companions, and his heroes, great and small.

Walafrid soon learned the history of this house of religion in which he was to live. It had been founded in 724 by one Pirmin, around whose name vigorous controversy has arisen. It seems probable, from hints given us by his writings, the *Dicta Pirminii*, that he was of Roman origin and had fled from the Arab invasion of Spain or southern France to Aquitaine, then on to the Rhine and this island in the lake. There he had built a rough dwelling for himself and for others who joined him in the monastic life, and there he had ruled a little community for three years. Then Theobald, duke of Alemannia, angry at the protection given to Pirmin by the Frankish government, had driven him from his cloister, and he had wandered into exile, to found other abbeys in Germany and never to return. The monastery, however, and its abbots, one after another, lived to make history in Reichenau. The Benedictine Rule was firmly established; and at the beginning of the ninth century we find one Waldo in command.

Waldo had come from the abbey of Saint-Gall, about nine miles southwest of the Boden See and a house closely linked in tradition with Reichenau. It had sprung from a little settlement made on the bank of the river Steinach about 612 by Gall, a fellow countryman and fellow monk of Columban of Luxeuil, who had gone with him from Ireland into the wilds of Burgundy and Switzerland. Not until long after Gall was dead did his venture on the Steinach win the name of monastery. During many years pilgrims from Ireland continually came in reverence to visit the cell of this man, renowned for his labor among the heathen, and more and more of them decided to stay and to carry on his work. Here, also, the Rule of St. Benedict became the guide of monks, supplanting the harsh Irish discipline which Columban and Gall had brought to France. Early in the eighth century the community of Saint-Gall was at last in regular functioning under its Abbot Othmar.

When Walafrid arrived in Reichenau, or "Augia," as he knew

it, both its foundation and that of Saint-Gall possessed flourishing schools of learning, not only for the oblates, the boys who came to be trained for monastic life, but also for "external" students, the sons of men of noble rank, who sent them to one or the other that either community might prepare them for a distinguished career in Church or in state. Before this time Waldo had left the island to become ruler of the royal abbey of Saint-Denis, near Paris, where he is found corresponding by letter with Charles the Great. At the time of Walafrid's coming the abbot of Reichenau was one Haito, who not only ruled this monastery but was also bishop of Basle. He, like Waldo, was known to Charles; in 811 the king had sent him with Hugh, count of Tours, and others, on a mission of peace to Constantinople. The envoys carried official confirmation of that yielding of territory by the Frankish ruler which was to pave the way for his eagerly desired salutation by Constantinople in the following year as brother in imperial dignity. In 822–23 Haito, longing for peace in contemplative prayer, retired from his bishopric and his abbacy to live quietly in community at Reichenau until his death in 836. He was followed in the abbot's chair by Erlebald; and it was probably under this Erlebald that Walafrid was professed as monk.

To his abbots Walafrid was consistently loyal; but it was to certain teachers at Reichenau that he gave his devoted affection. There was Reginbert, known far and wide as librarian and as copyist of valuable manuscripts for the increasing culture of his abbey. For many years he had been adding to its collection. On each of his manuscripts, as he brought it to its close, he inscribed lines of counsel and warning, a warning apparently as ancient as it is modern:

> For honour of the Lord God and Our Lady dear
> And many holy men by Augia's house revered,
> This book with loving care, attentive to command,
> Was made by Reginbert the scribe; in earnest hope
> That long it should endure, long serve his brethren's need.
> He prays you all, lest vain his labour die,
> In Heaven's most gracious Name to offer it to none
> Outside our walls; save should the seeker pledge his word

Our property in sound condition to return.
Good friend, ponder this well: a writer's task is hard;
Take, open, read, harm not; finish, refold, RESTORE!

Day by day, also, Walafrid sat in the abbey listening to its monks Grimald and Tatto, who had themselves been trained by Reginbert. Both had been taught as boys in the Palace School at Aachen before they entered Reichenau. Perhaps Walafrid was already in its cloister when the two set out together, in 817 or shortly afterwards, on a visit to one of the leading Frankish abbeys, probably that of Kornelimünster, recently built by Louis the Pious for his spiritual adviser, Benedict of Aniane. The Synod held at Aachen in July 817 had laid down the principles of discipline according to that code of St. Benedict of Nursia, which henceforth under command of King Louis was to govern the monasteries of Frankland; and Reichenau, in common with many other religious communities, was already in fear lest the inspectors sent out by the king to examine into conditions in Frankish monasteries should find something amiss in their communal life. We have two letters sent back to Reichenau by Grimald and Tatto during their absence. One, sent to Reginbert, brought him a copy of the *Rule* of St. Benedict; the other, written to Abbot Haito, gave a careful report of their visit and minute detail concerning all that they had observed. This report ended with an earnest suggestion that the abbot maintain in regular practice the discipline thus noted and described.

2

In the midst of the study of Latin and of some small amount of Greek (probably inspired by Irish members of Reichenau and Saint-Gall), of the Bible and the Latin Fathers, of secular subjects—history, geography, astronomy—all very new and attractive to this young barbarian, as Walafrid was afterward to call himself, he now discovered the delight of metrical verse. Soon his teachers were sure that they had among them a boy with a genuine poetic gift, and they were not slow to foster it. At the age of fifteen we find Walafrid sending verses, in the name, it is true, of his teacher Tatto, to Ebbo, archbishop of Reims. The verses, of course, express dutifully their admiration of this high prelate, who had not yet come forth in condemnation of Louis the Pious, his Emperor. Other verses go to Thegan, a bishop in the diocese of Trier, whom Walafrid was to know well later on. Now he writes humbly to him, "as a mouse to a giant." In one of these youthful productions he refers to his own disfigurement: " 'Tis the boy, Father, with the twisted eye who writes these words to you." At times, too, he describes the joy, mingled with awe, with which he is filled as he stands looking upon his monastery's church, of Saints Mary, Peter, and Paul, or tells the thoughts that come to him within his own little cell.

Gradually, his ambition grew. At the request of three of his friends he set to work at a *Life* in hexameters of the monk and martyr, Mammes, an undertaking which shows the influence of the Greek East and its religious life upon these monks of the West. Of Mammes we know very little. In tradition he appears as a shepherd of Caesarea in Cappadocia, Asia Minor, who witnessed to his Christian faith by enduring torture and death about 275 A.D., and who was deeply revered by Fathers of the Eastern Church, St. Basil the Great and St. Gregory Nazianzen. His name still keeps its place in official martyrologies.

Among the long descriptions of his constancy under trial we come upon stories of that power over wild life so commonly found in Celtic tradition. Walafrid tells of Mammes as a fugitive in the mountains, fed with milk from wild ewes that flock to aid him; of bear, leopard, and lion rushing upon him before the crowds in the public arena, only to crouch at his feet and obey his commands.

Of still greater interest is the request of Felix, a priest of Reichenau, that Walafrid tell in verse the story, at the time still fresh in men's minds, of an Irish saint, Blaithmaic. Irish annals record against the year 825 that Blaithmaic, the son of Fland, was killed by the Danes on the isle of Iona; and about a year later Walafrid wrote his poem from accounts given him by the Irish pilgrims who visited his abbey. Here he told that Blaithmaic was of the blood of Ireland's kings, but that, like Columba himself, he had preferred the monastic calling to his Irish heritage. In the course of time he had become abbot of an Irish monastery; and at length, filled with desire for a martyr's reward, he had crossed the sea to Iona, which, as he well knew, was frequently visited by Viking pirates from the North.

He had won his desire. Early one morning, just as the sun rose, the Danes came down upon the island. Before the altar of Iona's church stood Blaithmaic, priest of the mass. At the sudden tumult he turned around to face whatever was coming, and in time to see the Northmen strike down his monks. None was armed, none could resist; and he, their abbot, stood alone. "Where are the bones of Columba?" shouted the pirates, greedy for the jewels which adorned the saint's coffin. "Buried in the ground, and I know not where," was the reply. "And if I did know, I would not tell." Blaithmaic, in truth, did not know, for the relics had been buried for their safekeeping long before he ever saw Iona. Now he was at once killed on the altar steps.

About the same time, in or near the year 826, Walafrid composed the most important work of his student days at Reichenau. This was the *Vision of Wettin,* containing nearly a thousand hexameter lines. It was one of those medieval narratives of foresight in man's spirit: visions of Fursey and of Drythelm, told long before by Bede; of the Monk of Much Wenlock, told by Boniface; of the English Priest, told by Prudentius, bishop of Troyes, against the year 839; of St. Anskar, told by Rimbert in this same ninth century; and so on to the very crown of all, the *Divina Commedia* of Dante more than four centuries later.

Wettin was a monk of Reichenau and a teacher in its school. From evidence discovered by him in Codex Bern, 584, Dom Germain Morin has seen not only Walafrid among his pupils there, but also the young Gottschalk whom Walafrid was to know later on at Fulda. Wettin's zeal for learning, we read, excelled his enthusiasm for spiritual discipline. His final lesson was a bitter one. In 824 he was suddenly seized by sickness and in his bed underwent various terrifying experiences. In the first of these an evil spirit appeared by his side, dressed in clerical habit, eyeless, dark and hideous to look upon, who in his hands was brandishing instruments of torture. Soon he was joined by a jostling crowd of his fellows, armed to the teeth and filling with horror the cell in which Wettin lay. Having given their warning, they blessedly all fled; and Wettin's Guardian Angel came in sight to bid him implore his brethren to plead for his forgiveness from the Lord, whom by his negligence he had so grievously offended. This his brethren did, with much chanting of penitential psalms, until at last, exhausted, the sick man fell asleep.

His sleep, however, was anything but peaceful. Once more his Guardian Angel appeared, and after a stern command to read and ponder the hundred and eighteenth psalm, "on moral virtues" (Psalm 119 in the King James Version), he caught Wettin up on a flight to a river of flame, in which a vast multitude of sinners, especially clergy of lesser and higher order alike, were fast bound, suffering chastisement for lust and foul living on earth. Next he was borne to a happier place of purgatory, where many souls, monks and layfolk, were doing penance in the hope of Heaven at the last. Among these to his astonishment he saw King Charles the Great himself. "But surely you know," he cried to his angelic escort, "King Charles was Defender of the Faith and of Holy Church. In this, our 'modern' time, he was a ruler almost without equal in his world! What is he doing here, bound to this punishment of shame?" "Ah," answered the Angel, "in truth many wonderful things he did, and for these in the end he shall find his seat among the elect. But now, for that in his old age he fell to lust and smeared his record of good, he must needs find purifying in this pain."

(The word *modernus* is of interest here as used by Walafrid for the describing of the new era brought to pass by Charlemagne.)

After these visions of pain and penance the Angel led Wettin to catch a faint sight of Heaven. The vastness, the splendor, which he seemed rather to conceive than even dimly to see, filled him with fear, and the more so when his guide turned to him and said: "Tomorrow you will depart from life on earth. While time still remains for you, let us pray the Lord for mercy on your soul."

Of himself Wettin could do nothing. Three times, instructed by the Angel, he implored help from the company of Heaven, and three times his prayer was heard. First the Priests, prostrate before the seat of Judgment, cried aloud for his forgiveness, but in vain. A voice from the throne of God came in dreadful answer: "It was for this man to show example of good works to others;

and that he did not do." Then came the Martyrs to plead for him, but all once more to no end. Finally, the Holy Virgins drew near. Before they could even touch the ground in humble supplication, the glory of the Lord shone round about them, and He raised them up, granting consent to their unspoken petition. Thus did judgment yield to the grace of purity.

The vision now faded, and Wettin awoke in his cell at Reichenau. As had been foretold, he died at the hour of Vespers on the following day, after he had told to Haito, now no longer abbot but a simple monk, all his dream of terror.

Haito sat down and wrote out in Latin prose what he had learned from Wettin in his last moments on earth. Not long afterward Adalgis, an older monk of Reichenau, asked Walafrid to tell the story in verse. This request brought the young novice into a state of immense tribulation and fear. Wettin had been his beloved teacher, and he missed him more than he could say. How could he describe in any decent fashion the visions of so great a man? What would Haito say? Things were even worse with him because Grimald, whom also he revered and loved, was absent from Reichenau, in service as chaplain at the Court of Louis the German, king of Bavaria. Already he had written to Grimald of his misery in Wettin's loss. Now he appealed to both Grimald and Adalgis for their sympathy in his plight, for his release from this fearsome task of turning the prose of Haito—once his abbot —into his own miserable lines. There was little enough sympathy for the writing of poetry in the mind of either his abbot Erlebald or of the monk in charge of the school of Reichenau, now Tatto, even though Tatto had at times ordered him to write greetings in verse to various dignitaries. "Of course," he wrote to Grimald, "Abbot Erlebald, who now rules us, and Tatto, my teacher here, will have to know what I have done; for it is not right for a monk to conceal any act of his from his abbot. And so, if they judge my verses to be foul with lies, they will punish me. They will show no mercy, I am afraid, for my scarce eighteen years, and I shall get a sound beating. Well skilled are they in the art of metre, as in other arts; but they like it little. I pray you, come to the rescue of my faulty lines!"

Adalgis and Grimald, however, comforted him, bade him gather up his courage and fulfill this labor with all the diligence and all the skill within him. The monastery of Reichenau would be proud of his tribute to Wettin. And so Walafrid did, and his work is still ours to read.

3

In 826 Abbot Erlebald and his school at Reichenau decided that it was time to send Walafrid to a more distinguished center of learning for his further progress. He was now eighteen and of sufficient promise to justify selection of the best. At Erlebald's command he set out for the abbey of Fulda where Einhard had read and learned forty years before.

He was to find in it one happiness which Einhard had not known. Since 822 Fulda's abbot had been the great scholar Hraban Maur. In the intervals of ruling his abbey and striving in the Emperor's cause, he was now engaged in compiling volume after volume of his vast collection of commentaries on the books of the Bible. For the greater part these consisted of excerpts from the writings of the Fathers, of whose works Hraban possessed a knowledge exceedingly wide. His method, indeed, does not offer great excitement or joy to the modern reader of his tomes; but to many students of the ninth century it was a source of delight.

Among these students was Walafrid, who soon became one of Hraban's favorite pupils. Together they pored over the Scriptures and searched for their interpretation by the Latin Fathers in the library of Fulda, far better furnished than in the days of Einhard's reading there. Hraban, too, was a lover of poetry; and although he himself was no poet and simply put together dull concoctions in meter, he gladly encouraged his young pupil to write his own lines in his leisure hours. Perhaps it was from Fulda that Walafrid sent verses of gratitude to Agobard, archbishop of Lyons. Agobard was already complaining of evils done by Jews and of superstitions current in his land; but the critical years of 830–33 and his determined stand against Louis the Pious had not yet come to pass. Walafrid wrote to Agobard to thank him for kindly words concerning his own *Vision of Wettin;* and in his verses he did not forget to praise the learning of that friend of Agobard, Florus, who in a few years was to appear at Thionville and at Quierzy as bitter enemy of the words of Amalar.

Walafrid's mingled love of study and of verse soon brought to him another happiness. One of his fellow students in the cloister of Fulda was a youth of about his own age: Gottschalk, son of Bern, a Saxon count who had offered his boy as a child-oblate to Fulda and with him a goodly endowment. Under Hraban as abbot, Gottschalk was initiated into Benedictine discipline, and in due time he received monastic tonsure.

But he was not at heart a monk or even patient of monastic discipline. He was too ardent a follower of devious paths of enquiry; he loved passionately to feel his way through new fields of thought, both in theology and in secular arts; obedience and reverence for authority imposed upon him were not his firm desire. Together he and Walafrid enjoyed the spell of Latin books, especially of the Latin genius in poetry. So keen, indeed, were they on Virgil and his verse that to Gottschalk Walafrid was, it seems, another Servius Honoratus; to Walafrid his friend was another Fulgentius, names given one to the other in remembrance of two of Virgil's best-known interpreters. Soon they were allied for life, in a bond which through years to come was to cause Walafrid deep anxiety and sorrow.

4

For the present, however, he felt only an uneasy fear for the future of his brilliant, but unstable friend. They were together only three years. Walafrid's repute for learning and quickness of mind, for honest and lovable character, was already reaching beyond Fulda's walls; and early in 829 he received a call from the Court of Louis the Pious at Aachen. The son of Louis and the Empress Judith, little Charles, to be known long afterward as Charles the Bald, was now nearly six years old. He needed a tutor. Some one, very probably Hilduin, archchaplain of the Court, suggested Walafrid; and to Aachen he went in excitement and delight.

Nine years he was to live there, from about his twenty-first to his thirtieth year, from 829 until 838; and it gave him far more joy even than it had given Einhard. Walafrid was, to be sure, a monk; but he was not naturally a recluse. Some of his leisure time at Aachen he spent in study. To these years belong, we may think, abridgments made by him of Hraban's *Commentaries on the Pentateuch.* In his preface he writes that he has made them lest all this wealth of learning should slip out of mind, especially his own mind. But alas! the readers of the future did not appreciate his labor of love. At the beginning of his selection of excerpts from Hraban's *Exodus* we find written by a later critic, as he laid down the manuscript in apparent disgust:

> This book Hraban explained, a scholar good and true;
> Strabus did nothing but paltry headings add.

To these years at Court may also perhaps be assigned Walafrid's *Life of Gall,* done in Latin prose. It, too, is a rewriting. Of the oldest *Life,* dating from the eighth century, we now have only fragments. In the early ninth century Gozbert, abbot of Saint-Gall from 816 until 836, asked some one—Wettin, it is thought, our monk of visions at Reichenau—to make another version; and a nephew of this Abbot Gozbert, a deacon of the same name, wrote yet another account of miracles due to the intercession of holy Gall. Neither the *Life* ascribed to Wettin nor the narrative of miracles by Gozbert Junior satisfied the abbot's ambition; and finally he requested Walafrid to make new versions of both. Walafrid did what he was asked, relying strongly upon that old *Life* of the eighth century. He informed his readers that he "had omitted the names of the writers from whom he had drawn his material, fearing that the dignity of the Latin language in which he had written might be impaired by those barbarous sounds." "I am sure," he added, "that the faithful will have no doubt as to the truth of my narrative."

This was not the only time that Walafrid came to the aid of Abbot Gozbert. The same nephew had written for the abbey of Saint-Gall a *Life* of its first abbot, Othmar, who died in 759. Here, also, his style had failed to please his uncle. Walafrid—we do not know exactly when—wrote it anew for him, and this narrative of Othmar's life and work is the only one now left to us.

These *Lives* have their importance; but it is not difficult to turn from them to Walafrid's growing delight in verse, verse addressed to many whom he had met in the royal palace:

> No service mine, no merit, yet lo! suddenly
>   Poor and unworthy, this honour I receive.
> Nothing can I return for all that you have done,
>   God from His heaven will give you recompense.

To the Emperor, Louis the Pious, he offered his homage and his loyalty at Christmas time, praying that the Child of Wonder, the Counsellor, the Prince of Peace on whose shoulders rests the ruling of the world, will keep and protect this, his dear lord. To his boy pupil, Charles, he wrote of the glory of his heritage. But it was to the fascination of intellect and grace by which the Empress Judith drew around her the young scholars in her Court that Walafrid gave his devotion, in anxious hope for her favor:

> Lover of peace, Seeker of light, you who hold in mind
> All things of good, with kindly thought my verses read.

To her service, as mother of Charles, he felt himself especially bound; and his reverent love for his Lady held firm throughout all the troubles which darkened the years at Court between 830 and 834. In 834, when her husband was again restored to his throne and reconciled with the Church, Walafrid told her in verse of a dream which had upheld him himself in those terrible days. While ill-omened power of evil—so he wrote—and device of fraud were oppressing all loyal men, the people and their king, while hatred was seeking, by violence, by prison and the sword, to banish faith from the land, while all was full of grief and treachery, one night, it seemed to him, he was reading a book. It told the deeds of the Frankish kings, and on one of its pages he found his Emperor's name, inscribed "Louis the Just." Then, as he sat rejoicing over this honor done to his lord, within his dream some hand snatched away the book. But before he lost it he caught sight of two lines upon its last page:

> Too sad these tears; such misery ill suits our hearts;
> No long time shall we suffer overthrow and loss.

The prophecy, he wrote, has been fulfilled. Let Judith now turn to joy!

Yet often Walafrid felt, as did other men, the force of Judith's arbitrary, changing moods. His was a Lententide of the heart as of the soul when he wrote:

> Many delights are mine, though nothing I deserve,
>   Which cheer the heart within me by their grace.
> Then some things turn the mind to unauspicious chill,
>   As thou dost know, though silent I remain.
> Not least of these that no command to serve your cause
>   Binds me to you nor calls me to your side.
> Your face I do not see, drink in no words; I hang
>   In hope, in fear; do I displease or please?
> My mind withal, knowing its constant loyalty,
>   Bids me despair not; better things shall come.
> Let proven faith suffice, and I shall pray the while
>   As I have ever prayed, a prayer most right
> (For so I hold), that life, protection, peace and joy
>   Christ give for evermore to you and yours.
> So yet more fully shall I still entreat throughout
>   The happy, holy days which now approach.

In the same loyalty he wrote his high praise to Rodbern, probably some secular officer of the Court, who had braved the perils of the Alps, defying capture by Lothar's garrisons, to enter Italy and penetrate as far as Judith's prison at Tortona to give her reassurance of rescue.

The wholehearted enthusiasm of Walafrid's allegiance to the Frankish Court is best shown, however, in some verses which he wrote soon after his arrival in Aachen. They are cast in the form of a dialogue between his own two selves, the outer man and his inner spirit, guide of his understanding. In this dialogue he thinks back upon himself as, not long before, he had stood in the courtyard in front of the Palace, looking thoughtfully at the statue of the Gothic king, Theodoric the Great, which Charles, also the Great, had brought from Ravenna in 801. There before him sat the barbarian monarch in his pride, while the pigeons flew in and out of their nesting in the nostrils and wide-open mouth of his war horse, and, all around, trees, flowers, and sky

were radiant in the sun of springtime. It was a sight of wonder
and beauty. Then Walafrid had remembered that he was looking
upon a heretic, an enemy of that Catholic faith to which he himself, his Emperor and Empress, and all their Court and people
were vowed. Where now was Theodoric's pride and glory? Consumed by eternal fire, imprisoned in the pit that holds no hope of
release!

Thus spoke in Walafrid his ninth century. Yet just after his
inner self had declared its judgment upon this Arian unbeliever,
just then had come suddenly before the eyes of his mind all the
true and orthodox splendor of the Frankish Court: Louis the
Pious, a man like Moses, a man most mild, but endued with power
through his converse with God; Lothar, also of imperial dignity;
the younger sons, Louis and Pippin; the Empress Judith, like
Rachel, leading Charles, her little Benjamin, by the hand. In their
train marched Hilduin, "the Aaron" of the Court; Einhard, skilled
in all artistry, little of stature but great of mind; and Grimald,
lover of verse, chaplain of Louis the German, his king in Bavaria.

The sun of Frankland, Walafrid knew, would banish by its
radiance the black night of Gothic heresy. The Christian would
conquer. "As the wild things of this forest of Aachen, bear and
boar, timid hare and fleeing deer, dread the hunter's bow," he
wrote, "so shall all nations—Bulgar and Spaniard, the dull Bretons,
shrewd Danes and savage tribes of Africa—so shall they yield
their power to the Frank."

Such was the dream of Walafrid on this spring morning. To
his verses he added a postscript, which concerned himself and
his name as writer of them. "Strabo," he observed, was his name
in holy Rule at Reichenau; but for his own self he willed it to be
"Strabus." The meaning is the same in either case; and as "Strabo"
the world, like the cloister, has known him.

5

Now and again the political events of his time are reflected
in Walafrid's verses. His sixty-fourth poem tells in exultation of
"the coming of Charles, son of the Emperor and Empress." Could
this have honored, as Dümmler in his edition has suggested, the

granting in 829 to Charles of Rhaetia, Alsace, part of Burgundy, and Walafrid's own land of Alemannia? There is no proof that it did; and such homage would have been strange for a writer like Walafrid, eager for the cause of unity in imperial rule. If, however, it did praise that grant, Walafrid in his simplicity must have disregarded the resentment and the foreboding to which it gave rise. The same thought applies to a song of delight in which he hailed "the arrival of the Emperor Lothar," a song which Dümmler dated between 830 and 840. That period included the years of tragedy for Louis the Pious. Could it be that Walafrid was hailing here the arrival of Lothar from Italy after Easter in 830? If this were so, he was perhaps hoping that this son and heir would aid rather than attack his father. The very thought of Lothar's attack upon the Emperor and the consequent internal strife would have been too fearful for him to conceive.

More than once we catch a glimpse of his grief in the misery of this time. To Modoin, himself a poet, he wrote in the sadness of the years which followed 830: "I would hope for the comfort of your verse, were not evils rife throughout the realm. Now the teacher has become soldier, the patron a warrior. Alas! how clearly is Satan's honour served! Peace is driven far from the earth."

Another letter, in elegiac verse, went to Prudentius, then chaplain of the Court and later, as we have seen, bishop of Troyes and annalist of the Frankish state. Prudentius was a native of Spain, and as a young man he had been known as Galindo. In after years his literary ambition had led him to borrow the name of Prudentius, the well-known Spanish poet. He, too, loved the Empress well. It has been thought that she was the noble lady who asked him, as he tells in one of his letters, to make for her a "Flores psalmorum," an anthology of passages from the Psalms, to comfort her in her troubles, probably those of 830–33. Walafrid wrote to Prudentius to beg for a commentary on the epic of Lucan and a copy of the minor poems of Virgil.

Verses, too, full of affection, went to a curious character named Bodo. It is Prudentius who tells of Bodo in his *Annals*. He was Alemannian by birth and, therefore, of Walafrid's land, educated at the Court of Louis the Pious, where Walafrid knew him as deacon of the Church. In 838, the year in which Walafrid left the Court, Bodo, now one of the royal chaplains, gained permission from Louis to leave Aachen for a pilgrimage to Rome. During his absence he astounded and horrified all men by boldly declaring himself a convert to the Jewish faith. Henceforth, circumcised, wearing long hair and beard, he elected to be called "Eleazar" and to live in marriage with a wife of Jewish race. The affair caused great scandal; for long the Emperor refused to believe the news. Prudentius declared that Bodo had been tempted by "wretched greed." As "Eleazar" he made his home in Spain, at Saragossa. Of course, the verses sent to him by Walafrid were written long before this strange apostasy.

6

In 838 Prince Charles was fifteen, a knight of the Frankish realm and lord of much of its western portion. He no longer needed a tutor's care; and, in gratitude for Walafrid's service to the young prince, Louis the Pious bestowed upon him the rule of the abbey of Reichenau, that "Augia" which he knew so well.

The nine years of his work for young Charles had been a heavy burden of responsibility; but, had Walafrid only lived longer, he would have found his reward. Extravagant praise, it is true, was lavished on this favorite youngest son of the Frankish royal house. Freculf, bishop of Lisieux, in a "Mirror for a Prince," sent to his mother, saw in him a vision of another Charles the Great. In years to come, as king of the western Franks, as "Charles the Bald," he was to show himself ambitious, persevering, and determined. He came, indeed, to a sad end, overcome by his own political ambition and by events and circumstances too strong for him. He could not hold the support of his nobles; he offended his bishops; he was conquered by rebellion within the lands he accounted his own and by the unceasing descents of the Northmen from without. Yet he stands out in his day as one of extraordinarily keen mind whenever he turned to books; he loved the learning in which he had been trained by Walafrid and which he so eagerly encouraged among his people. Not only did his own Frankish scholars look to him for support, for his interest in their labors, whether of theology, philosophy, or Biblical exegesis; he also called to his kingdom men of genius from countries abroad. Especially the Irish brought their quick minds to find security under him, in refuge from Viking invaders of their shores. Sedulius, the Irishman, who about 848 came across the sea to Liége and there drew around himself a colony of his Irish friends, all happy in royal patronage, poured out verses of gratitude and praise for Charles the Bald. As Freculf of Lisieux had prophesied long before, so now Sedulius declared: "A new Charles has arisen, bearing the power of the old." Scribes and artists worked at this king's command, offered to him their skill in picture, prose, and verse. Another Irishman, John the Scot, the most brilliant thinker of his time, however deservedly he incurred the censure of Catholic critics, formed at Laon in the kingdom of this Charles another settlement of the Irish and for many years led the teaching at his Palace School. For King Charles—"my Charles" he called him— this John translated from Greek into Latin the works of the pseudo-Dionysius, and in his preface wrote of his patron as the support of all researchers into the mysteries of the Christian faith. Since it was the Irish who knew the secrets of Greek, the study of its language and literature on the Continent owed a vast debt to Charles the Bald.

This vast debt Walafrid did not live to realize. At Reichenau he ruled as abbot for two years, from 838 until 840. Then, just before the death of his friend, Louis the Pious, trouble came to him. As we saw, Louis in the last months of his life made division of Frankish lands between his eldest son, Lothar, and his youngest, Charles. Only Bavaria was left to their brother, Louis the German. The resentment of Louis sent him on a raid of plundering into Alemannia, and he drove the abbot of Reichenau from his monastery's seat.

7

From 840 until 842 the abbot was in exile, while hostility, rising into war, divided Lothar from Louis and Charles. From afar Walafrid watched the ever-growing rift in that unity of Empire which was his ideal; and earnestly he hoped that in Lothar, as appointed Emperor by Louis the Pious himself, supremacy of rule might at last be restored.

The history of the crisis of these years in the Frankish Empire, a history which cannot be disregarded in any attempt to
portray men of its time, is given in detail by Nithard, a cousin
of Lothar and his brothers. In his vivid narrative—Nithard himself, as he declares, had a "not inconsiderable part" in its action
—we see Lothar, after word of his father's death reached him in
Italy, cautiously advancing across the Alps to claim the title of
Emperor and the lands bequeathed to him, with all those which
he could seize from his two brothers. His, he now reflected, was
by right of inheritance the royal Palace at Ingelheim on the Rhine.
One of his first acts on arriving there was to issue, in August 840,
an edict reinvesting the banished Ebbo with the see and diocese
of Reims, with "that power, Ebbo, which for Our sake you lost
by hostile force." Men of rank hurried to Lothar's support. Drogo,
that loyal half-brother of the late Emperor, now signed this Act
in favor of Ebbo, and so did a line of bishops, all eager that in the
spirit of 817 Lothar should hold supreme control. Not one of
these bishops, however, belonged to the ecclesiastical Province
of Reims; and the act after a while fell dead. The Pope refused to
confirm it, and Ebbo held his regained see of metropolitan dignity
only a bare ten months.

Of this we shall hear later. Now Lothar marched out to conquer. Nithard—and his story here is confirmed by the Frankish
annals—shows him crossing the Rhine to attack, first his brother
Louis, then Charles. Charles was godson of Lothar, one whom
Lothar had sworn to protect. Now Charles pleaded with him for
peace, but in vain. In a short while Lothar was crossing the Seine,
invading the realm given to Charles by the edict of Worms in 839;
and Hilduin, abbot of Saint-Denis, with many others, was yielding
him homage.

Neither Lothar nor Charles, however, was ready for open
breaking out of war between their forces. Lothar was at enmity
with Louis the German; Charles was worried by rebellion in his
land of Aquitaine. Near Orléans in November 840, the two brothers
met and made terms for temporary peace. By this "Truce of
Orléans" Lothar allowed Charles the rule, or nominal rule, over
Aquitaine, Septimania, Provence, and part of the region between
the Seine and the Loire; and with this diminished dominion
Charles felt obliged to declare himself content. But only for the

present. Lothar promised to meet this brother of his again, in May 841, at Attigny, for a permanent arranging of division.

On the day assigned, May 8, Charles was waiting at Attigny; Lothar did not arrive. Another mission was sent off to him, this time by both Louis and Charles; it was one, we are told, of "men of noble rank, bishops and laymen, prudent and of good intent." If Lothar would not listen to their counsels and prayers, they were ordered to say, his brothers would turn to Divine aid for the justice they desired and intended to gain. This invasion by Lothar, they agreed, must by all means be stopped. All that Louis and Charles could do they had done, and all had ended in nothing.

Then at last they took action. They broke camp, prepared for battle, and with their armies, on June 21, 841, they came within sight of Lothar's forces, drawn up near Auxerre. The next day he suddenly left his position, a very unfavorable one for fighting, and took up his stand at Fontenoy-en-Puisaye, near the Bois de Briottes. His brothers followed him. On the twenty-third a truce was made, to last until the twenty-fifth when, Louis and Charles sent word, they would deliver assault by arms.

Messengers came and went, but brought no word of decision for peace. From seven in the morning of Saturday, June 25, the battle of Fontenoy was fought. Each side won advantage, each side suffered defeat; the result gave conquest to neither. All three brothers lived to see the end. Then Lothar fled, leaving the field to Louis and Charles, and many held them to be the victors.

The memory of this field of Fontenoy lived on in horror. "So great slaughter was wrought on either side," declared the annalist of Fulda, "as never can our memory recall at any time before among the Franks." Regino, in his *Chronicle,* published early in the tenth century, mourned that "by this battle the power of the Franks was so diminished and their glorious strength so weakened that not only were they unable in the future to extend the bounds of their realm, they could not even protect what they had."

Most striking of all these Latin records of the battle and its issue is the verse of one Angilbert, who himself was present, fighting on the side of Lothar:

> *Fontaneto fontem dicunt, villam quoque rustici,*
> *ubi strages et ruina Francorum de sanguine;*
> *orrent campi, orrent silvae, orrent ipsi paludes.*

Gramen illud ros et ymber nec humectat pluvia,
in quo fortes ceciderunt, proelio doctissimi,
pater, mater, soror, frater, quos amici fleverant.

Hoc autem scelus peractum, quod descripsi ritmice,
Angelbertus ego vidi pugnansque cum aliis,
solus de multis remansi prima frontis acie.

Karoli de parte vero, Hludovici pariter
albent campi vestimentis mortuorum lineis,
velut solent in autumno albescere avibus.

Maledicta dies illa, nec in anni circulo
numeretur, sed radatur ab omni memoria,
iubar solis illi desit, aurora crepusculo.

Noxque illa, nox amara, noxque dura nimium,
in qua fortes ceciderunt, proelio doctissimi,
pater, mater, soror, frater, quos amici fleverant.

Ploratum et ululatum nec describo amplius;
unusquique quantum potest restringatque lacrimas;
pro illorum animabus deprecemur dominum.

Fontenoy they call its fountain, manor to the peasant known,
There the slaughter, there the ruin, of the blood of Frankish race;
Plains and forest shiver, shudder; horror wakes the silent marsh.

Neither dew nor shower nor rainfall yields its freshness to that field,
Where they fell, the strong men fighting, shrewdest in the battle's skill,
Father, mother, sister, brother, friends, the dead with tears have wept.

And this deed of crime accomplished, which I here in verse have told,
Angilbert myself I witnessed, fighting with the other men,
I alone of all remaining, in the battle's foremost line.

On the side alike of Louis, on the side of Charles alike,
Lies the field in white enshrouded, in the vestments of the dead,
As it lies when birds in autumn settle white from off the shore.

Woe unto that day of mourning! Never in the round of years
Be it numbered in men's annals! Be it banished from all mind,
Never gleam of sun shine on it, never dawn its dusk awake.

Night it was, a night most bitter, harder than we could endure,
When they fell, the brave men fighting, shrewdest in the battle's skill,
Father, mother, sister, brother, friends, the dead with tears have wept.

Now the wailing, the lamenting, now no longer will I tell;
Each, so far as in him lieth, let him stay his weeping now;
On their souls may He have mercy, let us pray the Lord of all.

After Lothar had ridden away in flight, his brothers on the
morrow, Sunday, buried the dead, cared for the wounded on both
sides without discrimination, and went their ways, each to his
own land. Whatever dispute attached to other portions of the
Empire, its Carolingian tradition steadily held Lothar as ruler of
Lombardy, Louis of Bavaria, Charles of Aquitaine. Many men of
Aquitaine, it is true, did not acknowledge Charles as their lord;
they looked upon the nephew of these three brothers, Pippin II,
as their rightful ruler. Had not his father, Pippin, that brother of
Lothar and Louis, and half-brother of Charles himself, been
solemnly assigned the kingship of Aquitaine by Louis the Pious
in 817? From this division of allegiance long strife was to come.

On his way to Aquitaine Charles was met at Soissons by
monks of the abbey of Saint-Médard, who prayed to him as their
sovereign for permission to transfer into a new church, lately
built by them, the relics of certain saints, among them some
relics of the martyrs Marcellinus and Peter so dear to Einhard.
Nithard's manuscript has here received addition from a later hand;
nevertheless, it may be that Hilduin, abbot of Saint-Médard, had
not returned quite all those stolen relics which Einhard demanded
from him.

Negotiations continued between the royal brothers, but to
no end. Then, on February 14, 842, Louis and Charles met in
Strasbourg. Already their kingdoms were becoming distinct from
one another, in both character and language. Two distinct peoples
faced them in a great assembly at Strasbourg: the one, of the west,

speaking Old French; the other, of the east, speaking Old High German. Since it was necessary that both peoples should understand all that was being done, the elder brother, Louis, in Old High German, the speech of his realm, told his subjects of the evil deeds of Lothar and of the resolve which he and Charles had made to enter into sworn and lasting alliance. After him Charles declared the same decision to his people in their own Old French. Then each king swore fidelity, not only in his own tongue, but also in the language of his brother's kingdom, so that everyone might be clearly informed and satisfied.

In March the two moved again in the direction of Lothar, who hurried from Sinzig, near Coblenz, to the Palace at Aachen, which he held his by imperial right. He stayed long enough to carry off valuable treasure from its store, especially a great disc of silver, bearing, within three concentric circles, plans of the earth, sun, moon, planets, and stars. It had been greatly prized both by Charles the Great, who named it particularly in his will, and by Louis the Pious, who had reserved it for his own pleasure when he distributed his father's legacy. Now Lothar broke it into pieces for the sake of its silver.

Still there went on from one camp to another the business of parley between the brothers. On June 15, however, all three found themselves face to face in a meeting near Mâcon, on an island in the river Saône. Here they took oath henceforth to keep the peace and decided upon the manner of its ensuing. On October 1, so they solemnly agreed, their deputies, forty for each brother, were to convene at Metz, there to divide the Frankish Empire into three portions, excluding those realms of Lombardy, Aquitaine, and Bavaria. Each brother was to receive one of these three portions; and Lothar was to have the first choice. Even this tentative move on the Saône was only brought about "with great difficulty, indeed scarcely reached at all." Not until August 843 was the division in any way settled.

8

It was during these years and their tragic happenings, from 840 until 842, that Walafrid knew the burdens of exile. At first he took refuge in Speyer. From there he may have gone on to Fulda, his old school, where Hraban Maur, like himself, desired the establishing of Lothar as Emperor. To Hraban, at any rate, we find him writing. He was in dire poverty and need, in misery of mind and suffering of body. No sandals even had he for his feet. Would Hraban not do something for his relief?

To Lothar he wrote in enthusiastic praise: "The hope of our fatherland lies in you," his verses declared. "Cease not to toil; all things shall fight for your cause." Then comes another prayer for aid to himself: "Much have I suffered in your father's death. Forgotten are the fields of Alemannia. I have fled from lands ruined by division within the Empire. Put out your hand, hallowed Emperor, to help those who have followed you."

But, poor as he was, and miserably homesick for his "happy island," he found comfort in study. Perhaps it was in Fulda's library that he now wrote his most interesting endeavor in prose, his work called *On the Beginnings and on the Growth of Observances in the Church.* Reginbert, the learned librarian at Reichenau, he said, had urged him to carry out this work.

It is a little manual of instruction concerning the outward and the inward building up of churches, explained by reference to philology, to history, and to custom, with copious quotation and illustration from the Bible and from patristic authority. "Nothing, indeed, do I attempt to set forth which I have not read as it stands, and from my reading have concluded to be truth; or which I have not gathered from the words of honest men; or which I have not learned from prevailing tradition." Explanation of names of the church and its furnishings is traced by derivation; description is given of customs dating from ancient days. Here Walafrid's knowledge of Greek, scanty as it was, served him well; even the barbarians of the German race, he reminds us, when they were fighting in the Roman armies learned and brought into permanent use Greek names for the church and its contents. The mention of pictures and images in the church allows him to state his own position in regard to their cult; like Einhard, he was neither iconoclast nor iconodule. If God, he argues, did not want to draw men toward Himself by means of beauty, why did He give the stars their splendor, the flowers their fragrance?

From material things Walafrid passes to spiritual, from buildings to ritual, from pictures to prayer:

Let us pray as those who have entered the presence of God and His angels, and let our minds attend upon our voices. At times we shall pray aloud in men's hearing. Did not Solomon bless all the congregation of Israel with a loud voice when he dedicated the Temple of the Lord? And did not the writer of the Apocalypse hear crying from under the altar the souls of them that were slain for the word of God? Yet the Lord heard Hannah, too, as she entreated Him for a child of her womb, though only her lips moved and no sound was heard.

God is worshipped most truly where there is least of vanity and pride. Even St. Augustine, in his *Confessions,* told of his wishing, now and again, that all the charm of the chanting of psalms might be far from his ears. Delight even in music, he knew, music in the service of God, could become a hindrance to the devotion of the heart.

It avails nothing, indeed, that the church be noble and its chanting a joy, if the hearts of those gathered there are not with God. From that church He departs with all His servants, and with Him go the angels who stand before His throne on earth. Nadab and Abihu, in the Old Testament, offered strange fire before the Lord, and they died, devoured by fire itself. Punishment came upon Uzzah, who touched the ark of God; and upon Uzziah the king, who desired to burn incense in His Presence, usurping that right which pertained to the priests alone, the consecrated sons of Aaron. Yet the Lord delivers from misery and peril those who reverence Him with a humble offering. Job rises from the ashes, Jeremiah from the mire; Daniel comes forth from the lions, Peter from prison, Paul from storm at sea. Evil cast down the angels from heaven, just as righteousness has rescued men from hell.

Let those who build and adorn churches give of their wealth honestly acquired. Let them offer of the fruits of hard toil, following the example of David, who would not give to the Lord his God of that which cost him nothing. Let them give, too, in love, not as the Pharisees, who rendered in barren scruple of convention their tithes of mint and rue and every other herb. The poor and the suffering are of more value in the eyes of God than even a magnificent Cathedral built by the pride of men. Did not holy Jerome point out the folly of those whose churches shine with gold while Christ lies hungry and naked at their doors? Moses built the tabernacle, but angered the Lord at the water of strife; Solomon raised his temple, and sinned, seduced by the face of woman. What doth the Lord require of thee, O man, cries Micah, but to do justly and to love mercy and to walk humbly with thy God?

Is not bread made of many grains of flour kneaded with water into one whole, and is not wine pressed out from many grapes? So is the

Body of Christ one union of the multitude of the saints. In this thought our fathers decreed that wine in the chalice should be mingled with water in order that the waters of the vision of the Apocalypse, "which are peoples and multitudes and nations and tongues," should not be separated from the consecrated wine which is Christ Himself.

How often should one receive this gift? Some Christians in time past, so Walafrid has learned from his reading, judged it meet to communicate once a year, fearful lest briefer preparation should send them to the altar unready and unfit; and they chose Holy Thursday for their devotion. Others, in their need of spiritual healing, came to the altar once a week, and allowed themselves to say the Lord's Prayer only at this time, for they held that its Bread for the day was of the soul rather than the body. Some now are bold to make their communions daily, conquering the thought of presumption by their desire, and mindful of the apostles, who, "continuing daily with one accord in the temple, and breaking bread from house to house, did eat their meat with gladness and singleness of heart."

Bound up with this question is that of the priest's offering of the Holy Sacrifice. In Walafrid's ninth century a priest might celebrate its ritual twice, three times, or even more often in one day, did he wish to do so. It was a matter of his decision and his desire. Did he do better, Walafrid asks, to celebrate once, remembering that the Lord of the living and the dead died once for all to take away the sins of men? Or should he believe that the more often he pleaded the Passion of Christ at the altar, the larger the mercy gained by this offering from God the Judge?

"Surely"—and here Walafrid puts in a word of his own— "surely it is better that a priest celebrate two or three times in a day than that Masses decreed by authority, as on Christmas Day, be omitted. Moreover, Masses are offered for very varied intent: in universal observance of special days, in private intercession for the living and the dead. If several of these intents call for Mass on one and the same day, and only one priest is available, either they must be united in the offering of one Mass, or several Masses must be said by one and the same celebrant." "Let every man decide, then," he writes, "in obedience to the will of the Church and the faith of his own inner spirit." And at what time should

Mass be celebrated? This, Walafrid states, may be morning, noon, evening, and sometimes at night.

After much detail of instruction on the canonical hours of prayer, the history of the chanting of psalms among the Franks, the use and practice proper for the administration of holy baptism, we then come to a few forceful words concerning the giving of tithes in alms. "The children of Israel gave tithes in oblation to the priests of the Lord; and this was only proper, since the Lord struck the Egyptians with ten plagues for their release from bondage. And should not those who live under the teaching of the Gospel show even greater zeal, seeing that they have more priests and a truer sacramental worship? Indeed should not tithes be given by Christian men in order that priests and ministers of the Church may be released from material necessity, set free from worry, free for meditation on the Divine law, free for teaching, free for the glad fulfilling of spiritual service, and in order, too, that the poor may be supported and that churches may be restored?"

At the end of his treatise Walafrid observes: "I have not found all the information which I was keen to find, nor have I reported on all that I found. It was all of interest, but there was so much that I could not tell it all. At least the reader who wants to know more will find here a goad to drive him on."

9

In 842 Louis the German, king of Bavaria, was weary of strife. Walafrid's former teacher, Grimald, well known in service at the Court of Louis, since 841 had also been abbot of Saint-Gall; and it was probably through his intercession that the king now allowed Walafrid to return as abbot to Reichenau. Seven years he was to rule there, and for him there now was peace.

Outside his island, however, the world was still unsettled. In August 843, the long-awaited division of the Frankish Empire between the three royal brothers was finally made and confirmed in the famous Treaty sworn at Verdun. As had been planned, it fell into three parts. To Louis, with the exception of Frisia, went the land east of the Rhine, and also the counties of Speyer, Worms, and Mainz, on the river's western side; to Lothar went the title of

Emperor and the rule over Central Frankland, extending from the northern coast of Frisia southward west of the Rhine, on to Provence and the Mediterranean, and eastward to include north and central Italy; to Charles, the portion west of this, stretching northward to the Atlantic and southward into Spain.

To Lothar went both capital cities, Aachen and Rome. His it was to work as Emperor with the Pope for the safe and secure functioning of the Catholic Church. In this, in his imperial heritage, and in his rule over the largest of the three portions, his dignity and power excelled those of his brothers; in other respects their standing as kings equalled his.

The partition sorely vexed those who longed for unity of rule over Frankland, and their grief found voice in a lament by Florus of Lyons, who added verse to his diatribes in prose against the evils rampant in his time:

> Lost to the Empire is now both name and glory,
> The realm, once one, hath fallen in triple lot;
> No man is Emperor, assessed in thought or honour,
> For king a kinglet, for realm the realm's dividings.

But the three kings all swore loyalty to one another before they departed from Verdun, each to rule his own realm, while Lothar again made haste to establish his imperial title.

In 844 the Pope, Gregory IV, died; and his rule came by election to Sergius II. Now Lothar sent his son Louis to Rome, accompanied by Drogo, recently raised from bishop to archbishop of Metz. Both were honored by the new Pope. Sergius anointed and crowned young Louis as king of Italy, and appointed Drogo as his vicar apostolic for Frankish lands of France and of Germany. In October of the same year Lothar, Louis the German, and Charles once more met, outwardly, at least, in brotherly concord, at Yütz, near Thionville, made their resolutions for union in peace, and listened to the godly and stringent admonitions of a Synod of bishops assembled at Thionville under the presidency of Archbishop Drogo, vicar apostolic.

Not only Drogo himself, but also the Emperor had been delighted by the conferring of the honor upon Drogo. Lothar hoped that by this power in the hands of his supporter his own control might increase. Soon, however, it came to nothing, since a Council of bishops assembled at Ver, near Senlis, in December 844, referred it to possible action in the future, and eventually Drogo ceased to preside.

The light of harmony kindled at Yütz was to be extinguished and to be renewed time after time in the coming years, while wars of rebellion, strife of rivalry, and assault from without racked and plundered Frankish lands, especially those of Charles, that pupil of Walafrid at Aachen. War, intrigue, and discord will meet us in their abundance later on, when we come to think of churchmen personally and vitally concerned with them in this ninth century. Abbot Walafrid, living in his monastery of Reichenau under the kingship of Louis the German, turned from tidings and rumors of these horrors, first to his prayers for Charles in his manifold perils and problems, then to the care of the brethren entrusted to his ruling, to the comfort and well-being of his friends, to the writing which still awaited his labor. Diplomatic and political missions he would fulfill if called upon by his king; but they were not in themselves part of his life. Probably to these later years belongs his editing of two *Lives:* of Charles the Great, by Einhard; and of his son, Louis the Pious, by that Thegan, bishop in Trier, to whom Walafrid had written verses in his schoolboy days.

The *Life* by Einhard we have already observed. Walafrid now divided it into chapters, provided these with headings, and placed at the beginning a preface of his own. As we also have marked, Walafrid's praise of Einhard in this preface, as in the verses inspired by the statue of King Theodoric the Goth, was great and generous. There is, however, in the same preface a passage which has been keenly discussed. Here Walafrid wrote: "Not only in the days of Charles himself, but—which is a greater marvel—under Louis as Emperor, when the Frankish State was tossed by storms and in many places was falling into ruin, by some wonderful gift of poise, bestowed upon him by Heaven for his protection, Einhard so guarded himself that neither by untimely action did he lose his repute for high and noble character—as many men did, at the cost of ill-will and peril—nor did he bring himself into dangers too great for remedy."

Does there lie hidden in these words a sting of bitter sarcasm, of scorn for Einhard's withdrawal from politics in the crucial years of Louis the Pious as Emperor? It may be so. But, if the scorn be there, it is singularly out of keeping with the generous and ever-kindly character of the writer and singularly different from his praise of Einhard's "unbroken honour and splendid repute" in the time of Charles the Great.

There is, indeed, one lament by Walafrid in this preface which is clear for all to read. He has been describing in glowing words the work of Charles the Great for the advancement of learning in his kingdom. He then writes: "Now, since enthusiasm for study is slipping back from high to low tide, the light of wisdom through lack of love is growing pale in many minds."

A very different tone appears in the treatment of Thegan's *Life of Louis the Pious,* also provided by Walafrid with chapters, headings, and preface. Here he writes: "This work Thegan, a Frank by birth and a bishop of the church of Trier (*chorepiscopus*), wrote in annalistic fashion, briefly and with more of truth than charm. Now and again he seems to give his opinions too fervently, extravagantly. He was a man high-minded and keen, who resented the bestowal of office on low-born persons and who could not keep his anger silent. Also, his exceeding passion for justice and for its wielder, the Most Christian Emperor, increased this natural resentment of what was wrong. But since his work is written in an honest spirit, it must not be scorned for some show of crudity. He was a student of wide reading, we know, but much occupied in his duties as preacher and administrator."

With this view of Thegan's anger and his loyalty to his king the critic will agree if he reads Thegan's chapter forty-four on the humiliation of Louis the Pious at the hands of Ebbo and his fellow bishops in the church at Saint-Médard, Soissons.

10

Yet these, important as they are, are not the writings of which men think first when they remember Walafrid at Reichenau. More often they see him, not laboring in his cell among his books, but in the open air outside, stooping to peer closely at his fragrant herbs, to gather their fruits for the healing of his brethren. It was this delight which brought from him not long before 849 twenty-

seven brief poems, now assembled under the general title of
Hortulus, or "The Little Garden." Their hexameter verses are not
so easy to read as the lyrics which he wrote in so many different
meters. The science of curative properties, the description of
growth and appearance, mingled with many glances at myth and
folk tale, tend at first to hide the love of Nature, the devoted care
for living things, which a second reading reveals so clearly.

In these verses we see Abbot Walafrid one winter day, looking out from his monastery upon a little courtyard before its door,
rough, long neglected, full of nettles, of tangled stems buried
deep below the ground. And as he looks, a thought is born within
him. Come spring at last, in his leisure hours he will dig and hoe
and fertilize, he will sow and plant. Surely here his abbey shall
have, like other houses of monks, its own garden of remedies for
sickness brought about by cold and damp, for casualties of wounds
and bruises, for troubles of indigestion due to coarse food. It shall
have, too, its own store of savory herbs to cheer a palate so long
inured to monotony.

Spring came, and the resolve held good. The abbot's back
ached as he toiled, pulling, plucking, digging. His hands were blis-
tered as he tore out the long, stubborn roots, entwined in the soil
like woven work of wicker, as he broke up the clods with his hoe;
they were stained dark and dirty as his spade spread rich manure
over the opened ground. Then he sowed and planted, then he
watched through sun and rain as the days grew longer and
warmer, until to his joy green shoots began to appear. Now he
worked more busily than ever. In dry weather he brought water,
cask after cask, the purest water in the largest casks he could find,
and let it fall upon his nursery drop by drop, fearful lest too sudden a rush might drown his tender seedlings. Many were the
problems of his care. The little courtyard faced east and the early
sun; but the jutting roof of the monastery kept part of it from its
due share of rain, while elsewhere a wall threw deep shadow, and
darkness hindered growth.

Yet the toil brought full reward. At length it was high summer,
of this year and the next, and Walafrid was pacing from plant to
plant, from shrub to shrub, all alive with promise of abundant
harvest. The herbs now rising sturdily in this little enclosure were

those regularly found at the time in kitchen gardens. All except five of these described here are named in the instructions given by Charles the Great in a Capitulary, dated about 800, for the provision of necessary stock on his imperial estates.

Did ills of the stomach, writes Walafrid, distress the brethren of Reichenau? * Here was fennel, pleasant to taste and pleasant, too, to smell; its seeds dipped in goat's milk made rapid cure. Here was chervil, to mix with pennyroyal and poppy leaves; or a concoction could be made from the clump of clary, rising high with stout stems and ample foliage. Parsley, too, was here to aid this "lord of the body," the stomach, if one only mixed its juice with water and sharp vinegar. Here was the sword-lily, gladiolus. Grind to powder its roots, and an ailing bladder would promptly be relieved. Did a brother complain of a racking cough? On the garden's edge tufts of feathery foliage marked radishes in plenty. Crush their roots, and healing, pungent but sure, would be his. For hoarseness and loss of voice there also grew mint of various kinds. Did headache trouble a novice, beset by problems of life? The abbot would make syrup of wormwood, would bathe in this the patient's head, and then bind the plant's leaves, well washed, around his brow and soon comfort would return once more. If poison taken by accident was causing crisis, juice of horehound, boiling hot, could be administered: a nauseous draught, but quick to act; or a potion from the cluster of rue, opening wide its leaves and panicles of flower. You could tell it afar by its scent. Near at hand were spreading the fragrant fibers, long and fine as a woman's hair, of southernwood, useful for rheumatism, for relief in fever, for the healing of wounds. So, too, for wounds the abbot could seek out his betony, plucked in summer and applied fresh, as poultice, or dried and stored against the winter's need; or his rows of tall agrimony, a lovely sight, from which he would make ointment with mixture of vinegar. Should the wound lie in the scalp, wash it, he bade, in a bath made from his catmint, very efficacious, especially if enriched with oil of roses. And along the front of the garden grew sweet-smelling sage, powerful against unnumbered troubles.

* The modern reader unacquainted with herbs, their uses and their poisons, is warned not to try any of these medieval remedies!

Yet Walafrid was cautious in his praise of his herb garden. One must be careful, he would say, in use of lovage. Better mix it with other remedies than apply it alone, because folk had long claimed that too frequent use would bring a cloud of darkness over the eyes.

Other of his plants provided food for Reichenau's community. The vine climbing over the trellis-work and weaving a web of twisted chain as it rose from stage to stage bore gourds in plenty. These, gathered while tender and succulent, sliced and cooked in a bubbling pan of rich fat, made a delicious dish for dinner. Their shells, empty, dry, and hard, made wonderful jars for wine. Walafrid's melons, too, ripened well on the ground in the sun. So juicy were they that the sap poured forth when a knife cut into them. Easy were they for an old brother's eating and full of goodly nourishment.

Two flowers in this garden were especially dear to this gardener monk. They were, of course, the lily and the rose; and when Walafrid reaches them in his verse, he turns from thought of sick bodies to happy souls. Not Parian marble gleams with greater radiance than the lily, not spikenard breathes a fairer fragrance. The lily brings to mind the purity of virgins; the rose tells of the blood of martyrs. Both are loved by the Virgin Queen of Heaven, the roses for the war against evil which the saints have waged, the lilies for joyous peace after toil.

When this story of his labors and of their fruits was finished and ready, in twenty-six divisions, Walafrid sent it to the monastery of Saint-Gall as a gift for Grimald, his teacher, friend, and protector, now abbot of Saint-Gall and of Weissenburg, or Wissembourg, in Alsace. Before his offering left him, however, he added a dedication, a picture of Abbot Grimald, a picture both tranquil and gay:

> A gift of little worth and service, Grimald,
> My Father of great learning, your Strabo sends to you,
> A gift of no importance, but offered with his love.
> That while you sit within your garden's closure
> Under the orchard's dim and leafy shadow,
> Where peach trees cast unequal light from quivering leaves;

While for you, Father, fruit with tender down of bloom
Your boys are plucking merrily, your happy school,
Grasping huge peaches in their hands outstretched,
Trying to hold within their palms each swelling round;
That, Father, by this gift you hold in mind my toil,
In reading what I gladly send; and reading thus
May cut away the bad, I pray, approve what pleases you.
Heaven fill you with the sap of its eternal energy
To reach reward hereafter, never-fading life;
God, Father, Son, and Holy Spirit, grant this of His grace.

11

In 848 Abbot Walafrid received a letter from Gottschalk, once his fellow pupil in Fulda. Many years had passed since they had studied there, and Gottschalk had known much trouble. Rumors of his doings had reached Walafrid from time to time, and now this letter, written in verse, both comforted and distressed his heart.

In June 829, before a Synod of bishops gathered at Mainz, his friend, weary of monastic discipline and eager for new fields, for debate and discussion outside his abbey, had pleaded for release from his life in religion. He had been brought to it as a child by his parents, he said; he had, in fact, been driven by pressure to accept it. Against him the abbot of Fulda, Hraban Maur, had vehemently contended that "it was lawful for a Christian man to dedicate his offspring to God in religion; that a vow vowed unto God could not be broken without great sin." Argument had been urged on both sides. Hatto, who was to follow Hraban in office at Fulda, had supported Gottschalk; but most churchmen had been of the mind of Hincmar, who, writing many years afterward from his archbishop's see of Reims, declared that Gottschalk had solemnly been offered as a child to the cloister, had been trained according to Rule, and in outward observance had obeyed it day by day. Hincmar had added, however: "In choir he sang with his lips. In his heart he could not perceive the meaning of what he sang, since wisdom entered not into a soul of evil desire, nor dwelt in a body subject to sin."

The Synod in 829 had debated and in the end allowed Gott-

schalk his freedom; but so great had been the feeling against him
and so powerful the influence of Hraban, that after a stay in the
monastery of Corbie, near Amiens, he had entered the cloistered
life again, at Orbais, southwest of Épernay, in the metropolitan
province of Reims. There he had spent all the time he could gain
from duties of the monastic round in reading St. Augustine and
in writing hymns for the relief of his soul and for the delight of
verse. We have these hymns still, with much other poetry from
his hand. The words are simple and show intense feeling; the
rhythms are wrought with extraordinary art. Thus had passed the
time until 835, or shortly afterward, when, without the authority,
without even the knowledge, of his diocesan bishop in Soissons,
he had been ordained priest by one Rigbold, then serving as
bishop in the cathedral of Reims.

This, Walafrid knew, was serious enough; but it was by no
means all. During the many hours that Gottschalk had spent on
Augustine and on Augustine's follower, Fulgentius, a learned
bishop of Ruspe in Africa of the sixth century, he had considered
long and deeply their teachings in regard to the future life of the
souls of men, good and evil, throughout eternity. This cogent
matter had, indeed, after the death of Augustine, been in constant
dispute among theologians of the fifth and the sixth centuries.
Did the Lord God will to leave "a mass of perdition," the great
multitude of the souls He had created, to suffer eternal damnation
in hell? Was this really the teaching of Augustine? Or had men
misinterpreted him? If it was his teaching, how should one reconcile with it the Church's doctrine on grace and love?

In 529, at the Second Council of Orange in the south of
France, the bishops, assembled under the leadership of Caesarius,
archbishop of Arles, had followed the authority of Augustine for
the condemning of semi-Pelagian error. After laying down twenty-
five canons drawn from his writings, they had concluded their
pronouncements with a general declaration on the doctrines of
grace, free will, and predestination. It contained these words:

*Hoc etiam secundum fidem catholicam credimus quod, post ac-
ceptam per baptismum gratiam, omnes baptizati Christo auxiliante et
cooperante, quae ad salutem animae pertinent, possint et debeant, si
fideliter laborare voluerint, adimplere. Aliquos vero ad malum divina*

*potestate praedestinatos esse, non solum non credimus, sed etiam, si
sunt qui tantum mali credere velint, cum omni detestatione illis anathema dicimus:*

This we believe according to the Catholic Faith: that, after receiving the grace of Baptism, all the baptized, with the aid and the cooperation of Christ, are obliged to fulfill, and, if they are willing to
labour faithfully, are able to fulfill, the things which pertain to the
salvation of the soul. That some are predestined to evil by Divine power
we do not believe; and, if there are those who are willing to believe so
great evil, upon such with all abhorrence we declare anathema.

On January 25, 531, Pope Boniface II had confirmed the
words of this Second Council of Orange. They had then become
part of orthodox Catholic doctrine, and controversy had died
away.

But in the ninth century doubt and dispute rose again, and
this doubt rankled in the restless mind of young Gottschalk. In
his thought, as he read in his cell at Orbais, there had been truly
born, as he judged from his study of Augustine and of Augustine's
study of St. Paul, a theory which had slowly grown within him
into an impassioned belief. Long afterward his great opponent,
Hincmar, archbishop of Reims, was to sum up this belief of Gottschalk in five sentences:

1. That the Deity of the Holy Trinity is threefold, just as there are three
   Persons of the Holy Trinity;
2. That there is a twofold predestination of men by God. Some men He
   predestines to eternal life, others to eternal death;
3. That God does not will all men to be saved. Those who are saved,
   He has willed to be saved; those whose salvation He has not willed,
   are not saved;
4. That Our Lord and Saviour Jesus Christ did not die upon the Cross
   for all men; but only for those who are saved;
5. That the words of 2 St. Peter, 2, i: "Denying the Lord Who bought
   them," are to be explained by teaching that the Lord bought such
   evil men by the sacrament of Holy Baptism, but did not for their
   sake undergo death upon the Cross nor shed His Blood.

Gottschalk, therefore, held that, from the beginning, God had
foreordained the souls of men to separate and different destiny:

some to eternal joy in His Presence, others to eternal misery in the final and lasting loss of Heaven.

As time went on and his belief became more deeply rooted, he had begun to teach what he held, and men had not only listened, but had accepted his words. Fearful they were. Yet Gottschalk had spoken as one who knew; he had woven a chain of logic which to some of his hearers appeared irrefutable. And had he not argued from the words of Holy Scripture itself? Some were drawn to join him when, before 840, he escaped from Orbais and fled to Rome. From Rome he had traveled here and there in northern Italy and had then settled down on an island under the rule of Eberhard, count of Friuli, where he had stayed more than two years. To all whom he met he had told of what he had come to believe, and of his struggle against monastic life. Banishment from his former companions had cost him much; and we still have lines of appealing sadness which he wrote in this island refuge. Perhaps they were sent to a young friend of his; perhaps they tell us of himself as addressed to his own soul in his solitude:

> *Ut quid iubes, pusiole,*
> *quare mandas, filiole,*
> *   carmen dulce me cantare,*
> *   cum sim longe exul valde*
> *   intra mare?*
> *   o cur iubes canere?*

And most certainly toward the end he cried to that Lord God Whom in his heart he loved:

> *Exul ego diuscule*
> *hoc in mari sum, domine:*
> *   annos nempe duos fere*
> *   nosti fore, sed iam iamque*
> *   miserere.*
> *   hoc rogo humillime.*

His unorthodox doctrine had so worried the Church in northern Italy that Noting, bishop-elect of Verona, had written off to Hraban Maur, begging him to set down in writing the Catholic teaching in regard to predestination, for all to read. This Hraban had done and in 840 had sent his treatise to Noting. Six years later he had felt compelled to do more. About 846 he had sent an urgent letter to Gottschalk's host, the Count of Friuli: "Word is being spread abroad here that you have staying with you a dabbler in books called Gottschalk. He is asserting, people declare, that a predestination by act of God binds men; that even if one wills to be saved and in this faith of salvation strives with honest and good words to attain eternal joy, he labours to no purpose and in vain if God has not predestined him for that joy. As though God by His predestining compels men to perish! He, the Author of our salvation! And more. The teaching of this Gottschalk has brought many men to despair of themselves. They are saying: 'What good is it for me to toil for my salvation and for eternal happiness? If I do good and I am not marked down for Heaven, it avails me nothing. If, on the other hand, God *has* destined me for happiness throughout eternity, then I can do all the evil I like on earth and I shall reach Heaven just the same!' I trust that you, my dear and honourable friend, are a good Christian, and do not want to have anything in your land which is enemy to the gospel of Christ."

Without delay Eberhard had driven Gottschalk from Friuli in disgrace and shame. He had gone forth, to wander through what is now Yugoslavia, Hungary, and Austria, always teaching as before, and finally had returned to eastern Frankland. From there, at Christmas of 848, it would seem, Walafrid received the letter noted above, written in verse. He wrote back to express —also in verse—his happiness in hearing from this dear "father and brother." "Your words," he said, "came to lift the cloud now hanging over us in this realm of Louis the German." But with this very natural expression of delight in receiving Gottschalk's letter, whatever his present circumstances, came a rebuke. Gottschalk, Walafrid complained, was not using for the aid of the world the talent with which God had endowed him. He added a warning: "I would not have you think that I want to hurt you, only that I would not willingly be silent concerning the danger in which, if I know the truth, you find yourself. Be unto me a friend, as I in all loyalty shall be a friend to you."

Evidently Walafrid was well aware that Gottschalk stood in peril, and he was deeply distressed; but at this Christmastide he did not, it seems, know all that by this time had happened. Already, in October 848, in the presence of King Louis the German, the bishops of eastern Frankland had met in formidable array at Mainz under the leadership of Hraban, since 847 archbishop of its see. To them Gottschalk had offered a long, passionate defense of his belief. It had fallen on horrified, angry ears. He had been condemned as heretic and had been sent to Reims, which was the metropolitan authority holding jurisdiction over Orbais, the monastery from which he had fled. At Reims he had been delivered for judgment to Hincmar, its archbishop, and Hincmar had promptly returned him to Orbais, and, as he hoped, to a life of penance and penitence.

Walafrid heard of these tragic happenings some time later, probably in the spring of 849. He heard at the same time of further trouble, lately come to pass. For Gottschalk had not shown penitence. He had continued unmoved by either force or persuasion; and Hincmar, after conference with Hraban Maur, had decided to bring him before another, even more august council of Frankish prelates. It had been called into session by the king of the western Franks, Charles the Bald, at his Palace of Quierzy in the spring of 849. Once again with all firmness, this time indeed with open defiance, Gottschalk had maintained his views. "Heretic," once again, and "incorrigible" he had been declared, and he had been punished accordingly. He had then and there been scourged until, as those who were present had told, "he was nearly dead," and he had been driven by sheer exhaustion to obey the order to cast a "Confession" of his belief upon a fire blazing in front of the assembly. He had been deposed from the priest's office so irregularly conferred and sent into strict keeping of imprisonment in the monastery of Hautvillers, near Épernay. This was in the archdiocese of Reims and therefore subject to Hincmar's ruling. Hincmar had made no move to send this heretic of "irrevocable self-will" back again to Orbais. The monastery of Orbais was under the immediate jurisdiction of Soissons, a suffragan see under Reims, and the bishop of Soissons at this time, Rothad, was, in the opinion of Hincmar, "a lover of novelty who could not be counted on to resist Gottschalk's arguments."

12

The Council of Quierzy sat until well into April 849. We may believe that Walafrid heard of Gottschalk's trial and sentencing at Quierzy from King Charles the Bald himself. For he had left his abbey of Reichenau—sometime during the previous year, 848, in all probability—at the request of Louis the German, to travel on a mission to Charles the Bald. In his reply to Gottschalk's letter Walafrid had said that it had reached him "in a Palace," which may well have been that at Quierzy, or some other residence of Charles. He was, no doubt, in close touch with the king through the spring and summer of 849; and he was, we know, in the realm of Charles in late summertime of this year, about to start on his return journey home, when by some accident death fell upon him as he was crossing the river Loire on August 18.

We learn of this untimely happening—he was still in his early forties—from Ermenric, a monk of the abbey of Ellwangen in Württemberg, who had been studying under him at Reichenau shortly before he had left there in 848. We learn of it also from Hraban Maur, who wrote in verse his epitaph. His body was laid to rest upon his beloved isle. Much must have been in his mind of plans for the future, much thought of more writing to come. We know that he was thinking of a version in meter of his prose *Life* of holy Gall. This version was eventually made, the achievement, unsatisfactory enough, of a monk of Saint-Gall whose name we do not know.

Walafrid's name lived on, as of one who loved his books; who loved all things created by God for life and happiness; who, above all, loved his friends. It is this threefold love which gave to the Carolingian age his poetry, and with it light to the bleak darkness of much mediocre verse. Among its records Walafrid and his friend Gottschalk, who bent their heads together over their Virgil in Fulda's library, still stand as witnesses to the passion of their delight in the human and the humane. No one who once has read the Latin lines which he wrote "To Luitger, cleric" can entirely forget Walafrid:

In love's dear service and with heart's devotion true
    To Luitger, Strabus sends this little note.
Though small perhaps appears affection on my part,
    Yet, I believe, thou holdst me well in mind.
All that thou hast of joy I want for thee; thy grief,
    If grief there is, is pain within my soul.
As mother loves her only boy, as sun to earth,
    As dew to grass, and stream to thirsty fish,
As air to birds that sing, as purling brooks to meads,
    So dear thy face, my little one, to me.

Nor can one forget his verses "To an absent friend":

When from on high the moon's pure splendour shines,
Stand then beneath the sky and think enthralled
Upon that glory's far-thrown radiance;
How its pure splendour holds encircled those
In body far apart, in love fast bound.
If face can see no more the face that cares,
At least this light shall tell us of our love.
Abiding friendship sends these little lines;
If, too, in thee the chain of faith stands firm,
For thee I pray forever happiness.

Chapter VI

LUPUS OF FERRIÈRES

1

If there are still those who describe the ninth century as a "Dark Age" of the mind, they will do well to study the life and letters of Lupus, surnamed Servatus, monk of the abbey of Ferrières in France. In his lifetime he was known far and wide as a learned scholar, consulted by many on problems of literature. The Latin classical writers were always in his hands. Not only did he know the works which the best libraries of his time offered him on the Scriptures and their interpretation, on theology and its anxious argument, but he discussed these clearly and in detail for those who sought his aid. From his pen we still possess verses, biographies, and more than a hundred and twenty letters, full of references to the history of his active years, from 836 until about 862. And more: We still have manuscripts, written or worked on by him, lying in London, in Bern, in Rome, in Paris. With a passion all his own he enlarged his abbey's store of books by begging and borrowing texts wherever he could, bent on collating, on criticizing, on copying, for the wider knowledge of himself and of those whom he loved to teach.

As a Frank of the western lands, he was a subject, and a most loyal subject, of Charles the Bald. He faithfully supported his king in his effort to maintain or to enlarge his realm and in his struggle with those who disputed his sovereignty and rose in rebellion against his control. At one moment Lupus was following Charles in expedition from place to place; at another he was leading out his retainers to fight, to stand fast in the path of battle, to face death or capture at enemy hands. Now he attended assemblies of the military host of his people, or Councils and Synods of state and Church, where on occasion he acted as official secretary; now he was traveling for the king on some special mission; now he was deep in plans for saving the treasure of his abbey threatened by the raids of Danish pirates.

A devoted priest of the Catholic Church, an abbot who ruled his monastery with zealous and unceasing concern during years of strife and of sharp division in matters political and spiritual, he took boldly the part he judged the better, against the highest in the land. Outspoken, even with menace and condemnation, in his words to king and commoner alike, he seasoned his letters to the friends he held most dear with a wit and humor, sometimes sharp and pungent, that reveal the inner warmth of his heart. His days were darkened by treachery, by crime, by assault from within and without; but over their darkness he has shed a welcome and enheartening light for all to whom his almost Ciceronian Latin still yields its spell.

2

His native country was the region around Sens, in the northeast of that western Frankish realm which we now call France. There he was born about 805. Tradition, given us by his pupil, Heiric of Auxerre, claims that his father belonged to an aristocratic East Frankish family, once settled in Bavaria, and afterward in the west. We first come upon him as a student, learning to read Latin books in the abbey of St. Peter and St. Paul, also known by the name of Bethlehem, at Ferrières-en-Gâtinais, near Montargis and the river Loing and in the Archdiocese of Sens. Its importance in the world of letters ranked high, and it was a home where memories of Alcuin lingered. Alcuin himself had been its abbot; and after him his pupils, Sigulf, Adalbert, and Aldric, in succession carried on its rule.

Adalbert, Alcuin's *magus meus niger*, his "black scholar," dark of hair and eyes, was in command when Lupus entered Ferrières. Under him the boy grew up, to show himself so keen for learning and so sharply intelligent that in 828 or early in 829, when he was in his early twenties, his abbot, now Aldric, from 829 archbishop of Sens, sent him, too, eastward to study in Germany under that master of his time in Biblical research, the abbot of Fulda, Hraban Maur. At Fulda we have already

seen Walafrid Strabo and his friend Gottschalk, whom Lupus may
have met in its school, although both left it in 829.

Even more strongly than Walafrid, Lupus was fascinated by
Hraban's passionate love of books. Constantly he talked with
him, asking him questions, whenever he could find the Father
Abbot free to sit down with a moment to spare. More and more
Hraban, on his side, learned to trust this young man's unwearying
energy and accurate skill and to make use of these for the checking
of statements and details of his own work. Manuscripts of his
commentary on the Book of Numbers bear the note: "At Hraban's
bidding Lupus and Gerwolf [another student of the Father at
Fulda] corrected this work, so far as the difficulties of their time
and their understanding allowed." Later on Lupus asked his
master to compose a Commentary on the Epistles of Saint Paul.
He received it from Hraban, some years after he himself had
left Fulda, with a letter addressed as to an equal:

"I missed you badly, brother, when you were no longer here;
but, as you may be sure, I have ever borne you with affection
and respect in my mind. Often I have remembered the zeal
with which you studied the Divine Law and that pleasant modesty
which you showed as we talked together on many things. And
therefore, remembering your petition and my promise, I have
done my best to make the Commentary on those Epistles of Saint
Paul. So far as has been possible for me, with the aid of those
who shared our reading, I have collected from different works
of the Fathers of the Church the teachings which concerned
these particular Epistles. I have added nothing of my own
thought, as has been my custom in other works of mine; for the
serious reader will find enough to satisfy him in the Fathers themselves. Of your dear charity pray for me; and may the Eternal
Majesty of Christ keep you strong in holy virtue for evermore."

At Fulda Lupus found time also for work of a different kind.
Already during these youthful years he was busy in that copying
which was to give him and his monastery so many books by
Christian, pagan, or barbarian writers. For that count of Friuli,
Eberhard, who some ten or twelve years later was to drive Gott-
schalk from a refuge in Italy, he made a thick roll of manuscript

containing a copy, written by him, of the national laws of German peoples: Franks, Ripuarians, Lombards, Alemannians, and Bavarians. His name and that of Eberhard were given in verses of dedication, and pictures of his own drawing illustrated his texts.

Probably it was at Fulda, too, that he wrote the first of his *Lives* of holy men. At any rate, in 836—a date which he himself gives us—he yielded to the request of Abbot Bun and his brethren of the monastery of Hersfeld, near Fulda, that he put together what was known concerning the saint, Wigbert, whose relics were the pride and glory of their cloister. "Busy as I am," Lupus wrote them, "I will put off the very serious calls on my time and for love's sake will do as you ask."

Wigbert was dear to all who knew Fulda. From his native England, where he had been a scholar of note, he had come to Germany at the call of Boniface to share in its missions. About 732 Boniface had sent him to be abbot of a monastery of St. Peter recently founded in Hesse, at Fritzlar on the river Eder. At Fritzlar, after some years of toil here and there, he had died, and in its church his relics were held in great reverence. Then, while Charles the Great was in full campaign against the Saxons, the terror of the enemy had driven Fritzlar's monks to carry these relics to the neighboring town of Buraburg, where Boniface had established a bishop's seat. The date of this flight was 774; and some years later the bishop of Buraburg ordered that the relics be enshrined in Hersfeld.

This abbey of Hersfeld on the river Fulda looked back upon its founding by Lull, successor of Boniface in the see of Mainz. To Lull it was as beloved as Fulda had been to Boniface. He was glad to welcome the relics of this English compatriot of his, this fellow worker under Boniface; and he had enclosed them at Hersfeld in a magnificent shrine of gold and silver work. Now, in 836, Lull had been dead for fifty years; but his name with that of Wigbert was still remembered in Hersfeld's daily prayer. Great was the satisfaction of its monks when the young student of Fulda sat down to write their saint's *Life*.

In its preface Lupus pleaded his excuse for the describing of events so far removed from his own day. Yet had not writers of classic Rome, Sallust and Livy, told of many things which happened long before their time? Had not holy Jerome in a Christian age written the *Life* of Paul, the hermit of Thebes, "a matter surely most remote in time from him?" Lupus already knew well what was due to history! Later on in the same preface he declared: "I hope that the cultured reader of this *Life* will forgive me for introducing into suave Latin prose the roughness of native German names, of people and of place. Will he please remember that I am writing history, not poetry, and that history cannot allow the colouring of poetic licence in its narrative?" This scrupulous adherence to truth gains interest when we compare it with the contrary scruple of Walafrid Strabo, who about the same time was omitting the "barbarous sounds" of German names from his Latin story of St. Gall, "lest he spoil the dignity of the Latin language."

But the most exciting hour of Lupus as he worked at Fulda arrived when, searching eagerly through its library sometime after his entry into its school, he came upon the *Life of Charles the Great* by Einhard. He read it through, from its preface to its final words, and he knew at once that he must talk with its author, both by letter and face to face. Would the writer of this wonderful book perhaps give him the chance? After much eager thinking, he seized his pen; and this, in substance, was his prayer to Einhard:

I have hesitated long before writing to your Excellence. Above all, among other very good reasons, I have been afraid that, since I am quite unknown to you, my very real desire to win your friendship might give you offence. But I want so much to write, and your gracious, modest words in that *Life* of King Charles, words filled with the true spirit of philosophy, have encouraged me to hope. Please will you read with patience and goodwill what I want to say? For indeed I am impelled by no unseemly, youthful whim.

I have loved books since I was a little boy. Never have I despised them, in the fashion of so many people of our times, as a frivolous indulgence of leisure hours. Perhaps, if teachers had not been lacking and the study of ancient classics had not almost died away through constant neglect, before now, God helping me, I might have been able to satisfy my longing to learn.

In the days of Charles the Emperor, as you must be well aware, the desire for knowledge did revive for a while. Nowadays those who want to learn are a burden upon society. The average man thinks of scholars as aloof and apart upon a high mountain; and if he has discovered some failing in them, he puts it down, not to human weakness, but to the life they lead, the work they do. So what follows? Some men of learning receive no reward worthy of their attainment; others, in fear of unpopularity, have thrown their noble calling entirely away.

To me, at least, knowledge is to be sought for its own sake. Through Aldric, now Archbishop of Sens, I found a teacher to instruct me in the art of grammar. But then, when I wanted to go on from this to study rhetoric and the other liberal arts, I discovered that in our days this study is a mere pretence. For some time I did dally with modern writings, and I found them altogether different from the dignity of Cicero and those other classical writers whose influence the great Christian scholars show so clearly in their style.

Now your splendid *Life* of the Emperor Charles has come into my hands. Please do not think that I want to flatter you; but your writing is so wonderful. It has all the sensitive, aristocratic thought of the Latin classics, all clearly defined in short paragraphs, with none of those long and complicated passages. Of course I knew your reputation for learning before. Then, directly I read your book I felt that I must see and talk with you, now or at some time in the future.

There is, too, a chance of this; for I have come from the western Franks to this country across the Rhine, and so I am not so far away from you. Aldric sent me to study the Bible under the great Hraban at Fulda. Would you be kind enough to grant me what I ask?

In the meantime—now that I have once for all crossed the bounds of decent modesty—could you lend me some of your books? Truly, I would far rather have your friendship than your books; nevertheless, I would be glad to see Cicero's treatise on rhetoric. I have, indeed, a copy of my own, but it has so many errors. And when I compared it with a manuscript which I found here, I discovered that the Fulda one is far worse even than mine! Then, too, I would like to borrow Cicero's *On the Orator* in three volumes. I think you must have them, for I have seen a list of your books. And, also, could you let me have the Commentary on the writings of Cicero, and Aulus Gellius, *Attic Nights?* When I have sent these back to you, there are many other manuscripts in the catalogue of your library which, if only God grant me your favour, I am terribly anxious to copy while I am here.

All this would make me grateful to you for life. There is much more which I could say; but you have heard enough by now of my trifles. I know that you are busy in your own affairs, perhaps deep in problems of philosophy.

Letters which we do not possess passed between the student of Fulda and the recluse of Seligenstadt; and early in 836 Lupus visited Einhard and his wife Imma in their home near the church of Sts. Marcellinus and Peter. Shortly afterward came word of the death of Imma, and Einhard for long was inconsolable. Within their bond of religious devotion the two had lived at Seligenstadt more truly as brother and sister than as husband and wife; yet Einhard had depended upon his faithful partner for comfort and support far more than he knew. At once Lupus wrote to him, now a "most dear teacher":

"I am shocked to the heart by this tragic news. More than ever would I now be with you, to lighten your sorrow by my sympathy or to remind you of the words of God. As it is, I can only ask you to bear it as a wise and disciplined man. You who have always bravely conquered the allurements of happier times must not now yield to misfortune. Call forth in yourself that strength of endurance to which you would rightly guide a beloved friend suddenly stricken by trouble such as yours."

Einhard, however, would not be comforted. His grief, he wrote Lupus in answer, had banished all memory of his own affairs and of those of his friends. Never would he forget it. Worst of all, and a very inflaming of the ulcer of his misery, was the thought that all his prayers, all his hopes for help from his holy martyrs, had come to absolutely nothing. And therefore words of encouragement, so often a solace to other men, were only causing his sore to break out afresh, when friends bade him bear calmly trouble which they themselves had never suffered, when they expected him to find consolation where there was for him no comfort or relief. What man on earth of sane and sober mind would not hold himself most wretched, even to tears, when in his affliction he found inexorably turned away from him the Face of that God to Whom he had looked for answer to his prayers?

Only, he admitted, the teachings of the Fathers, Cyprian, Augustine, and Jerome, had saved him from utter despair. Imma was not dead, he knew; only her time on earth was over. Yet, do what he could, his sorrow was always with him. At every turn, in the running of his home and household, in the ordering of all things, things of God and things of man, he looked for Imma, and she was not there. Surely his suffering would last until God saw fit to end it by his own passing from this world. One thing, no doubt, was salutary. By this sudden loss his mind had been jerked and pulled back from happy, peaceful days, from hope and love of long life, to remember that he was now an old man, that his years would soon be over. Far better to spend in sorrow rather than in joy the brief, uncertain time which was left. Did not the Lord declare, *Blessed are they that mourn?*

Answer came quickly from Lupus. It throws some light upon the earnest concern of its writer, exhorting and counseling from his standpoint of some thirty-one years a man about sixty-six.

I read, Reverend Sir, with deep distress your letter lamenting your late bereavement. Friends who are far better than I have tried to relieve your pain; clearly they have not succeeded. And so, turning away from my inexperienced youth and from any confidence in my ability, I will presume to hammer out on the anvil of my thought some words for your consoling. Oftentimes common, ordinary remedies succeed when those of value, conceived by high skill, have failed.

For I venture to believe, to believe firmly, that God even of His goodwill towards you and your wife allowed this untimely death. Why? I can hear you ask. In this way: Husband and wife, though no more twain, but one flesh, do not die at the same time; one must survive the other. They must, therefore, if faithful one to the other, desire that the one destined to survive shall be the stronger of the two to endure, the more able to carry out duties in a truly Christian manner. Courage is not a matter of sex, but of mind.

Now, although your good wife had gained much from marriage with you, so much indeed that she far excelled not only the average woman but also the average man, although, a frail woman in physical nature, she had grown into masculine power of thought, yet she never could have hoped to reach the height of your wisdom. Never would she have equalled that great and consistent strength which all men admire in you; never, if she had survived you, would she have been able to do so much for your eternal salvation as you can do both for her and for yourself.

Toward the end of his letter Lupus turned from a long stream of excellent and orthodox counsel, garnished with many texts of Biblical and patristic authority, to an energetic appeal to his master to continue his intellectual work. He concluded:

managed, also, at the repeated request of his friend Waldo,
onk of Trier, to rewrite an old *Life* of St. Maximin, a bishop
hat city in the fourth century. Maximin had given shelter at
r in 336 to the great Athanasius, bishop of Alexandria, ban-
d from his see by the Emperor Constantine in a crisis of bitter
moil through the East. The work had appealed to that sense
istory which we have already marked in Lupus. The old *Life*
Maximin then current contained, he said, "little enough of fact,
stories next door to legend." Besides, here was a chance to
trast the courage of Maximin with the flabby spirit of this
th century.

"O! the degenerate ways of this, our time! Almost all the sinews
ur former stoutheartedness have fallen into decay. Endurance
yielded, broken by puny alarms; money matters now, not
tice. I have no doubt at all that no one, or hardly anyone,
ong men now living would welcome to his home a refugee,
en so noble a refugee as Bishop Athanasius, fleeing from the
cked wrath of an Emperor! He would be too scared for his
n skin."

This *Life* was finished in 839. The next year saw the death of
e Emperor Louis the Pious, confusion and rivalry among his
irs, and invasion of the western kingdom of Charles the Bald
his brother Lothar, now possessed of the imperial title. Odo,
bbot of Ferrières, was greatly worried. To whom should he give
legiance? To the Emperor, Lothar? Or to King Charles? His
bbey lay in western Frankland, in the region between the Seine
nd the Loire. Which of the two would ultimately hold it, the
ing who claimed it by title and deed, or the invading Emperor?
t would be highly desirable to be on the conquering side. In his
orry Odo wrote to Marcward, once a monk at Ferrières, now
bbot of Prüm in the German Rhineland:

"I am hesitating, caught between two possibilities, and I
on't know what to do. I cannot find out who is going to rule
ur part of the land; and, as I hear from your messengers, opinions
differ about this. I do beg you, Father, that, if the general feeling
turns to Lothar and if, as I hope and believe, Divine mercy gives
you a chance to influence him for the advantage of this abbey,
you will kindly remember us."

How I admired your *Adoration of the Cross* which you sent to me!
Would that you might make me happy by unravelling all the knots of
argument which I have constantly sent you! I have decided to leave
Fulda in the middle of May, and, God willing, I shall then make that
visit to your home of which I wrote to you. I want to return your books
to you and enjoy the great delight of listening to your talk.

3

We do not know how the visit, which had to be postponed
until June, passed off with all its talk and argument. But in this
same year, 836, we find Lupus home again from Germany and
back at his monastery of Ferrières in France, writing to one Immo,
probably that Immo who was to become bishop of Noyon five
years later:

"Well, Heaven helping me, I have returned safe and sound.
Some of my friends have died while I have been away, among
them my lord and patron, Aldric. That does hurt. Otherwise,
nothing very bad. Why you wanted me to tell you what books I
copied or read in Germany I could not make out, unless perhaps
you wanted to see whether I would boast of my study or show
myself a young fool. Frankly, I spent most of my time reading. I
did copy a few books, to help my memory and add to my store
of knowledge. No! I did *not* take on the long, slow grind of learning German because, as some idiots have said, 'I fell in love with
that language.'"

The abbot of Ferrières was now one Odo. He welcomed
the young man back, now not only monk but deacon of the
Church, and soon saw him advanced to the priesthood. The next
few years were spent by Lupus among his books, in teaching the
novices of the abbey, in dealing with problems, philological and
astrological, for various questioners, and in writing letters concerning these problems. To Altwin, a monk whom he had known
in Germany, he wrote on the proper accenting and pronunciation
of certain words, and added an interesting paragraph on comets:
"A subject rather to be feared than discussed. Divine authority
has told us nothing about them; and they have won their sinister
reputation from the experience of pagan men, who declared that
they portended famine or pestilence or war. I myself, this very

April, at an hour shortly after midnight, saw a star drawing behind it a tail, which extended from the Sign of the Lion to that
of the Virgin."

This was the comet which Einhard also had seen in this
year of 837. Einhard had been much troubled, we remember,
since he feared that it foretold ill about to befall the Emperor,
Louis the Pious.

"That manuscript which you wanted me to send you," Lupus
continued to Altwin, "many other people also asked to borrow,
and not the kind who should have it in their hands. I almost
decided to put it away somewhere lest it should get lost. Perhaps
you may have it when you come here for a visit. I am surprised
that you should want it entrusted to that cleric of yours, however
faithful you find him. He is travelling on foot, and that isn't
really a safe way of carrying books."

Many years afterward Lupus was to write to the great
Hincmar, archbishop of Reims, about this same danger:

"I was afraid to send you the compilation made by Bede
from Saint Augustine's writings on the Apostle Paul. It is so big a
book that it could not be hidden in the bearer's dress or carried
very easily in a wallet. Whichever one did, robbers might well
seize it, through greed for so beautiful a prize, and then it would
be lost both to me and to you. I shall be glad to let you have it
when, God willing, we meet together somewhere, safe and sound."

Gradually our young monk's leisure for study, with all this
correspondence, became less and less. To Altwin at last he wrote
again, in something of the tone of our own day:

"If it were as easy to discuss questions as it is to raise them,
long ago students would have reached perfect wisdom. Now,
when research in literature is almost out-of-date, who is there
who is not complaining about the ignorance of teachers, the
scarcity of books—yes, and even the lack of time? So you ought
not to be angry with me if I think that I should spend my few
free hours in following up the things which I don't know rather
than in discussing those which I have already learned. Nor do
I think that I do wrong when I point out, to those to whom I
have already opened or made clearer the path of understanding,
that they must by their own effort follow where I have led the

way. Surely I cannot be blamed when I declare t
whom I talk, or when, upon those who *will per*
me, I try to impress it by my determined silence

It must have come as a rather pleasant in
in the autumn of 836 friends obtained for Lup
to visit the Court of Louis the Pious and his E
and when, in 837, he was invited by her to appea
Perhaps she felt especially friendly toward Lu
both had drawn their forebears from eastern,
Abbot Odo in 836 escorted and presented his yo
Court. The journey was marked by a serious mish
was attacked by a painful abscess in the groin. "I
me with death," he cheerfully wrote to Altwin;
prayed for me that the Lord gave it cure." The Lo
to Lupus, healed this abscess through the interces
who was at this time, and is now, a saint of the Cl
seventh century he had been bishop of Meaux, north

In 837 Abbot Odo was absent for a long time fro
and more and more responsibility fell upon Lupus.
him declaring to his friend Altwin, still eager to co
of problems: "If you had suddenly arrived, you woul
your journey for nothing. You would have found me
up in all sorts of necessary duties that many days
passed with scarcely an hour in which I could listen at
The Abbot is away, and that, too, would have greatly
plans. Well, there we are. As I said before, I am busy, a
Abbot isn't expected back until the autumn, if then. So
you *must* come to Ferrières, you will have to await you

Yet, whenever he could, Lupus gave generously of
To a fellow monk, possibly his own brother in family ki
sent this counsel: "If no change in my position takes
had been half-expecting a summons to the Imperial
you had better come to stay with me and make good pr
your study of Virgil. You will have plenty of time, and
be eager to help you. If you try to work alone, your pa
be greater than your profit."

No further call, so far as we know, had by 838 arrive
the Court, and Lupus continued to carry on his manifold

This petition, in practical effect, acknowledged Lothar as the probable source of aid for Ferrières in the future. Odo did more. About the same time, in the autumn of 840, he wrote in the name of his community to Lothar himself, praying him to help the brethren to recover possession of a small house of religion, once attached to Ferrières. This was the cell of Saint-Josse in the Pas-de-Calais, given by Charles the Great into Alcuin's keeping as a hospice for pilgrims. Down the years the cell had prospered. It owned wide fields, and its harvests were of great benefit to Ferrières. Now Odo was lamenting that this useful dependency had been handed over by the Emperor Lothar to one of his vassals.

"Even," he wrote, "had your father, Louis, our sovereign, not conferred this gift upon us, so earnestly have we laboured and still do labour on your behalf that we believe, all of us at Ferrières, that this cell should be ours, Sire, through your bestowing—if not indeed some greater gift."

His inclination toward the Emperor Lothar was to cost Abbot Odo dear. In November 840, as we have seen, by the "Truce of Orléans" Lothar conceded to his brother Charles as his right, the rule, at least for the time being, over part of the land between the Seine and the Loire. This part included the domain of Ferrières; and henceforth Charles the Bald was established there as king and lord. The abbey, like so many abbeys of this time, was in the gift of the ruler of its domain; and in return for this gift its abbot was pledged to prove his loyalty to his secular patron in every way open to him, spiritual and secular. Charles, now acknowledged king in its territory, did not forgive Odo for favoring the invader, Lothar. He decided that Odo should at once be replaced as abbot of Ferrières by the loyal Lupus. The date of the "electing" of Lupus by the monks of its community was November 22, 840, and he received confirmation of his appointment in a visit to King Charles at Court.

What happened afterward may be told in the words of this newly elected abbot, written to Jonas, bishop of Orléans:

I hear that false reports have reached you concerning our former head, Odo, and so I am giving you the exact story of what actually occurred. Our Lord King Charles gave order that he should not remain in our monastery, and with this order he said some things which I had better not repeat. So, when I returned from Court to Ferrières, I told Odo this as pleasantly as possible. I arranged for an escort of men to see him on his way, for horses and clothing and money for his journey. Our Lord King had told me to get him out by the thirtieth of November, but I decided that he should have until December the third. I expected to see the king again on that day.

I did see the king, and after a very correct and formal welcome of me as now head of Ferrières, he asked me what I had done about our late ruler. Of course I told him that Odo had gone, according to order, and I honestly believed that he had. Then, upon my arrival home, on the twelfth of December, I found him still here! It worried me terribly, because I had told the king just the opposite. At once, that very night, I sent Odo word to leave at dawn; I told him that I would not even set foot inside the abbey until he was out of it. So he departed, taking with him all that I had given him, and some other things, too, which I threw in for good measure. Promptly I announced this to my friends at Court and explained the whole matter to the king. They all agreed that I had acted in every way correctly. Let those who have spread around different stories look to their own conscience. My eye in this business is certainly single; and I trust that, as the Bible declares, my whole body will be full of light.

4

From this time onward, as before, Lupus steadily followed and supported Charles the Bald. First of all, he wrote a fervent letter of gratitude:

Though of necessity for a while I must be absent from you, yet my spirit so closely adheres to you that I hold you and yours always before my eyes. Without any tinge of falsehood I confess to you the truth: I embrace you with a love scarcely comprehensible. Surely the reason why all good men love you is clear to see in your own self. With all my being, with all my power, with all my mind, I am your faithful man.

In his delight he wrote off also to Louis, chancellor of King Charles and his cousin, and to Ebroin, archchaplain of the king and bishop of Poitiers. To Ebroin he sent a gift, an ivory comb: "I beg you, keep it for your own use, that while you comb your hair you may think of me." And, of course, he sent the good news speedily to Fulda, to his beloved friend, Hraban Maur.

The duties of Abbot Lupus under royal appointment were

many and exacting. There was service, military, political, diplomatic, to his king, beset by rebellion in Brittany and in Aquitaine,
by the perpetual discord between himself and his royal brothers,
each of the three constantly maneuvering for his own ends, by
the frequent raids of Danish pirates upon the coast. There was
the rule and the upkeep of the abbey of Ferrières, threatened by
poverty. There was the fight against unrest, against plotting and
intrigue, among his brethren, many of whom had been ill content
with his being installed as their abbot. There was his duty, or
what he held as his duty, to be rendered to his Church at large
by his writings on theology; and there was the continual correspondence with many on many things, both small and great.

In August 843, Charles the Bald and his two brothers, Lothar
the Emperor, king of Italy, and Louis, king of Germany, swore
their consent in peace and harmony to the dividing of the Empire
among them. The meeting, as we noted in the chapter on Walafrid
Strabo, took place at Verdun. Before he reached Verdun, Charles
held an Assembly of his army near Châlons-sur-Marne; and Lupus,
as in service bound, led out his men to the mustering. On his
way there he stayed to rest at the monastery of Faremoutiers-en-
Brie and wrote from there to Marcward, abbot of Prüm, of his
joy in the repentance of one of his rebel monks. This brother
had fled from Ferrières, had left monastic rule and habit for
secular life, and had won employment as clerk in the service of
the Emperor Lothar. Lothar himself had actively encouraged the
deserter's change of heart, and Lupus on his return home sent
him grateful thanks. With his thanks, however, he did not hesitate
to mingle words of monastic authority.

"By us of this community to you must be attributed, Sire,
after God, our brother's rescue from error; by him himself the
saving of his own soul. As to his continuing to hold office as clerk
to your Imperial Court after his resuming of the religious habit,
that would not become you as Emperor and would be impossible
for us. Our monastic rule is scarcely kept in any decent way even
within our walls. Far less could it be fulfilled by any one, let
alone one inclined to negligence, amid the distractions of the
world."

The distractions of this world day by day bore more heavily

on the abbot's mind. Within the royal dominions of Charles the Bald dwellers in Aquitaine were giving stubborn and persistent allegiance to the man they held their king, Pippin II. As we saw, his father, Pippin I, son of Louis the Pious, had been given Aquitaine's crown by the solemn ordinance of 817. After the death of Pippin I, his son had been entirely ignored by the same Louis in the partition declared at Worms in 839, when Aquitaine had gone to the favorite son of Louis, young Charles. Many men of Aquitaine resented this decision. They looked upon Charles as an intruder; in their view the neglected son of their former king held the right to rule over them.

In January 843, Charles had been forced to march hither and thither in Aquitaine in an attempt to hold his own. While he was there, Brittany had flared into battle. Nominoë, Duke of the Bretons, whom Charles claimed as his vassal, and Nominoë's son, Erispoë, pushed on by Lambert, a Frank once in high office of state under Louis the Pious and now driven to revolt in bitter resentment of what he thought unjust action by King Charles, were urging their Breton people to seize complete independence. In May a Breton force had killed Rainald, duke of Nantes, in the Frankish kingdom, with many of his followers who defended the cause of Charles. In June pirates from Scandinavia had descended on Nantes to seize and plunder the city and had then settled for the autumn and winter with their booty upon the isle of Noirmoutiers at the mouth of the Loire. As a result of these evils, agriculture and trade were neglected and famine was rampant. "In many parts of France"—so recorded Prudentius of Troyes in his *Annals*—"men were eating a kind of bread made of earth mixed with a little meal. It was pathetic, it was an abominable crime, that the horses of the pirates had abundance of fodder, while human beings hungered for mud as their food."

Amid all these troubles the bishops and lay nobles of the realm of Charles the Bald met in November 843 at Coulaines, near Le Mans in France, and issued a declaration, their own, though put forward in the name of the king. It was of note for its significance.

There was no one, this declaration proclaimed, who did not lament the discord of past years, discord still present and in need of healing. This healing must be sought by a proper recognition of the power, privilege, and authority of the bishops and abbots of the Church, of the king, and of his nobles alike. This the king acknowledged. Let none endeavor to wrest gifts from him through greed or any unworthy motive. If such honor or gift had been forced from him, contrary to the dignity of the throne and the well-being of its subjects, then it was for the bishops and nobles of the realm to correct this evil. Whosoever should show himself unwilling to mark and obey these injunctions, with him episcopal authority and the majesty of the Crown would deal as reason and necessity should demand.

As in the days of Louis the Pious, here again the power of the bishops of the Church to deal with affairs of state was clearly shown. Here again the king depended on the authority of his leading men in Church and state for the protection and the administration of his land and people. A bishop, an abbot, or a noble of secular rank might now again boldly rebuke, admonish, and chastise his sovereign in the cause of his sovereign's good. It is therefore not surprising that about this time we find Abbot Lupus of Ferrières severely admonishing that king, Charles the Bald, whom he had so enthusiastically thanked for the gift of his abbot's chair:

"That you may reign in peace and happiness, these precepts, which with faithful devotion I have put together, must be observed by you. When you were a child, you spoke as a child, you understood as a child. Now that you have become a man, put away childish things, refuse all that is foolish and senseless, follow that which is according to reason, that which will profit your salvation, present and to come. Do not so subject yourself to any man that in all ways you do his will. Why do you assume the name of a king if you do not know how to *be* a king?"

5

The next year, 844, saw Charles once more in Aquitaine, encamped before Toulouse and laying siege to its walls. He was badly in need of reinforcement, and in June his main army marched to his aid. In its line marched Lupus, leading his abbey's retainers to support their king in his war. On June 14 troops of

Pippin II swept down upon the army as it was hurrying through the province of Angoumois, near Angoulême. Many were killed, among them Hugh, the uncle of Charles; many were captured, among them Lupus himself, with his friend Ebroin, bishop of Poitiers and archchaplain to the Court of Charles.

In three weeks' time, however, they were once more free, thanks to the intervention on their behalf of Turpion, count of Angoulême. July saw Lupus safe and sound in his monastery, writing to Marcward of Prüm to give him the good news. What, indeed, to Lupus was capture for three weeks, compared with books which live in permanence? Would Marcward kindly send one of his monks, one who knew his business, to Fulda to ask its abbot, now Hatto (Hraban Maur had resigned in 842), to give over to him Fulda's manuscript of Suetonius, *Lives of the Caesars,* in its two small rolls? "And, then, Marcward, when this messenger of yours brings those rolls to Prüm, have a copy of them made for me there, and get the copy conveyed to me here at Ferrières, either by you yourself, which would be wonderful, or, if my sins won't allow me that joy just yet, by some really trustworthy person. I am sending some boys, sons of a noble family, to Prüm to learn German. I want them to be of use here in our abbey some day."

Soon afterward trouble broke out in that abbey itself, for an attempt was made to depose Lupus and make one Egilbert its head. Lupus poured out his indignation to Louis, the chancellor of Charles:

"Be mindful of our friendship, and try to help me as you have always done. Especially when you know how faithful I have been to the king and his service, and you realize what a disgrace it is that I should be compared with that Egilbert, to say nothing of his being actually *preferred* before me!"

It has been suggested, by Lot and Halphen in their work on Charles the Bald, that suspicion had been cast upon the fidelity of Lupus to his king. Why had he been so quickly released from captivity that year? And, of all men, by Turpion, that count of Angoulême? Was not Turpion a supporter of Pippin, enemy of Charles? Lupus made haste to send to King Charles another fervid declaration of his loyal devotion.

Yet, loyal as he was, he knew that things were not going well. In December of this same year, 844, he was putting into official record further counsels directed toward the king, since he was acting as secretary for a Synod gathered at the royal palace of Ver, near Senlis. Among these counsels he recorded one which concerned abbeys of France under Charles.

"We see," wrote Lupus for the bishops assembled at Ver, "we see the wrath of God hanging over you, our king, and over us, your bishops, when the endowments of the Church which kings and other Christian men have offered for the maintenance of monks, for the aid of the poor, for the reception of pilgrims, for the redeeming of captives and the restoring of the houses of God, have passed into the control of secular hands. For this cause many servants of God in monasteries suffer lack of food and drink, the poor lack alms, pilgrims are neglected, captives are left without hope of ransom, and the good name of us all is wounded and rent apart."

Lupus must have enjoyed the duty of writing these words. His heart was bitter within him because that cell of Saint-Josse-sur-Mer in the Pas-de-Calais, on which Ferrières depended for its supplies of daily food, was again in the grasp of lay hands, sure to turn its working to their own profit. Charles himself had handed it over to one Odulf, a count of his realm, as a bribe for the continuance of support which he so badly needed at this time.

As the years passed and no return of Saint-Josse-sur-Mer was made, letter after letter went from the abbot of Ferrières, not only to the king, but to men who held influence over him: to the chancellor, Louis, to Hincmar, since 845 archbishop of Reims. To Louis the words of Lupus were extremely frank:

We are so driven here by poverty that to our intense sorrow we have had to sell the very altar vessels and ornaments in our church, few enough as they were. I do implore you to impress our need, our real misery, upon the king.

Yes, and you must warn him, not only in regard to this, but to the whole Church in his lands. This Church he received whole and entire when he became our king. Who knows—God forbid!—whether he may not be forced to leave it torn and mutilated, while we weep and his enemies laugh aloud? Pray Heaven he may not learn the truth of those words of the Apostle: *It is a fearful thing to fall into the hands of the living God.*

So, too, Lupus wrote for Hincmar's reading:

To such great want have we come that this year we have supplies of corn for scarcely two months; our servants—and we cannot get along without them—are almost naked; our brethren are in the same case, their habits threadbare and torn. We have had to cut down our giving of alms; we have spent what those who lived here before us had saved; and in these days of tumult we ask humanity from the king and the gift of patience from God.

The worry of it all is driving me continually to consider whether I should resign my office. The only thing, indeed, which keeps me here as abbot is the thought of leaving my monks to face the greed and disorder of seculars, who would be only too glad to lay hands on this house. King Charles has given over our cell of Saint-Josse to Count Odulf. And what good has that noble layman done him? Has *he* conquered for the king any of the pirates? Has *he* brought peace to this rebellious land? If only the king had kept the vow he made to return that cell to us, if only he had obeyed the admonitions given him by the bishops at Ver—admonitions drawn up by my own pen and justly declared, as men will admit—then God would surely have given it him to dwell in peace.

And, to the king himself:

The monks of Ferrières have to buy their vegetables; they hardly ever get the comfort of fish or cheese; all these things were brought us from Saint-Josse. We are hungry and we are cold; we have no means of caring for our boys, for our aged brethren and our sick.

Nothing happened. At the turn of the year 846–47 Lupus brought forward the witness of his community of seventy-two monks against their king:

Listen to their own words. They say it is not right that they should be tormented by you in hunger and cold when they are bound to make perpetual prayer for your wellbeing throughout time and eternity. They say that you will never win the felicity for which you long until you return into the good grace of our poor little Saint Peter's. Do not think this a jest. Our older monks are seriously declaring that they know, by tradition and by their own experience, that any one who has hurt our monastery here has invariably run into great harm.

Do not, then, I beg of you, risk the loss of your own soul. You, too, as well as we, are hastening day by day to that dreadful hour of Judgment, which will mete out to each of us what he deserves, without respect of dignity or person. Life here on earth is brief and uncertain; younger men than you die every day.

To his friend, Marcward of Prüm, at the same time:

On November the thirtieth I saw the king and pleaded with him; it cost me enormous effort and expense. It was no good. He would hear nothing for the present; Odulf was away, he said. There is a report that Odulf is ill, not ill enough to repent, as I would wish, and not in danger of death, either. I should, of course, be sorry if he died, for he most certainly would land in hell.

Thus vigorously spoke the abbot of Ferrières. Nevertheless, he continued conscientiously to render service to his king. He went twice, in 844 and 845, on mission as inspector to Burgundy, a province which Charles desired to hold firmly in his grasp and to which his claim was weak. Lupus complained that in this labor —and "labor" was the word he used—he had lost ten horses through lack of fodder, and that in the disaster of the Angoumois he had lost all those which he had with him.

By 845 matters for the king were turning from bad to worse. In March a band of Northern pirates under the command of Ragnar Lodbrok, a Danish chieftain, sailed up the Seine, captured and "did their will" in Rouen, and proceeded toward Paris. There Charles sat encamped on the bank of the river, determined at all costs to save from destruction the royal abbey of Saint-Denis. Along the bank marched the invaders, dragging with them a collection of wretched captives whom they hanged on trees just outside the abbey walls. At this the Frankish soldiers fled; "and Charles, most noble king, seeing what had been done, he who had been ready to die for the defence of the Holy Church of God, grieving and sad and beating his youthful breast, retired from the scene."

At dawn on March 29, Easter Day, the Northmen entered Paris and did not leave it until churches and roads were robbed and rent. By a bribe of seven thousand pounds Charles persuaded them to withdraw to the sea. They went, despoiling on their way many places near the coast, and among them the renowned abbey of Saint-Bertin.

The end of June or the beginning of July 845 found this king of France in the monastery of Saint-Benoît-sur-Loire, near Orléans. There he received homage and an oath of fidelity from Pippin II and in return yielded to him rule over the whole of Aquitaine except the eastern lands of Poitou, Angoumois, and Saintonge. Pippin had no intention of keeping his word; but "all the Aquitanians at once deserted Charles and zealously turned to him." In the late autumn Charles led in haste a small force into Brittany against the rebel chieftain Nominoë. On November 22 he was not only forced to retreat ignominiously into the marshes around Ballon, near Redon, but he barely escaped with his life.

Various reports and rumors reached Lupus concerning this Breton expedition. He had been ordered by the king to meet him at Saint Martin's abbey in Tours. Then, just as he was setting out, word had come that he was to stay at home. Charles, it seemed, had heard that many of the Bretons were dissatisfied with the rule of Nominoë and were ready to desert to him; therefore, he was hurrying to Brittany instead of to Tours. Next, Lupus heard that the king himself and his chancellor, Louis, had been killed in the battle, and, finally, that both were safe. Of course he wrote off at once to both to tell of his horror, grief, and joy. The following year, 846, Charles made peace with this duke of the Bretons, and, as in the case of Pippin, in exchange for an oath of loyalty to himself as overlord, declared Brittany's freedom from subjection. But neither did Nominoë prove true to his oath; and Breton raiders continued to ravage Frankish lands.

6

The years rolled on, from 846 until 851, bringing with them an ever-increasing burden of trouble for Charles the Bald and his realm. Lupus continued to do what he could. He was present in 847 at the First Conference of Meersen, near Maastricht in the Netherlands, when once again the three brothers swore peace one with another; when they sent warning both to Nominoë and to the Northmen that they cease from invasion and assault. The oaths and the warnings came to nothing. In 848 the Danes invaded Aquitaine and burned Bordeaux. The "sloth and negligence of Pippin" drove the men of Aquitaine back to an appeal to Charles;

at Orléans he was solemnly crowned by the archbishop, Wenilo of Sens, who now held jurisdiction over Lupus and his abbey of Ferrières. But in 849 Charles was once more on campaign in this province which had acknowledged him as king; once more Nominoë of Brittany was "rioting with his accustomed insolence."

Now, sick at heart and bereft of hope, Lupus was trying to win release from military service. In a letter to Pardulus, bishop of Laon, he made his protest:

"As you know, I have not learned how to strike and to escape from an enemy, nor how to carry out the other duties of a soldier on foot and on horseback. Our king needs more than warriors. Through your counsel, I beseech you, and, perhaps, through help from Hincmar, if men really are again going out to fight in Aquitaine, do make the king see sense. True, he doesn't think much of my way of life. But make him deem it worthwhile at least to try to understand and to give me duties which do not utterly jar against it."

Charles did see sense. He himself, in his heart of hearts, would have delighted in more time and peace for study. That same summer of 849 Lupus was preparing to leave France for Rome, sent by his king on a mission to the Pope, Leo IV. It was a signal honor; and careful preparation was advisable. To a bishop, a friend of his, he wrote without delay:

"I shall be passing through your city shortly on my way to Rome, and I have no Italian money. I am told that this is the only currency in use there. Would you of your kindness assist me?"

From Marcward of Prüm he could ask more special favor:

"I am off to Rome. I shall need the aid of the Apostolic See in carrying out my business, and that means, of course, that I should carry with me gifts. I hurry to you as to the arms of a father—no! a mother! I pray you, who have never yet failed me, please, if you possibly can, send me by these messengers of mine two cloaks of deep blue color and two linen vestments. I hear that the Pope admires and likes these immensely. If you cannot send all, then send part! My worldly training has taught me to hope for little, but to ask for much! Also, in case you imagine that my mind cannot think up any further ideas, if you could

help me on my journey by sending me a horse to trot along with
—a really good trotter—or some other sturdy beast, I should
honestly be most grateful."

In 850 Lupus was back in France and facing a crisis in
Brittany. For a long time Nominoë had realized that one of the
chief obstacles in the way of Breton independence was the stubborn loyalty of Brittany's seven bishops to Charles, the West
Frankish king, and to their metropolitan, the archbishop of Tours
in the realm of Charles. Nothing had seemed able to shake this
allegiance. At last, urged on by one of his abbots, Conwoion of
Redon in Brittany, Nominoë decided to bring a charge of simony
against these bishops, among whom were Susan, bishop of Vannes,
and Felix, bishop of Quimper. His decision once made, he turned
to act; and in 848 he called a Synod for the examination of the
accused. There they maintained against all questioning that they
had merely received presents from their clergy, gifts given volun-
tarily; that *never* had they ordained anyone at the price of money!

The Synod hesitated. Its clergy were reluctant to condemn
bishops; and a matter so grave as simony demanded an accurate
and thorough knowledge of canon law. The wisest course, surely,
would be to submit this charge against their prelates to the judgment of the Pope at Rome. To Rome, therefore, Conwoion, with
Susan and Felix in his company, now journeyed across the Alps.
When they returned, they brought with them a letter from Pope
Leo, which he addressed to all the bishops of Brittany. In it he
informed them that, detestable as was the crime alleged, the
accused could only receive sentence of condemnation from twelve
other bishops, after these twelve bishops had heard and had carefully weighed the testimony of seventy-two competent witnesses,
given under oath upon the Gospels. Moreover, no bishop thus
accused was to be prevented from coming later to Rome to lay
his case before the Papal Court. Lastly, gifts to bishops from their
clergy were not unlawful, if given of free will and under no com-
pulsion.

Nominoë, however, was not quelled. He gathered, still in 848,
another Synod, packed with lay delegates, at Coëtleu, between
Redon and Vannes. Soon, in terror for their lives, four of the seven
Breton bishops, Susan and Felix among them, declared themselves

guilty. They were expelled from their sees and from Brittany itself; and Nominoë replaced them by men on whose support he could rely. Henceforth, he declared, Breton bishops would owe loyalty to a Breton metropolitan see, placed at Dol; they would yield no allegiance to Tours. Brittany, he boasted, now possessed its own national Church.

In 849–50 for good measure he showed his independence by invading regions belonging to the realm of Charles: Rennes and Nantes and the country around Angers. This he did because further motive for rebellion had struck him. The bishops whom he had dismissed had appealed promptly to the Pope, and Leo had sent him a strong letter of rebuke. At least so he supposed, although he had not even deigned to receive the letter when it arrived.

It was high time for Charles to take action. For the moment Aquitaine was quiet, subdued by the campaign of the year before. Now in 850 the king raised an army, then marched into Anjou, and, probably in that province, assembled a Council of his Frank-ish bishops. The Council passed severe censure upon Nominoë and entrusted to Lupus the composing of a letter which should convey this censure to him in no uncertain terms.

The letter, as Lupus fashioned it, was worthy of him. It was frank, bold, determined, yet expressed the Council's readiness to accept penitence and peace. It told of bitter wrongs done to churches; of afflictions brought upon high and low, rich and poor, widows and orphans; of damnable greed and hideous cruelty; and all laid firmly at the door of Nominoë's conscience. It accused the Breton chieftain of laying waste Christian land, of destroying the houses of God and burning the sacred relics of His saints; of robbing the humble of their living and the noble of their heritage; of slaughter and slavery spread far and wide; of adultery and rape; of driving bishops from their sees and introducing hirelings in their stead; of stirring up tumult and confusion throughout the Church of Brittany; of receiving with high welcome Lambert, rebel against King Charles; and, finally, of casting scorn upon the Pope, holder of the seat of blessed Peter and Primate over all God's earth.

"Sufficient, and more than sufficient," wrote Lupus, "hast

thou done for thy perdition. If, nevertheless, thou shalt receive and hearken to the words of the Holy See, thou shalt find mercy with God and blessed Peter and aid and intercession from us. But if thou shalt scorn our kindly warnings, of a certainty never shalt thou find home in heaven, and soon no home on earth. Expelled by thine own fault from fellowship with the Apostolic See, from fellowship with us of France, overthrown by just judgment —may God avert it!—at the last thou shalt find thine own due place among those damned forevermore."

In 851 Nominoë was dead, unrepentant to the end. His son, Erispoë, in return for an oath of fidelity lightly given, gained acknowledgment as king of Brittany, with an addition of Rennes, Nantes, and Retz. A treaty, signed and sealed at Angers in Anjou, was destined to keep the peace for Charles with the Bretons for a brief while. Account of the celebration of this dubious achieving went from Lupus to the abbot of Prüm:

"I am just back from the expedition to Brittany, and a most magnificent banquet, which cost my digestion anguish indescribable. At last our Lord King Charles, your foster-child, set me free from those delights which were killing me.

"You have sent, I hear, some of your friends gifts of wonderful cups, made of wood, excellent to use in travelling. I am dying with envy. Do send me some, too."

7

It is pleasant in the midst of such battle and conflict to turn to look for a moment at two letters of peaceful content sent about this time by Lupus to friends in England. Both contained a petition common in these days. We have seen Einhard praying the abbot of Fontenelle to arrange his purchase, at the price of fifty pounds, of lead for his church at Seligenstadt. About 852 Lupus wrote to Ethelwulf, king of Wessex, praising his "fervour in the worship of God." But that compliment was only a preliminary! He continued with the main substance of his letter:

"We are obliged to put a roof of lead upon the church of our monastery of Ferrières, or Bethlehem, as its founder named it, dedicated to Saint Peter and all the Apostles. In this work we pray you to share, if you will. Help us, for the honour of God, to finish our task, not for our own merit, but for your reward in heaven. We do make our prayers for you without any gifts in return; but we shall be all the keener in our intercessions if we have received a present which will be of aid, both to you and to us, in the saving of our souls. We shall be ready to fulfill all that you may bid us do to the limit of our power."

The second letter went to Felix, a Frankish secretary of Ethelwulf, long known to Lupus. It was on the same subject:

"I have asked your esteemed king to send us for our church such amount of lead as God shall inspire him to bestow upon us. If, through God's goodness and your cooperation, I obtain this, I leave it to your care to get it despatched across the Channel to Étaples."

8

Higher and higher rose the tension in France, even in spite of the fact that Lothar, Louis the German, and Charles the Bald met a second time in 851 to declare peace and concord between them in the Second Council of Meersen. Only some favorable opportunity was needed for the breaking apart once again of the frail bond which bound the royal brothers in this so-called union of harmony.

Pirates from the North were again distracting the realm of Charles; now on the Seine, now on the Loire they were carrying on their fearful work. November 8, 853, saw them burning the abbey of Saint-Martin at Tours; happily its treasure had been safely transferred to Orléans. The next year, however, the Northmen turned in the direction of Orléans, and were only stayed from assaulting the city by bold preparations for resistance made by Agius, bishop of Orléans and Burchard, bishop of Chartres. The abbot of Saint-Martin of Tours was another Hilduin, second of that name in our story, archchaplain of Charles the Bald. In his fear for his abbey's treasure, now lying at Orléans—a city which he was sure would soon be attacked and plundered by these pirates—Hilduin wrote to Lupus to beg him that the abbey's precious relics might be received for safekeeping at Ferrières. Lupus was a friend of Hilduin and his abbey; but he was keenly aware of uncomfortable facts.

"It is not surprising," he wrote in answer, "that you thought your treasure might safely rest with us, for you did not know our situation. If you had, you would not have dreamed of sending it here for even three days. Access to our monastery looks difficult, I know, for those pirates, although for our sins nothing far away fails to be easy for *them* to reach, nothing hard is for *them* impossible. To tell the truth, our defence is very weak; and their greed to seize is simply sharpened by the knowledge that we have only a few men able to stand against them. They can rush upon us from cover of our woods, to find no fortifications and only a handful of defenders. Then, once more hidden in the depths of the forest, they can flee with their prizes where they will. So be prudent and send your treasure elsewhere. We don't want you to repent of rashness, nor do we want charge of negligence brought unjustly against ourselves."

In the middle of August 856, other Vikings from the North entered the Seine, and after ravaging the countryside on either bank, especially its monasteries and towns for the wealth they held, settled for the winter months in a strongly fortified position on the river. From there on December 28 they attacked Paris, again the victim of this Northern terror, and set fire to its churches. In 857 Poitiers was sacked, and raiders rushed to ruin many other places of attraction in Aquitaine. On the Loire, Tours and Blois, each for the second time, were torn and mutilated by murderous descent. The following year, 858, saw Charles the Bald facing from his camp on the Seine pirates entrenched in its isle of Oissel near Mantes. From it they sallied out to capture Louis, chancellor to King Charles, abbot of Saint-Denis, and friend of Lupus. With Louis was seized his brother, who ruled the great abbey of Saint-Maur-sur-Loire. The king exhausted his treasury in the effort to raise the ransom exacted. When no more could be obtained from royal funds, bishops, abbots, counts, and many others who could lay their hands on ready money made up what was lacking.

About this time Lupus wrote to a friend who lived outside this kingdom of Charles the Bald:

"I long to see you here at Ferrières, but do be very, very careful to come by a safe road. In this realm revolution has broken out. Plunderings are rife, and the wicked are never punished. Nothing goes on with more security, more persistence, than attacks and raids of robbers."

Even more keen in their anger were the words of Paschasius Radbert, as he turned for a moment from his commentary on the *Lamentations* of Jeremiah to lament the sins of his own land:

"And so among us the sword of barbarian men rages, unsheathed from the scabbard of the Lord! And we, wretched creatures, live as though paralysed, not only among the hideous evils done by savages, but as well among the wars fought without pity between our own peoples, amid sedition and fraud. Day by day men's hearts burn with new ardour to commit greater and more wicked crimes!"

Paschasius might well write of pitiless war fought within his own country. For now discord among the royal brothers again raised high its head. During the days succeeding the death of Louis the Pious it had been the brother Lothar who had invaded the dominion of Charles; now it was Louis, king of the eastern Franks, of Germany. For long he had been scheming to increase his power. His chance of aggression had come first from Aquitaine. In 853 its rebels had turned to ask support from him. They had been without a leader to encourage their cause; for the year before, Pippin II had been captured by a Gascon noble, had been handed over to Charles and given for safekeeping to the monks of Saint-Médard at Soissons. Louis the German had gladly accepted their call. Now, he had thought, the way to Aquitaine was open, since Charles was absorbed in defending his land from pirate raids.

Louis had begun operations by sending his son, Louis the Younger, into Aquitaine, in the hope that its people would hail him as their king. The attempt had failed miserably, and he had looked around for another chance. While he had waited, events in the Frankish Empire had taken a new turn. The eldest brother, the Emperor Lothar, had died, in 855, wearied by illness, by long years of quarrel and intrigue; so wearied, indeed, that he had passed his last hours in the abbey of Prüm, clad in monastic habit, with a monk's profession on his lips. He had already declared his wishes for the sharing of his kingdom between his three sons. To the eldest, Louis II, he left the imperial title and Italy; to Lothar, next in age, was to come the central part of the Frankish Empire, that region of the Rhine, the Moselle and the Meuse, which was known in future days first as Lotharingia and afterwards as Lorraine, together with much of Burgundy; to the youngest, Charles, a mere child and an epileptic, Provence and the district around Lyons. In the same year Aquitania received as king another child, a son of Charles the Bald, and saw him crowned at Limoges. He will appear again later on. The claimant, Pippin II, had already escaped from prison and was constantly to seek his lost crown. But in vain.

In 858 the secret plotting of Louis the German at last found its hour of action. Nobles of high standing came to him, not only from Aquitaine, but from other parts of France, complaining that "they could no longer endure the tyranny of Charles the Bald, that he was ruining whatever was left to them from the destruction wrought by pirates; that if their own Frankish princes could not help them they would have to seek aid from those very pagans themselves." In August Louis marched to Worms and thence into his brother's territory: to Ponthion, a royal residence of Charles, then to Sens, and on to Orléans. Many who owed loyalty to Charles turned from him to this king of German Frankland. Among them was the nephew of both, the young Lothar II, king of Lotharingia.

Exactly at this time, in 858, Charles was facing the Danish pirates entrenched upon the isle of Oissel in the Seine. Caught between two imminent perils, he left his camp of operation against the Northern invaders and hastened to try to intercept Louis; but he found himself "deserted by his people" and after a while was forced to retreat into Burgundy. Not, however, for long. The bishops and clergy of his realm used their controlling power in rising to his rescue; and they saved the day for king and kingdom alike. As Frankish men heard their bishops denouncing Louis the German for his action against his brother, against the peace and unity of the Empire, they began to rally to the support of Charles. In January 859, while Louis was at Jouy-en-Laonnais, having held his Christmas revel at Saint-Quentin, Charles fell upon him, scattered his army, and drove him back to his own land.

Quickly the nephew, Lothar of Lotharingia, came to the victor, declared his penitence for his desertion, and marched henceforth with his uncle Charles.

The honor of rousing the Church of France for the defense of its king and country belongs to Hincmar, archbishop of Reims. The invasion of Louis had struck Abbot Lupus not only in his own country, but in his own personal relations; for one of those who deserted King Charles for his brother Louis at this time was that archbishop, Wenilo of Sens, in whose diocese Ferrières lay. He was a friend of Lupus. And Lupus was present, with Hincmar and seven other archbishops, with thirty-two bishops and two other abbots, at a Synod assembled in June 859 at Savonnières, near Toul, a Synod to which Charles the Bald presented a scathing denunciation of this same Wenilo, a leading prelate of his land:

"It was I," Charles declared, "to whom Archbishop Wenilo owed his consecration and his appointing to this metropolitan see in my realm. By solemn oath he swore to support peace and mutual aid between me and my brother Louis. At Orléans he hallowed me as king with holy chrism, and lifted me up on high with sceptre and crown. When rebellion began to rise and to run its course in our kingdom, and my loyal subjects acknowledged in written record their duty to render me counsel and succour, Wenilo was one of those who signed the assurance. Then, after all this witness, this protesting of fidelity, when I was face to face with attack by pirates on land and sea, Wenilo pleaded that he was ill and must return to his home. When my brother Louis, as you know, marched with a hostile force from his dominion into mine, Wenilo, with no word to me, went to confer with him whom he knew to be my enemy. So conferred none other of my bishops. No support did Wenilo give me when I went forth against that brother of mine. No! When by force of necessity I had to retreat, it was Wenilo who gave comfort to Louis against me. It was he who celebrated Mass openly in my palace of Attigny, in the diocese of another archbishop, and one, too, loyal to me; it was he who shared that holy rite with men forbidden the communion of the Church. It was Wenilo, also, who drew away my nephew Lothar from me by his weaving of lies."

Wenilo himself was not present at Savonnières, and action

following these charges against him by the king was therefore postponed. But the archbishop heard that Lupus was present, and Lupus was one of the abbots under his jurisdiction. Men were saying that Lupus had openly declared his wish that Wenilo might be deposed from his see. In great indignation the archbishop wrote to Ferrières, and Lupus as fiercely denied the rumor:

"How could I be guilty of so great wickedness," he protested, "that I should desire the deposing of one from whom I had received sacred consecration? I call to witness Him before whose Judgment-seat we both shall stand, that ever since you, Wenilo, have thought me worthy to be your friend, I have always desired your advancement in holiness and dignity. If, while fortune was mine, if aught of evil—the Lord forbid it!—had befallen you, I was ready to help you with all my power. Please let us meet as soon as may be, that by grace of the Holy Spirit I may regain that friendship which the malevolence of a malicious mind has disturbed."

We do not know whether the wrath of Wenilo ever allowed this. Nor do we know whether Lupus was truthful in protesting his unbroken regard for the archbishop who had deserted in an hour of need the king to whom they both had pledged their service. But Frankish record declares that Wenilo was not brought before a Synod in the kingdom of Charles the Bald to answer for his desertion, and that he finally won reconciliation from that king, in this same year of 859.

The year in its course even saw a war between classes. Misery and want caused by raids and plundering drove the peasants dwelling between the Seine and the Loire into a common rising against the enemy, Louis the German. The attempt was bold and brave; but it lacked preparation and means for its support; and tradition tells that it was put down with easy slaughter by the Frankish nobles themselves. In the distracted state of the land armed revolt of peasants on their own initiative was an omen not to be endured.

Now, also, a new peril was threatening. Another army of Danes, under a chieftain named Weland, had settled on the river Somme. Soon Amiens was in flames, and all the region around lay waste and bare. Lupus wrote to Odo, abbot of Corbie, a monastery very near the Somme:

"I do hope rumour is lying. We hear that in action against the barbarians some of your community have been seriously wounded, and our dear G. so grievously that we can hardly hope for his life. We are offering our prayers here every day. Please let me know soon how he is. I am also extremely worried about you, for I know that you are always ready to dash into danger, quite unarmed."

In 860 Charles despaired of driving away the Danish invaders from these two centers of attack, on the Seine and on the Somme. His nobles were giving him no adequate support; his army was no match for these hungry men from the North. He decided to turn to other means than battle and siege: to negotiation and even to bribery. His attempt seemed at first to promise success. The Danes on the Somme promised that in return for three thousand pounds of silver, established by accurate weight, they would proceed against their fellow countrymen on the Seine and either drive them from the isle of Oissel or slay them then and there.

The king again strained every nerve to provide this sum, from the funds of Church and charity, from resources public and private alike; but he failed. Weland's pirates in disappointment accepted hostages, and, feeling that for the time they had plundered to the full these Frankish shores, sailed away in the hope of fresh prize on English lands. Their hope was not fulfilled. Back across the Channel they sailed, and after some further marauding settled in a station of their own on the Seine, again under Weland.

There were now two encampments of Danes on this river. Those on the isle of Oissel in 861 once more descended on Paris and destroyed churches in the city. Both camps were dangerously near the abbey of Ferrières-en-Gâtinais. The situation for Lupus and his monks was critical. Already the pirates from Oissel had burned Melun, a town not far away. To Folcric, who had been elected bishop of Troyes after the death of Prudentius, Lupus wrote in 862:

"When you came to see us at Ferrières and you found me seriously ill and all of us terrified out of our lives, then straightway, without even waiting for our entreaty, without any horrid, worrying discussion, you saved us from shame. Of your own goodwill you offered us shelter on your estate at Aix-en-Othe [between Sens and Troyes] that we might in greater safety abide the evil of those days and in some sort find means to follow our profession. You showed to us the widest generosity in the gift of scarcely believable kindness. Words cannot thank you.

"But the mercy of God, in spite of our grievous sins, has now turned from us the menace and outspoken threatening of these ravaging robbers. May He do the like for all Christian men! Please, however, may we keep your offer in mind, should another such crisis come upon us?"

The monks of Ferrières, therefore, did not leave their home for Aix-en-Othe. But in 861 they had been driven to seek hospitality and shelter for themselves and the sacred treasure of their church from the brethren of the abbey of Saint-Germain in Auxerre.

9

The crisis, when Lupus wrote these words to Folcric in 862, had indeed passed, at least for the moment, and its passing had been in no slight measure due to Charles the Bald. Before the year 861 ended, he had gathered all his remaining courage and had once more approached Weland, now raiding with his pirates on the Seine. To them the king had offered five thousand pounds of silver, with other produce of livestock in great measure, if they would besiege and drive away the Danes upon Oissel. By what means he had managed to inspire in Weland the hope that he could raise this sum we do not know. Perhaps Weland was already keen to banish his rival countrymen so near to him. Dane, therefore, had entered into battle with Dane on the island in the river. The siege had not lasted long. Beset by famine and utter misery, the pirates of Oissel had themselves solved the matter by promising six thousand pounds of gold and silver as the price of freedom to Weland. Thus they won their freedom. They tried to sail away by sea and were prevented by winter storms. Eventually they returned to encamp once more upon the Seine.

There they were in 862, while Weland's men were stationed on the Marne and plundering the city of Meaux. News of this fresh outrage reached Charles as he was awaiting reinforcements at Senlis. Now he made his great effort. He threw a bridge across the Marne, posted all the fighting men he could muster on either bank of the river, and effectually cut off Weland's retreat. Nothing for the present was left to the Danish chieftain but to send hostages to the king who had outwitted him and to submit to his terms of peace. Charles ordered that not only should Weland and his men, after releasing all whom they had captured on the Marne, depart from the region of the Marne and the Seine, but that also those Danes should leave who had formerly made the isle of Oissel their base. If, indeed, this latter force proved unwilling to leave the Seine, Weland, so the command went, was to join Charles in compelling their departure. Before the year 862 was over, all of both companies "were sailing away whither they would" from France. Weland himself, before his welcome departure, gave oath of homage and received Christian baptism.

In this year, then, after unending battle on land and on river, against his own people and against pirates here and there, Charles the Bald knew at long last a moment of comfort and peace. On the Seine and on the Somme he had gained respite, even if only temporary, from prevailing terror; two years earlier, at Coblenz, he had once more made treaty of peace with his fellow kings, with Louis of Germany and with Lothar II, of Lotharingia. The cost to him had been great, in outlay of men and money, in shame, and in endurance; the peril to him and his people had been worse. But during all the struggle he had done what he had in him to do for the rescue of his country and his crown from rebellion, from cowardice, and from the menace of the seas.

10

All his days as abbot, in the midst of rebellion, raid, and peril, earlier and later Lupus carried on his work of scholarship and of writing. He carefully examined the varied meters of Boethius, and we still have his findings. He criticized and corrected the manuscripts he read; the modern student can still note his corrections, his insertions, his erasures. He wrung promise of a copy of a valuable text from Ratleic, that clerk of Einhard who had stolen for him sacred relics at Rome and who after Einhard's death had succeeded him as abbot of his beloved Seligenstadt. He compared with his own copy the readings of Cicero's *Letters* in a manuscript sent to him from Prüm. He wrote to England, in one of the last letters which passed between the famous school of York and the scholars of Frankland before the destruction of York by the Vikings. In it he begged Ealdsige, abbot of York, to send him works of Quintilian, of St. Jerome, of Bede the Venerable. He was worried because he could find only six books of Jerome's *Commentaries on Jeremiah;* the others were lacking. Would Ealdsige kindly send them? Hraban, we may note here, had the same trouble. Had not Cassiodorus stated that Jerome had written twenty commentaries? Nothing daunted, when the fourteen books continued wanting, Lupus wrote off to the Pope himself, Benedict III, humbly praying him to forward these from his great library. The fourteen books never arrived; Jerome, it seems, had died after writing the first six. Perhaps the confusion in the mind of Lupus was caused by the fact that Origen wrote fourteen Homilies on Jeremiah!

Of importance in these works of Lupus are five writings on theology. Many men consulted him as an expert in knowledge of the things of God. Among these was King Charles himself, always interested in such matters, as his grandfather, Charles the Great, and his father, Louis the Pious, had been. The king was especially concerned by the theories and beliefs spreading from the cell of Gottschalk, the captive in Hautvillers. In 849–50 Lupus wrote in answer to a royal request:

"Lately, when we met at Bourges, you asked me concerning predestination, free will, and redemption; and I briefly declared to your Majesty what I had learned from the Divine Scriptures and from the chief authorities on these subjects. But, since there are men who differ from me, who think that my belief concerning God is neither loyal nor according to true faith, since, moreover, many people boldly discuss these questions and few grasp them with intelligence, I will now write down for you my answer, in few words, but truthful and clear."

The statement which follows is only a little, if at all, less dour than that of Gottschalk. It was conceived by Lupus according to his own interpretation of St. Augustine and St. Paul:

Adam, as created by God, was good and pure, and in God's intention all human beings descended from Adam were likewise to be good and pure. Then Adam of his own will sinned, sinned so grievously that he ruined not only himself but all—all men and all women, who were born, and were to be born, down the ages in descent from him. Through Adam all human souls of all time came, and were to come, into the world doomed to a life of sin.

God did not cause the sin of Adam; but He foresaw it and its fatal consequence for all the human race. Therefore, before the foundation of this world, before Adam and Eve were created, God of His mercy chose out from the sum of human life those souls whom by gift of His grace He willed to deliver from sin and from the punishment due to sin, both actual sin, and that sin inherited from Adam's fall. The rest of His human creatures, those on whom He did not will to bestow this gift of saving grace, in His altogether just and righteous judgment He left to meet that damnation for all eternity which their guilt deserved.

This dividing into the saved and the condemned has been, is, and will be; and it will be revealed when time is over, at the Last Judgment. Those on whom God has pity are predestined to enjoy Him and His heaven. Those whom He hardens in spirit, that is, those whose hearts He does not will to soften, are left without hope in His sight.

The blessed will give thanks evermore for their creation and redeeming; the lost will acknowledge that their doom was rightly the penalty of sin. Shall not God do as He wills with what is His? He is under no necessity to cleanse and to free man from that evil which man's own fault brought upon his soul. The saving of some from the guilty multitude is due to His goodness alone.

We, then, His creatures, shall praise Him for His gift of life. The original befouling of man did not cause God to cease from creating human souls. He willed to use for His own good end even that which was bad.

"So," wrote Lupus, "so blessed Augustine did not hesitate to declare in many books."

In regard to free will, the truth is the same. Original sin took away from man, through Adam, his free will for goodness; it left him but a will for evil. Only the grace of God can restore to guilty man the power of his will for good. No one is driven by God of necessity to do either good or evil. Man is free. God simply omits to bestow the gift of grace where He does not will to bestow it.

And on redemption. Did the Lord suffer death for all men, or only for those who after this life shall enter into the joy of heaven, saved by His gift of grace? Saint Matthew wrote of the Blood "shed for many for the remission of sins." "For many" also wrote Saint Mark; Saint Luke wrote "for you." None of the three wrote "for all."

What, then, did the Fathers of the Church declare on this grave question? Saint Jerome wrote: "He did not say that He gave His life as redemption for all, but for many, that is, for those who would will to believe." So, too, wrote Augustine: "The Lord saw that they who believed not, who were not of His sheep, were predestined to everlasting death; they were not purchased for eternal life at the price of His Blood."

"This faith," wrote Lupus to Charles the Bald, "I hold and guard. This, to those who will, I reveal without boasting or conceit; to those who will not, conscious of my own littleness, I declare it not."

Such were the problems which split the theological thinking of the ninth century, aroused by the words of Gottschalk, into two camps of battle. Hincmar, worried by Gottschalk's obdurate stand, by the long imprisonment in that monastic cell of Hautvillers, by the following which Gottschalk had received as teacher, of his own impulse also wrote from Reims to Lupus to ask his views. The answer of Lupus was the same: "The elect, receiving from God the will and the power to act, do freely that which brings them eternal reward; the perverse, abandoned by God, also of their free will do that which deservedly brings them eternal punishment: a judgment just, though hidden to our eyes." A third letter went from Lupus to Pardulus, bishop of Laon. Neither Hincmar nor Pardulus agreed with him.

In 850, remembering the disturbance caused among Christian men of northern Italy by Gottschalk's words when he was living there, Lupus decided to compose a longer writing on these disputed matters. He called this his *De Tribus Quaestionibus*,

"On the Three Questions," and he sent it, also, to King Charles.

About the same time he had received a letter from Gottschalk. In it Gottschalk had carefully set forth, as he did at the same time to other learned men, what he on his side, and what the "followers of Hraban" on their side, believed in regard to the doctrine of predestination as interpreted by St. Augustine. In answer, it would seem, Lupus sent his "On the Three Questions": "a book," Gottschalk wrote afterward to Ratramn, monk of Corbie, "in which he does not identify himself fully with either side. Lupus is a cautious and a cunning man."

Gottschalk had also written in this letter on another subject. Would Lupus tell him how, by what means, will the blessed in heaven after their resurrection from the dead receive their Vision of God? With what eyes—of the body? of the spirit? Directly, or through some medium?

The answer here from Lupus was rather impatient. Gottschalk doubtless had plenty of time on his hands for abstruse questions and for letters; Lupus had not. These questions concerning the Beatific Vision, Lupus wrote, he could not solve; not even St. Augustine had arrived at their decision. But he would sum up what Augustine had said, and would add some interpretation of his own. This he did, rather fully, and then added:

"My reverend brother, do not, I pray you, wear out your mind to no purpose. If you busy yourself in problems of this nature more than you should, you will lose the power to think out and to teach truths which will bring more profit to you at present. Why should we probe so zealously into things which perhaps it is not yet well for us to understand? No! Nor do I have just now the time to examine into the meaning of those Greek words which you mention. And, please, if you write me again, do not heap upon me words of praise superfluous and untrue! Will you rather pray God that I may look to Him as both End and Source of all praise given to men?"

Lupus, it is true, went much of the way with Gottschalk in the thought which both deduced from Augustine; but he was not eager for full agreement with a mind of so daring and original a cast. Hincmar might and did differ from Lupus in regard to the predestination of man's soul; but in other ways the spirit of Lupus, that lover of tradition and of texts, could maintain friendship with Archbishop Hincmar far better than it could with the questioning, brilliant, but restless intellect of the prisoner of Hautvillers.

11

About 862 we lose sight of this abbot of Ferrières, no doubt on account of his death. It is pleasant, as one thinks of him, to recall a picture of goodly living which he drew for one of his friends. This picture is contained in a letter, and we do not know when Lupus wrote it. We know only that the monk, Eberhard, to whom he sent it, was related to him by family kinship. But in it there seems to beat the inmost heart of his persistent hunger for truth:

You keep on urging me, dear one, to write you something which, if not of use, may be of delight to you. This I might have done in some way worth while if you had told me on what I was to write. Since, however, you say that you will be glad to have anything at all, if only I will write it, I have not worried much about the subject, far less about polished periods. I will just put down whatever comes to my mind.

It is good that some men in our land are again striving in quest of wisdom, that once again among us wisdom returns to life. Yet it still lies heavy on my soul that men seek one part of wisdom and arrogantly reject another. Surely we are at variance here with our true selves; surely we think unwisely concerning wisdom. Many of us are now seeking from knowledge a mere cult of words; very few are to be found who would choose rather to gain from their books a high code of character, a thing greatly to be preferred. We are afraid of faults of speech, and we try hard to rid ourselves of them. We think little of the sins of our lives; in fact, we foster them.

All wisdom, as Holy Scripture affirms, is from the Lord God. Let us seek it in the right and proper order, and then without doubt we shall attain it. But those who live in evil, while they are ambitious to speak well, are those of whom Holy Writ tells: *All the labour of man is for his mouth; but his soul shall not be filled.* Truly he who seeks knowledge rather than holiness shall fast to his undoing; he shall not feast at the table of wisdom.

Various are the ways of those who love wisdom, and each one perfect of its own kind. Each may freely and safely bring its followers into the sanctuary of true understanding; for all are united in a harmony of difference. It is clear, then, that varying roads of life, followed in peace by different people of God, may lead each and all to that same end. The temple of Mother Church is open to all who come to it in loyalty; but each shall attain his end the more surely as he more surely places the things of God before the things of man.

Whatever, then, your own particular step on the ladder of the Christian life, respect all those who stand on others. By God's help gain more day by day and show yourself sound in Him. At the same time, do not neglect the noble arts of secular learning. Seek their skills, also, from Him Who gives to all abundantly without reproach; and according to the measure of your faith surely shall power be given unto you.

Chapter VII

HINCMAR OF REIMS

1

At the opening of his study, *Hinkmar, Erzbischof von Reims,*
Heinrich Schrörs names the three men who stand out and will
always stand out in the historical records of the ninth century:
Charles the Great, Pope Nicholas I, and Hincmar of Reims.
Charles we recalled in the beginning of this book. Here in its last
chapter but one we shall find the Pope and the Archbishop,
striving one against the other with all their force, spiritual and
intellectual, for the end which each man desired.

We have seen in this century Einhard, calling upon his
saints in his solitude; Amalar, absorbed in interpretation of the
liturgy; Walafrid, serving his king and governing the abbey on
his island; Lupus, the zealous collector of books. Now we come
to a man who rises far above them all: a prince of the Church, a
statesman, an administrator, a scholar; a man who worked his
will in Synod and in Council, in episcopal cathedral and in royal
Court; a man devoted to Catholic faith and learning, and a life-
long upholder of the throne of France; a man of energy incredible.
One who fought during thirty-seven years with all his knowledge
of canon law for causes ecclesiastical, with all his power of skilful manipulation for causes political; and who, in all his fighting,
never forgot his desire for himself, his insistent ambition, his own
aims and hopes.

We come upon him first about 814, a little boy of some seven
or eight years, brought by his kinsfolk to the abbey of Saint-Denis
just outside the city of Paris. There he was to be trained in the
discipline of learning, sacred, religious, secular.

He probably was born in northern France and came, we
assume, of a noble and aristocratic house; for the abbey of Saint-
Denis chose its pupils and its child-oblates with great care. Its
story was known to all. Had not Gregory of Tours himself told

that in the third century one Dionysius, better known as Denis, had been sent by Rome to become the first bishop of Paris? And had not this Denis proved himself as martyr, killed by the sword for his bold preaching? In Gregory's sixth century a church was hallowed in the name of Denis, at or near the place of his burial, and served by a community of clergy under an abbot. In the days that followed, Saint-Denis became the sanctuary of the Frankish kings, in which they learned as boys, received their anointing with holy oil, and were laid to rest in the tomb.

The Merovingian Dagobert I and in her widowhood the devout Bathild, once queen of Clovis II, endowed the abbey with splendid offerings. In 754 Pope Stephen II stayed a spring and a summer within it as guest of Abbot Fulrad, and marked his stay by anointing as king, or king of future time, both Pippin the Short and his sons, Carloman and Charles, afterward Charles the Great. Fulrad was still abbot when this same Pippin the Short built a new church for the brethren; there he was buried, in 768. Throughout his reign Charles the Great revered this royal sanctuary in frequent prayer; and by his gifts he enriched it only in lesser degree than his own Palace chapel at Aachen.

To his son, Louis the Pious, Saint-Denis was a source of some sorrow. Its discipline was not Benedictine in regular strictness; its clergy lived as canons rather than as monks, though they were ruled by an "abbot." The effort of Louis and his counselor, Benedict of Aniane, to bring the West Frankish abbeys under true monastic order had not succeeded here; and Hincmar tells us that his earlier years were spent "in canonical habit."

Just about the time of Hincmar's entering, Hilduin, whom we have met at the Court of Louis the Pious, became head of the abbey of Saint-Denis. Under him Hincmar was taught in its church and library. Then, when about 822 Hilduin was called to the honor of archchaplain of the Court, he carried off this pupil of his for further study in its Palace. Lessons were given to him there by Adalard, "an old man and wise," in the principles of unity of Empire and of loyalty to the throne; there he read eagerly in books which told of politics of the state and the canon law of the Church. He heard the talk of men when the king-Emperor Louis the Pious took Judith as his second wife; when, to the joy of all, Charles, their son, was born; and when Louis bowed his head in penitence at Attigny for the sins of his rule.

He did not follow his tutor, Hilduin, into the rebellion of 830; he was probably at this time once again living at Saint-Denis. Nor did he sympathize with Hilduin's march under arms into the assembly hall of Nijmegen. But when Hilduin was banished to exile among the Saxons, Hincmar went with him as his friend. From Saxony, too, he pleaded so strongly for Hilduin's recall that soon the abbot of Saint-Denis was again in his monastery, and Hincmar was once more at home.

Already a strong effort had been made to raise the brethren of Saint-Denis into Benedictine life. At the end of 829 or the beginning of 830, Aldric, Archbishop of Sens, and Ebbo, Archbishop of Reims, had come with their suffragans to the abbey for this purpose. "They made diligent inquiry concerning those who had offered monastic profession there. Some, they found, had forsaken their calling and had died in disloyalty. Others declared that they had never taken monastic vows; these were convicted of lying and placed under penance. The greater number, however, although also guilty of lapse, confessed this in all humility and received again the religious cowl and scapular."

This renewal soon broke down, however, and grumbling burst out in force. Some of the community even sent a deputation to the Emperor, Louis the Pious, complaining of the material austerities of their Benedictine rule of life. Once more a conference was held, in January 832, and a new scale of provision was introduced, strict enough for Benedictine standard, but reasonable in its supply of food and clothing.

For this end Hincmar had worked hard. In the distracted years which followed he could do so little for his land and its crown that he gave himself to study. Doubtless in 834, in his own abbey of Saint-Denis, he saw the Emperor Louis a prisoner, dethroned by his son; in Saint-Denis, also, he must have rejoiced to see him restored to royal and imperial dignity.

It was now that Hincmar came into close connection with his king and Emperor; for Louis, attracted by his quickness of mind and his zeal for work, took him into his service. From this time the young man, already professed monk and ordained priest, was present at assemblies of the Church, of the state, of the Frankish people in the West; in other words, of the people of France.

Year by year he gained experience, and in experience he found power. The change of ruler, from Louis the Pious to Charles the Bald, increased both his enthusiasm and his influence. As counselor, as a pillar of strength behind the throne, for many years he was to be for Charles a primary support. For his king his ambition worked as for himself. It was only when Charles refused to follow his shrewd policy or dared to prefer another man in honor of office that Hincmar in resentment went on his way alone.

2

We come now to 844, when Hincmar was close to forty years old. He was now known throughout the Frankish Empire for his learning and for his diplomatic skill. As he himself tells us: "After the death of the Emperor Louis, I laboured in the service of those who desired harmony between his sons. With all my power I toiled, in frequent journeys, in missions fulfilled by word of mouth or by written documents, for the restoration of due and constitutional order, in Church, in realm, in the royal household and palace."

His working brought material reward. King Charles assigned to him the rule and the revenue, as their head, of two abbeys, of Notre-Dame at Compiègne and of Saint-Germer-de-Flay, near Beauvais. In them he did much for the better ordering of their monastic life.

In 844 Hincmar was among the bishops and priests assembled in the royal palace at Ver, near Senlis, for consultation concerning grave problems of the Church. One of these problems was the forlorn state of the see of Reims, vacant now for nine years, ever since Ebbo, its archbishop, at Thionville in 835 had declared himself unworthy of its charge and had been deposed from office. For nearly all this time administration of the diocese had been carried on by one Fulco, a priest of Reims; but in this year of 844 another administrator, Notho, was in control. There was no episcopal head, some prelate being summoned from without for episcopal functions.

The bishops of France were worried, for they knew well that the reason for this long vacancy lay in the history of Ebbo. After the loss of his see in 835, Ebbo for some years had been kept in monastic imprisonment by Louis the Pious. Then, when Louis had died in June 840 and his eldest son Lothar had come marching across the Alps to claim the imperial title and to invade the kingdom of his brother Charles, Lothar had assembled in August a Council at the royal palace of Ingelheim. There he had ordered the reinstating of Ebbo in the see of Reims; and the bishops present at the Council had confirmed his order. To learn that the prelate who had worked to dethrone his father was now in possession of Reims would surely, Lothar thought in his malice, vex the heart of Charles! It would vex Charles more that for this cathedral of Reims, in his own realm, the invader should appoint any archbishop at all.

On December 6, 840, we are told, formal ceremony honored Ebbo at Reims. Suffragan bishops of the diocese were present, and others sent letters of excuse. The edict of restoration was read from the pulpit; *Te Deum* was sung; Ebbo, once more in bishop's vestments, was escorted to his high seat in the sanctuary; pontifical mass was celebrated; and to suffragans who had been consecrated during the years of his absence he now as head of the Archdiocese solemnly presented their croziers and their rings.

So, at least, we read; and these details of the story may be true. But their source, the "Narrative of the Clerics of Ebbo," cannot be held above suspicion. We do not know in certainty either the author or the date of this "Narrative." It may have been written by Wulfad, one of these clerics; it may have been written by him, however, as late as 866, twenty-six years after the event.

At any rate, Ebbo was restored to office and remained as archbishop in Reims for some ten months. Then, after Lothar had been driven from the kingdom of Charles, Ebbo left the city and its cathedral, never to return. He was terrified of the wrath of Charles, and he fled to Lothar's protection. It was given, and with it two abbeys for his shelter and support: the houses of Stavelot in Flanders and of Bobbio in northern Italy. Lothar also from time to time employed this refugee from France in missions of diplomatic concern.

Nonetheless, Ebbo still held himself lawful archbishop of Reims. His free hours were spent in concocting an "Apology," a defense of his acts, a glorification of Lothar, and a bitter attack upon the "persecution" which he had suffered from Louis the Pious. At last in 844 he hoped that his chance had arrived. Lothar was sending his young son, Louis, to Rome to receive formal blessing from a Pope lately elected as Sergius II. With Louis went Drogo, Archbishop of Metz, to receive the title of vicar apostolic for France and Germany; and with them both traveled Ebbo, to plead for his restoration to the cathedral which he still called his own.

He pleaded in vain. Sergius forbade his restoration to the metropolitan see of Reims. Moreover, for the future he was forbidden to receive communion at the altar as a priest of the Church. He must hereafter receive it only among the multitude, as a layman.

This failure in Rome quickly cooled Lothar's friendship; Ebbo, also, was failing him in work as diplomatic envoy. The two abbeys were taken away from him and presented to other, more successful men; and Ebbo in despair went off to try his fortune with Lothar's brother, Louis, king of Germany. Good fortune it turned out to be. Rembert, bishop of Hildesheim in Saxony, had lately died. His see was still vacant, and with the permission of German prelates Louis bestowed it upon the unhappy wanderer. It was now about 845, and Ebbo lived and ruled at Hildesheim for six years, the rest of his life.

The vacancy at Reims had thus lasted nine years because men were still in doubt concerning it. Had Archbishop Ebbo been deposed by convincing authority? On the other hand, had those bishops at Ingelheim any right to confirm a restoration, carried out by order of a king who was an invader of another's realm? Did the penance imposed by Pope Sergius upon Ebbo amount to a confirmation of his deposing in permanence by Papal decree?

The vacancy had lasted, also, for other and less valid reasons. Many had been glad that the great Archdiocese of Reims should lie in unofficial, irregular holding. Among them was King Charles the Bald himself. It had been for him a happy convenience to be able to draw upon the unused revenues of a vacant and a wealthy see in order to pay his monstrous bribes for the warding off of pirate raids.

Now, however, the bishops of France determined to end this scandal. Through the pen of Lupus of Ferrières, secretary for the Synod assembled in 844 at Ver, we can read the mind of its prelates:

"We cannot without sorrow speak of the Church of Reims, long destitute of a Pastor, recently despoiled of its property, overwhelmed by injuries. We implore that it be restored into wholeness, and that in accordance with canon law a bishop meet for its dignity be at once sought out and placed in charge."

The following year, in April 845, and in a Synod gathered at Beauvais, Hincmar was elected archbishop of Reims by general consent: of episcopal vote, of the king's majesty, and of assurance from the community of Saint-Denis. A few weeks later, on May 3, he received consecration from Wenilo, archbishop of Sens.

3

The time was critical for Charles the Bald and his realm of France. Only a few weeks before, in March 845, he had been forced to seek refuge in the royal abbey of Saint-Denis from the Northern invaders who sailed up the Seine to assault Paris on Easter Day. The following November he was to flee for his life before the conqueror, Nominoë, of Brittany. Now, as in the days of his father, Louis the Pious, power for the defense of both Church and state was held, and held increasingly, in the strong hands of the leading Frankish clergy. The king had acknowledged this power at that same Synod of Beauvais, when he had declared before his bishops: "May it not come to pass that you act for my condemnation through any deed of mine; and Heaven forbid that I myself act openly against God and you."

Hincmar, therefore, as archbishop of Reims, a see of primary importance in the realm of Charles, was to counsel, guide, and support his king. From the beginning his position was full of difficulty. In the first place, part of his diocese, and, in particular, its suffragan see of Cambrai, lay within the land ruled by the Emperor Lothar; and the brief harmony which had been restored in the division of kingdoms made at Verdun in 843 was again wearing thin. Now jealousy was once more breeding dissension between Lothar and his brother Charles, who was a younger man, more energetic, and far more widely recognized by those of culture than was Lothar. This resentment of Lothar and his followers was readily extended to include the archbishop, friend and loyal defender of Charles, Hincmar himself.

He worked hard for peace, writing letter after letter both to Charles and to his queen, Irmintrud. Unfortunately several causes of offense arose to stimulate ill-feeling. In 846 a vassal of Charles, Gislebert, carried off a daughter of Lothar into Aquitaine, no consent being asked or obtained from authority, and made her his wife. About the same time Hincmar was writing to the archbishop of Trier in regard to one Fulcric, a vassal of Lothar, whom, as resident in his Archdiocese, he himself had excommunicated for breaking the Church's marriage law, a law which Hincmar was to uphold with all his energy again and again. Fulcric, he declared, had cast off his wife for another woman; he was thus guilty of rape. Now in his fear of penalty he had fled for refuge to Trier. Would its archbishop, asked Hincmar, please send him without delay to Reims?

Yet another source of trouble for Hincmar was the sad state of his diocese. Its cathedral badly needed enlarging and rebuilding, a work which, indeed, Ebbo had begun. Far worse was the loss due to wholesale robbery of land and properties; the very administrators themselves, Fulco and Notho, had not hesitated to profit by their opportunity. Here again Reims came into collision with the Emperor. Lothar's daughter, Bertha, was abbess of Avenay in its diocese. Soon after the archbishop entered upon his rule, she wrote to him, complaining that by his order his men had done much harm to her abbey's possessions. His retort was quickly dispatched: "Your words are the words of the Devil himself, Father of lies as he is. That my men have done hurt to your convent I do not deny. But I neither knew this at the time, nor did I will it." On his side, too, Hincmar had reason for wrath. The abbess's men had been trespassing, taking over land that belonged to Hautvillers, one of his monasteries. Would she please

pay attention to this? Otherwise he would be compelled to bring
the matter before the Emperor, her father, and, if necessary, use
legal means of restitution.

Pressing more heavily, however, than these smaller worries
upon the mind of this archbishop as he walked in his cathedral at
Reims was the thought of Ebbo, banished from its seat. Ebbo
provided not only thought, but fear. People still remembered him,
and rumors of injustice done him were still heard. In 846 Lothar,
in his hostility to Hincmar, wrote on this matter of Ebbo to the
Pope, still Sergius II. In answer Sergius sent a letter to Charles the
Bald, requiring that Guntbold, archbishop of Rouen, should assemble at Trier a Synod of bishops to debate and to decide judgment. He also announced that legates from the Holy See would
be present; and he wrote especially to Hincmar, ordering him to
attend in person.

Guntbold obeyed; but the Papal envoys did not appear for
the Synod. We do not know why. Perhaps, it has been suggested,
the thoughts of Sergius and his ministers were full of the Saracen
menace against Italy. Neither did Ebbo arrive, although the archbishop of Trier had summoned him from Hildesheim. No action,
therefore, was taken at this time. Later on, in a Council held at
Paris this same year, the deposing of Ebbo was judged valid for
the past, present, and future. Hincmar now decided to hope for
peace and to pray that this disturbing question was settled forevermore.

The next year his hope seemed confirmed. Sergius II died in
January 847, and Leo IV was elected Pope. Now Lothar, who
was given to sudden changes of mood, decided to turn a friendly
eye upon his brother Charles and that brother's friends. A gracious
letter from him caused the newly consecrated Pope to send Hincmar official permission for his wearing on high days of Feast the
pallium, a vestment symbolic of metropolitan authority. Four
years later, in 851, again moved by Lothar, who had meanwhile
met Charles in amicable conference at Péronne, near Cambrai,
Leo forwarded to Hincmar a concession which, as he wrote, "he
never expected to grant to any other archbishop." This concession was permission to wear the pallium on any and every day!

Relief and joy overwhelmed the archbishop of Reims. The joy was somewhat dimmed, however, as he continued to read the Pope's letter. "Willing as I would have been," wrote Leo IV, "I cannot also grant you another favour desired for you by the Emperor Lothar, the office of Vicar Apostolic, of representative of the Holy See in France and Germany. This was given by my predecessor, Sergius, to Drogo, Archbishop of Metz."

The trouble in Hincmar's mind was not prompted by envy of Drogo, but rather by the knowledge that he himself could have raised that office of Vicar Apostolic to the high importance which it promised.

Pope Leo IV was not always so gracious in his letters to Reims. That vassal of Lothar, Fulcric, was still busy in his own defense. He had even made the long and difficult journey to Rome that he might lay his case before the Pope; and now, about 851, another and very different message from the Holy See reached Hincmar: "We have questioned with great diligence this man whom you so harshly deprived of communion," wrote the Pope. "He tells us quite frankly that he did once live with a mistress, but he was not then married. After a while, so he declared, both of them fell to quarrelling, and he gladly saw her depart of her own will to the peace of a convent. Then, as he could not live without a woman—this was his admission—he found another, and promptly made her his wife in Holy Church. Now he wants to know why you, without any reasonable cause in law, canonical or civil, have banished him from the altar. We are deeply distressed about it, and we bid you reconcile him at once. If, moreover, we hear that you step again outside the bounds of the mercy freely extended by the Church, we shall bring down upon you with all our power our sharpest censure."

Hincmar did not yield. He wrote in all respect, in all firmness of conviction, to the Pope, to the Emperor Lothar, to Fulcric, to Trier. Not until 854 was the matter settled and the victory his. Fulcric finally confessed and submitted to penance. The archbishop at once restored him to the rights and privileges he desired and wrote to commend Lothar for his "humility" in heeding episcopal advice.

4

In 851 Ebbo died at Hildesheim; and Hincmar at last felt secure. Ebbo's ghost would not haunt his days as his living person had done. In spite of Ebbo's sentence from Pope Sergius, in spite of his own receiving of the pallium from Pope Leo, Hincmar had always feared that something might occur to threaten his seat at Reims.

There was still some reason for this feeling. While Ebbo, restored by Lothar, was holding the archbishop's rule in Reims during 840–41, he had ordained there certain men as priests and as deacons; and thirteen of these were still living. Some were now canons, others monks, and some belonged to the abbey of Saint-Remi at Reims. Was their ordination valid? Had Ebbo the right to ordain these men after his deposing? The question had come up directly after Hincmar had begun his rule as archbishop, and he had faced it with determination. At his first important Council, held at Meaux in June 845, six weeks after his consecrating, he had issued, for himself as president of the assembly and, as he said, for his fellow bishops, a decree of suspension from office against these clerics until further examination could be made. This had caused bitter feeling; and Hincmar told of "persecution" of himself by his critics.

Time did not stop this "persecution." The men concerned were constantly in Reims and making constant complaint. At last, in 853, the archbishop, with the consent of his king, Charles the Bald, decided to bring the matter before a Council of the West Frankish Church at Soissons.

It opened on April 22. From five provinces of the Church the clergy had come, high and low: three archbishops, including Hincmar himself, some twenty bishops, and a great many abbots and priests, to speak, to listen, and to judge in the monastery of Saint-Médard and its church of the Holy Trinity. The suspended clerics were all there except one, Wulfad, who was ill in bed. Hincmar, who was presiding, began proceedings by asking what they wished to say for themselves? They answered that they had not come of their own free will; but, since they were there, they desired to pray for mercy and compassion at the hands of their judges. They had no consciousness of guilt in the matter of their ordaining, or of their work as priests or as deacons. They had fully believed their orders to be valid.

Hincmar replied to this plea with a brief reminder that this was a trial and that it must be conducted according to the form prescribed by canon law. He therefore demanded from the twelve men, as plaintiffs, a written statement of their case, which at last after much hesitation they provided. The archbishop of Reims then named judges for the trial, appointed by himself as president of the court: Wenilo, archbishop of Rouen, Amalric, archbishop of Tours, and Pardulus, bishop of Laon, one of his own suffragans. The plaintiffs, he decided, might also choose judges on their side. This was not strictly required by law, but he was anxious to appear impartial. Only one name was put forward by them, that of Prudentius, bishop of Troyes, who was no friend of Hincmar.

In the next session Hincmar stepped down from the president's chair and sat as one of the general assembly. Arguments were vigorously carried on, arguments against Ebbo and in favor of the present archbishop. Hincmar rose to support his own cause from the floor. The end was soon clearly to be seen: the archbishop of Reims, the Council judged, was rightly and properly ruler of his diocese; the thirteen clerics were sentenced to regular and permanent loss of their functions in the Church.

In vain they protested. Their protest was quickly quashed as exaggeration, as false witness, as grounded on forgery. All they did was to arouse anger. A motion was made and carried by the Council, still in session, that they be not only deposed, but excommunicated.

This business once settled, Hincmar again took the chair, and the bishops turned to discuss other matters. But when the meeting drew to its end, the king himself, Charles the Bald, rose to plead that the ban of excommunication be lifted. Hincmar, in spite of the past action of the Council, led his colleagues in granting this; he could well afford, he thought, to be gracious. As soon as was possible, the archbishop of Reims sent the minutes of this Council of Soissons to Pope Leo at Rome, praying for their confirmation, a matter about which he had little doubt.

The answer which arrived in the summer of 853 vexed him

extremely. According to Hincmar himself, the Pope's letter was one "of excuse." He refused to confirm the Acts passed at Soissons. The bishops present there, he said, had not sent envoys to Rome for the explaining of their conclusions; no legates of the Apostolic See had attended the Council; the Emperor Lothar had not written to Rome in its support; and lastly, and most decisively, the deposed clerics had made appeal to Papal judgment.

Again Hincmar wrote to Rome. The Pope remained firm. Another Synod must be summoned, he now declared; the case must be tried anew. And if the accused were not willing to submit to the verdict of this new trial, they must freely be allowed to await decision at Rome, whither they must travel. In the meantime, a Papal legate, Peter, bishop of Spoleto in southern Italy, would journey to France to witness proceedings at the Synod which was to review the evidence.

Opinion in France was still divided. Archbishop Hraban Maur, friend of Hincmar though he was, wrote from Germany to Heribald, bishop of Auxerre: "As to the deposing and restoration of Ebbo of Reims, let those who were responsible decide whether they acted justly or unjustly. I found him in a Saxon diocese, and I did not forbid him to function there, for I had heard that he was allowed to do so by the Holy See."

Far worse than divided opinion was the news that the Emperor Lothar, at the request of one of his bishops, was himself praying the Pope not to confirm the sentence of deposition passed at Soissons. This petition he was forwarding to Rome through another Peter, bishop of Arezzo. It was now 855, and Hincmar in his anxiety sent off yet a third letter to the Pope. Its bearers were still hurrying to Rome when they heard of the death of Leo IV on July 17, 855.

They continued their journey and they found reward. In October of this same year the next Pope, Benedict III, in one of the first acts of his rule, gave Papal approval of the action of Soissons. This was contained in a letter borne back to France and read by Hincmar with great joy. He hardly noted the words added by Benedict: "On condition that all proceedings have been carried out as you have reported to the Apostolic See."

These words of caution he regarded as a matter of conventional form. He could not, alas! see into the distant future.

5

September 855 had seen the death of the Emperor Lothar. As we have noted, he had left to his eldest son, Louis II, the imperial title and the throne of Italy; to his second son, Lothar II, the crown of Lotharingia, a kingdom lying between the realm of Charles the Bald in France and that of Louis the German in Germany; to his youngest son, Charles, Provence and the Lyonnais.

The loyalty of Hincmar and his power in France were never more needed by his king than in the years from 853 to 859. In 853 the nobles of Aquitaine and, indeed, of other parts of France, had forsaken Charles the Bald and had sent envoys to Louis the German to declare their adherence to his crown; and Louis, hard pressed by Slavic invaders, had gladly welcomed this advance. For the time he could think of nothing but the protection of his own frontier, while for five years Aquitanians begged him to invade his brother's kingdom, and for five years Charles sent messages to his rebellious magnates, trying to win them back. Four times in 856 the king sent out his appeals. During February 857, he held a Council of bishops and nobles at his palace of Quierzy in a desperate endeavor to stay the havoc caused throughout his lands by the heathen rushing down from the North, by the desertion of his own people, by the riotous insolence "of those who ought to defend the Church of God and the appointed rule of the realm." To these words Hincmar as archbishop added his own admonitions.

It was all in vain. In August 858, Louis the German gathered his host at Worms and marched into his brother's kingdom, even to the royal estate of Charles at Ponthion. His motive was sheer greed of conquest, however vividly the German annalist in the records of Fulda pictured his pious concern for his brother's people, his anguish of conscience, torn by doubt as to what was right and needful. From Ponthion he went to Sens and on to Orléans, while Aquitanians, Bretons, and Frankish men swelled his force daily. From his post of guard against pirates on the Seine

Charles hastily marched to meet the invader. He tried to bring about a conference, but Louis was in no mind for peace. Day by day the ranks defending France grew thinner; at last on November 12 Charles ordered retreat into Burgundy. There he heard that Louis was triumphantly lavishing gifts of countships, abbeys, manors, and estates upon those who flocked to join him; that even their nephew, Lothar of Lotharingia, was feasting with him in Charles' own palace of Attigny.

But feasting was not all. There was also news of determined action. From Attigny Louis sent out letters to the bishops of his brother's kingdom, ordering them to meet him in Council on November 25 at, of all places, Reims, seat of Archbishop Hincmar.

Hincmar had watched all this progress with rising wrath. He had exhorted the nobles of Charles to stand fast; he had led them in loyal assurance of fidelity to the Crown in 858; he had written to Louis the German himself, warning him that he would violate the realm of Charles at the peril of his soul. Now he called the prelates of the dioceses of Reims and Rouen to assemble in Synod at Quierzy. From this Synod a letter went out to Louis, the enemy. Its words are those of Hincmar, and they tell clearly of the power held by the Church over the crown in France and Germany at this time:

We have received, Lord King, your letter commanding us to appear before you at Reims, to treat with you and your liegemen concerning "the restoring of holy Church and the safety of Christian men." The time you name is too early, and the approach of Christmas forbids it; nor can we journey to Reims in the confusion and tumult of these days. He who demands the impossible brings contempt upon himself.

You say that you desire to talk with us on the restoring of holy Church and the salvation of Christian people; for you it were more just and reasonable to desire to obey in us the sacred will of God. Again and again you have heard from bishops and Archbishops, from Hincmar of Reims and from Wenilo of Rouen, the things that pertain to salvation. If you did not listen to them in time past, we fear that you would not listen now.

No, Lord King. Look into your own heart, search thoroughly your own conscience, and in this light judge what you say and do. Judge what you are doing in the thought of that hour when you shall depart this earth, alone, naked and desolate, when your sins shall stand clear before you and devils rise to accuse you of broken charity and broken faith, never redeemed by penitence. That hour is nearer than you think. Then shall those who now receive your gifts make mockery of you and pass on to seek from other men.

The man, O King, who does the things we hear of you is hellbound for eternal fire. So great, so loathsome and cruel are the deeds done by your march through our realm that even the misery brought by the Northmen pales before them. Christian is fighting against Christian, Christian king against Christian king, brother against brother, in scorn of all laws human and divine. Your royal house of Germany, once sacred, is verily become sacrilegious. How now shall fugitives hope to flee from this land of France, beset by pagan pirates, to peace and shelter within your kingdom and country? Shall it not be as the prophet told: *As if a man did flee from a lion, to meet in his flight a bear?*

Do you desire to restore the House of God? Then keep and guard well the honour due to the bishops and to the churches committed to their care. Revere the rulers and shepherds of the Church, as Fathers, as Vicars of Christ. Did not the prophet Malachi declare: *The priest's lips shall keep knowledge, and men shall seek the law at his mouth?* Do not, we pray you, as a Judas betraying his Christ, do not rob the churches of their properties, nor dedicated communities of their rights. It was for this sin that Charles Martel, ancestor of your family and your line, was lost to all eternity.

Do you desire to heal others? Then, Physician, heal thyself! It is for you, O King, to shine forth as a lantern set on high; to you the eyes of all must look. Yours is the care of all men, high and low, poor and rich, governors and servants, who dwell under your crown.

Thus do we answer you. And when a time shall come, free from plundering, from confusion and from misery, then, if God will, we who are Archbishops and bishops of the Church shall be zealous to meet together that we may duly counsel you. Meanwhile you shall learn by heart lessons from holy writ. Read the Book of Kings, and you shall find there how proper it is for you to treat with reverence your brother ruler, as one anointed for his office with the hallowing of the Church. Did not Samuel honour Saul the king? And do not we, the bishops of this day, stand even now as Samuel before the Lord? He who scorns us scorns the Christ Himself. For the sake of your own soul, O King, do not try to augment your earthly realm by doing dishonour to Heaven in the hope that we, the keepers of the Church, shall aid or abet you. We are bishops consecrated to God, not secular men who should swear fealty by oath to any ruler, for such oath of vassalage is strictly forbidden us by authority apostolic and evangelical. The hands that bless bread and wine into the sacrament of the Body and Blood of the Lord, the tongue that by grace of God is the key of Heaven to men, they are not those of layfolk, that they should take oath upon sacred relics for any earthly cause. Of a certainty you shall know that as Christ founded his Church with our fathers, the Apostles, so, through us and with us— may it not be said for our undoing!—with us, their sons, day by day He holds, increases, and governs that Church. We are the bishops who hallow kings for their reigning. And so shall we pray for you, that you sink not amid the storms and raging waters with which the Devil is making shipwreck of our time.

In such words, and many more, Hincmar wrote to Louis the German. He wrote also on his own account, to forbid his coming to Reims. But he came, to find nothing but rebuke. Then he passed on to keep Christmas at Saint-Quentin.

At last with the new year came relief. Charles, pressed forward by Hincmar, gathered up his remaining force, broke in upon Louis at Jouy-en-Laonnais in January 859, and drove his brother back to his German lands.

The king of Germany was expelled from France, it was true. But his immortal soul was still in danger, still held by Hincmar and other archbishops as under the ban of the Church. It would be well, they decided, to send delegates to warn him of this, and to deliver to him the conditions under which he might find release. Even Louis, the invader, traitor, and plunderer, feared excommunication, they knew well. He had been brought up in the Carolingian reverence for things ecclesiastical.

Delegates, therefore, chosen by a Council held at Metz and headed by Hincmar, presented their credentials before the king at Worms on June 4. They carried with them the terms of reconciliation: Louis the German was to make full acknowledgment of his guilt, to promise peace on his part, and to live for the future in harmony with his brother Charles of France.

A detail or two of some interest, preserved in tradition, can help us to picture the meeting. The archbishop of Reims, we are told, was somewhat abrupt in his manner toward the king; but, admonished by Grimald, abbot of Saint-Gall and archchaplain of Louis, to "spare him, as he prays you," he became rather more polite. Louis listened while the terms set by the Church were read, and then said that he could do nothing before consulting with his own bishops of Germany.

There the matter seems to have been left. We hear nothing of confession of crime by the German king. Sometime later Hincmar wrote to Abbot Grimald, asking him to use his influence with Louis in the cause of peace. "If he had listened to my advice," the archbishop wrote, "this disgrace to his name would never have come about."

Hincmar continued to work incessantly for peace, from June 859 until June 860. Finally, in that month at Coblenz Louis of Germany and Charles of France swore a solemn oath of faith, each to his brother and to his nephews, Louis of Italy and Lothar of Lotharingia. Each, in the tongue spoken by his own people, promised that ravage and invasion, rape and pillage, should no more trouble the land.

6

The archbishop of Reims had saved France, his own country, by his power as ecclesiastic, by his skill as statesman, and by his high courage. He had punished a royal invader. Not inferior, however, in interest were the battles he fought against immorality, and, more especially, by violation of the Seventh Commandment. Marriage to Hincmar was a sacrament; abduction, rape, incest, adultery were of Satan and his slaves. Two of his experiences here are especially worthy of note, the more worthy because their story comes in large part from the pen of Hincmar himself, from his letters, from his learned works, and from the *Annals of Saint-Bertin*, which he recorded from the year 861 onwards. These *Annals*, in truth, give us a priceless insight into his life and character.

In 862 Charles the Bald was traveling from Reims to Soissons. He was both happy and troubled in mind, happy in a moment of relief from the perpetual Viking assault, troubled concerning his daughter, young Judith. Her few years had seen much experience. On October 1, 856, at the palace of Verberie-sur-Oise, near Compiègne, she had been married by Archbishop Hincmar in a splendid ceremony to Ethelwulf, king of Wessex in England. She was then about thirteen years old, and she had crossed the Channel to sit by Ethelwulf's side as queen, crowned and consecrated. In January 858 her husband had died, and the girl-widow had promptly married his son, Ethelbald, who now succeeded to his rule over Wessex. In 860 Ethelbald also had departed this life, and Judith had returned to France and to her anxious father.

Twice a widow at eighteen, and widow of her own stepson! What would she do next? Her father had decided to hold her under close guard in his castle of Senlis, near Verberie, until some suitable husband should be found to keep her and her royal parents from the whispers of scandal which were already rife. Unfortunately, her brother, heir to the throne as Louis the Stammerer, sympathized with her longing to enjoy life in these dire days.

At Senlis, then, Charles the Bald supposed her to be in 862, when he arrived at Soissons. Bad news, however, greeted him. Judith, dressed as a peasant girl and aided by her brother, had escaped by night from Senlis with one Baldwin, a bold and adventurous count of Flanders, a man of Frankish birth and a vassal of Charles!

The king's rage was furious. At once he summoned the leading bishops and nobles of his realm and obtained, from the former, excommunication of the count, from the latter, his condemnation in civil court. Baldwin and Judith fled for shelter to her cousin King Lothar of Lotharingia; whereupon Charles of France and Louis of Germany, together with Hincmar, archbishop of Reims, in solemn Council declared Baldwin an exile from all civilized peoples, and Lothar a sinner against the laws of both Heaven and earth. Quickly the count did a wise and a shrewd thing. He hurried to Rome to ask help from the Pope, now Nicholas I, since Benedict III had died in 858.

Here we come to that Nicholas the Great, who was to leave his mark for all the years to come upon the mind of Hincmar. At first, in 858, the archbishop of Reims had by no means foreseen this future, for Nicholas was not then a man of distinction in the Church of Rome. Prudentius of Troyes had written in the *Annals of Saint-Bertin* against that year: "It was through the presence and the support of King Louis [the second, king of Italy] and of his nobles rather than through the choice of the clergy that Nicholas was elected to follow Benedict as Pope."

The clergy of Rome were soon enlightened. During the eighth century Papal rule and authority had been rising in power; in this ninth century, through the stand taken by Nicholas, it increased both in intensity and in breadth. His conception of the Papacy required for it worldwide dominance. To Charles he wrote in this year of 862: "This supreme See, to which is committed the care of the flock of the Lord, in all parts of the world has charge in all things to provide and to fulfill." And again: "The Holy Roman Church which through the will of God we serve excels all others through the world by primacy of her privilege." And to Photius, whose consecration as Patriarch in the East Nicholas refused to recognize, he wrote in the same year: "The universal body of the faithful seeks its doctrine from the Holy Roman Church, head of all the churches. It calls to her for the integrity of faith. From her direction all the churches seek and follow justice and order in all provisions and institutions ecclesiastical. These are preserved by her inviolate and irrefragable, according to the sanctions of the holy Fathers handed down by canon and by council."

Nicholas, then, saw himself by the will of God holder, for his time, of supreme power over Church and world alike in all matters of faith and morality. He was not one to yield to any archbishop of West or of East, wherever he saw reason for dissent. Hincmar might indeed be renowned for his knowledge of canon law. Nicholas, however, had at his call in Rome men exceedingly able and learned, men whom Hincmar himself feared, especially the librarian and chancellor of the Pope, Anastasius, whose skill in many Papal letters of this time may be clearly discerned.

Yet this Pope Nicholas had a very human, a very humane heart. He was always ready, even passionately ready, to aid the troubled, the oppressed, the sinner who was penitent. So now, when Baldwin frankly admitted to him that he had done wrong in carrying off Judith from her father's castle, the Pope decided to intervene, to plead with Charles for the girl and for her count.

His words aroused no sympathy in the king and deeply angered Hincmar. Penance, long and strict, was proper for a man who had been excommunicated. In his wisdom, however, Nicholas had added a warning to his plea. If, he wrote, if Charles persisted in his wrath, Count Baldwin might well desert his liege lord for service with the Scandinavian pirates who were endangering the crown of France. Hincmar's anxiety increased. About the same time, he himself was writing to Rorik of Denmark, a leader among the pirates, but recently, so it was said, converted to the Christian faith. Rorik would speedily find himself outside the Church, Hincmar's letter threatened, did he dare to give solace or shelter to the man who had carried off a daughter of the royal Carolingian line.

The Pope's kindly persuading continued. In June 863, King Charles gave audience at the abbey of Saint-Médard, Soissons, to Rodoald, bishop of Porto in Italy, and John, bishop of Cervia, near Ravenna, legates dispatched to France on papal business. Through their adroit insistence the king was induced to give consent to the marriage of Judith with Count Baldwin. It took, however, strenuous debate in Council to wring consent from Hincmar and his supporters, without penance duly fulfilled by the guilty pair. Bishops in session at Verberie during October pointed out that the Pope had authority to release a sinner from his penance; that it was not wise thus obstinately to stand out against Nicholas; that Hincmar might find himself, too, under discipline. In the end he yielded, and early in 864 he wrote to the Pope: "The Council of bishops, with no infliction of penalty from the Church (though you yourself, Supreme Pontiff as you are, did mention penance before pardon), have allowed Baldwin and Judith to receive the sanction of the law. Our Lord King would not attend either the betrothal or the marriage. But he sent public officials of his realm to witness their union according to civil law, and he presented to Baldwin the honours which you had asked for him."

By the Church, by the law, Baldwin and Judith were united; and Nicholas had thus won his will. The "honours" were gifts of counties in Flemish lands near the coast, which were assigned to Baldwin for their defense against the Northern pirates. It must be admitted that he fulfilled all that was required of him. He beat off invaders boldly; he lived to attain high distinction in Flanders.

After his death his descendants won fame by their savage determination to add to his lands.

7

Yet Hincmar's endeavor to bring down penalty upon Baldwin was as nothing compared with the battle he carried on for nine years, from 860 until 869, against the most notorious scandal in marital records of this century. Here there was no forgiveness, for the sin lasted until the death of the sinner; and the learned periods of the archbishop of Reims, who exposed its manifold intrigue, were calm compared with the blast of damnation uttered by Pope Nicholas.

The sinner was again connected with Charles the Bald; in fact, he was his nephew, Lothar, since 855 king of Lotharingia. In that year Lothar had married a young woman named Theutberga, of noble family and a sister of Hubert, abbot of Saint-Maurice, the famous monastery in the Swiss Alps. It was a most unhappy marriage. To begin with, it had been induced by political motive: Theutberga's relations, dwellers of the Valais, had promised hope of aid in that region, and Lothar's father had needed this aid. Then Lothar himself wanted none of this wedlock; he was passionately in love with another woman, his mistress, Waldrada, and he cared for nothing but to make her his wife and queen. Soon he could not bear the sight of Theutberga. She gave him no hope of the son and heir for whom he longed, while Waldrada had already borne him a child, a boy with no right of inheritance.

After a year or two of this situation the king was secretly searching with his most trusted counselors for some means of release. Among the bishops of Lotharingia there were three who had vast ambition to stand well with the crown, and no scruple of conscience: Gunther, archbishop of Cologne; Theutgaud, archbishop of Trier; and Adventius, bishop of Metz. By 857 they had thought up a plan.

Rumors began now to circulate. Soon, so Hincmar indignantly said, "men's ears were buzzing and women were gossiping excitedly as they sat at the loom." They told one another what they had heard—that before her marriage to Lothar Theutberga had known in sexual intercourse another man, and that man her own brother Hubert. No doubt he had used force upon her; everyone understood that he was evil and unholy in his ways. Had not even the Pope himself, Benedict III, summoned him to Rome to answer for the crimes charged against him? Nevertheless, guilty or victim, if the story was true, Theutberga was no woman to be queen of Lotharingia. Still further details were added: that, through this raping by her brother, Theutberga had become pregnant, and that in her horror of discovery she had obtained and swallowed some powerful draught which had brought on abortion.

These sordid tales ran from the palace of Lotharingia to the markets and the looms, until in 858 some of the leading men of the kingdom rose up in their wrath and declared that in justice to herself the queen must be tried by the civil law of the land. A court was held, consisting of lay nobles who gravely pondered the matter, but could reach no deciding of its problems. There were no witnesses to prove the horrid story; and Theutberga continually denied it. At last all concluded that the only thing to do was to subject the accused to the Ordeal by means of one of the elements created by God and obedient to His will.

The Ordeal, of course, was a method of trial frequently used during these early Middle Ages, both on the Continent and in England. As Theutberga, however, was of royal rank, her judges could not allow her to undergo this testing in her own person; and a champion was found to act as her representative. In solemn assembly of clergy and people some small object—perhaps a stone —was dropped into a deep vessel full of boiling water. The queen's defender plunged in his arm, groped around, seized the object and brought it up. Miraculously he was unhurt. It was the doing of Almighty God, men cried, Protector of the queen's cause. She was declared innocent, and Lothar was ordered to receive her again in his palace. Kings, like humbler men, were subject to the law of Heaven. He obeyed. But he refused even to speak to his wife. She became a prisoner in her own rooms. In her misery and her fear of yet worse things to come, she awaited her chance and at last managed to send off secretly to Rome an appeal to the Pope. She knew, she said, that she would be made to declare herself guilty.

She had made no mistake in this fear. On January 9, 860, she was brought before a Synod of Lotharingian bishops, meeting at Aachen. At its head sat Gunther of Cologne, and near him were Theutgaud of Trier and Adventius of Metz.

We possess an account of the proceedings of this Synod, proceedings dark with lies. It was composed by Gunther for distribution, in the hope that its details might be believed strictly true. Hincmar received a copy, and through this, which he afterward published, we can read Gunther's narrative, in two forms. Form A, in eight chapters, was sent to bishops who, like Hincmar himself, had not been present at the Synod; and Form B, in seven chapters, to lay nobles of Lotharingia.

Form A describes King Lothar as coming before the episcopal assembly with tears and sighs, imploring counsel. In a voice choked with grief and drawing sympathy from those who sat around, he declared that his beloved queen had begged him to free her from their marriage. She was, she had confessed, unworthy to be his wife. Let her, she prayed, depart to spend her remaining years in a convent.

So had the queen in her fear recited the story which she had been ordered to tell. Shock, we are now informed, struck all the Fathers in God. They agreed to send for Theutberga, who threw herself at their feet and, also, prayed for advice. "We cannot aid you," said Gunther in the name of his brother bishops, "unless first you tell us what is troubling you. Be honest and confess. And take heed. Let no hope of gain or fear of penalty, even death, lead you to declare what is not true." "Nothing but the truth will I tell," said the unhappy woman, who, as this narrative does not say, had been well taught what to fear if she did declare that her words were an invention of Satan. "I give you as witness Archbishop Gunther, to whom I have already confessed what has happened." Then she turned to him and asked that through him "what must be known might be told." Gunther, "full of sorrow and pain, and wishing that he had never heard her confession," at last revealed its details. Account A then ends by inviting bishops who had not been present on this occasion to attend another Synod shortly to be held.

This is known as the Second Synod of Aachen, and it met at

the Palace in mid-February, 860. An attempt had been made to strengthen its influence by bringing in prelates from outside Lotharingia; and therefore, with the Lotharingians, two bishops from the kingdom of Charles the Bald attended and one from Provence, kingdom of his nephew Charles. Adventius of Metz had made a special visit to Reims to induce Hincmar to attend. He would not tell Hincmar the business of the meeting; but the archbishop guessed well enough. He pleaded illness and stayed away. Secular nobles were also present; but they had no part in the Synod's final decision.

Before all the assembly the queen with her own words declared what she had been brought there to say: that her brother Hubert had worked his will upon her in rape and violation; that she was confessing this of her own free will; that she was telling the truth before men in the hope of release from eternal punishment to come. Again murmurs of horror were heard. The bishops asked King Lothar, who was now presiding from his throne in Aachen's great hall, whether this admission had been brought about either by persuasion or by menace? "No, indeed," he answered, "the queen is confessing nothing but the truth. Just as you, when I first heard this unspeakable story, I, too, was overcome. I wanted to hide it, and I did so, as long as I could, for the disgrace of revelation was too heavy to face. But the foul thing could not be concealed, and I had to give way, especially when tidings of it reached Burgundy and Italy. Then it had to come up for examination before the bishops of my land."

Rightly did Lothar mention Italy. He had gone there himself to ask his brother Louis, Emperor and king of Italy, to help him in carrying out his design against Theutberga, and he had bolstered his asking by the gift of counties within his own rule: of Geneva, Sitten, and Lausanne.

Now indeed, our narrative tells, all were willing to give assent. An unheard-of crime, a pollution indescribable, they were to maintain, had been discovered in the royal House of Lotharingia. The sentence would be purgation by public penance. The queen would be allowed her "desire"; she would promptly be interned in a monastery. But the bishops who judged her as guilty did not allow a divorce to her royal husband.

8

Four events followed in this year of 860. First, Lothar, the king, wrote to Pope Nicholas a letter filled with assertions of his utter loyalty and devotion to the Holy See. For long he had been hoping to journey there; but, though defended by the Pope's gracious prayers, his land had been suffering greatly through the raids of the pagan Vikings. He was still hoping to come; but in the meantime he was sending his envoys to witness to his faithfulness and to seek Papal counsel in these difficult hours. Among the envoys was archbishop Theutgaud of Trier.

The letter ended: "If any enemy of mine should dare to tell in your most holy ears anything sinister concerning me, will your Apostolic authority cast it away as the venom of a serpent? And, I pray, should the pagan Saracens attempt attack upon the territory of blessed Peter, please with all speed let me know. I am ready to meet danger and death in your cause, which I hold dear beyond all things on this earth." So also wrote to Rome the bishops who had condemned Theutberga at the Second Synod of Aachen.

Second, in his desire for support, Lothar turned also to his uncle Louis the German, and held out to him the hope of gaining a very choice morsel, the region of Alsace.

Third, relations between Lothar and his other uncle, Charles the Bald, took a turn for the worse, when Queen Theutberga escaped from her monastery in Lotharingia and fled for refuge to the kingdom of Charles.

Fourth, even before Hincmar had succeeded in gaining peace between the Frankish kings at Coblenz in June 860, he had sat down to begin to write a learned criticism and survey of all the action taken by Lotharingia in regard to its queen. It went to the public, we may think, before the troubled year came to an end.

He had a direct reason for writing. Questions in two communications, one containing twenty-three, and the other one a further seven, had been sent in by various people, among them bishops who had been present at the Synods of Aachen and were feeling uneasy. Would Hincmar, the expert on canon law, they asked, please discuss their worrying problems as to this hideous situation?

The work which Hincmar put out in 860 is known to us as his *De Divortio Lotharii et Tetbergae*. It includes the two accounts of the First Synod of Aachen, and it republishes from "a lengthy volume, too diffuse to reproduce as a whole," some chapters describing the Second Synod. Like all Hincmar's writings, it is very difficult to read. Its Latin rambles on, eternally swollen with passages from the Bible, from authorities patristic and Papal, from the minutes of Synod and Council, quoted in place and out of place, and all thrown together in one confusing mass. Some, indeed, of these very vexing faults were caused by the multitude of other affairs of one sort and another with which its writer was dealing at the time: a common cause of trouble, as a glance at the table of events, of writings, and of dates given at the end of this book of mine will show. Indeed, in the middle of this *De Divortio* Hincmar laments: "I must not shut up the bowels of my compassion from the prayers of my brethren. So I snatch, rather than borrow, some brief hours from the unending and utterly different occupations of my day to give to this work. I have no free days for thought."

This scandal of Lotharingia, he warns his readers at the beginning, will attract the attention of all people, high and low, men and women, young and old, because of the sovereign rank of those concerned. In its judging, truth and honesty are required, "not a mousetrap baited with deceit of pleasant words." His own words will be frankness itself, and no one is to shrink from them in false modesty.

He then deals with the thirty questions in turn, one by one, and from his many pages the following details stand out:

1. In regard to the charges made against Theutberga, her trial before the civil court, and the Ordeal:

His own research, illumined by medical science, has convinced him that the story of the pregnancy is impossible and that the story of the abortion is untrue. As for the Ordeal by boiling water, that, he firmly believes, in common with the majority of his fellow churchmen, is a Christian rite, even in some degree comparable with the sacrament of holy baptism. Here, therefore, the judgment of God has revealed the innocence of the queen.

2. In regard to the Synods of Aachen:

The story of the confession of Theutberga is inconsistent with reason and is supported by no proof. The queen, he is quite sure, cannot be convicted on the evidence of a confession made in private to the Church, the "secret matter," told in confession to Archbishop Gunther. That pious and holy man, "so full of grief and regret that he ever listened to her words," ought never to have revealed her confession to anyone, even at her own request. There is grave reason, moreover, to suspect that her "confession" was forced from her; and a forced confession, true or not, cannot be admitted as legal evidence.

3. In regard to the marriage of Lothar and Theutberga:

There is one and the same standard of fidelity to nuptial vows for husband and for wife, and it has been shown that Lothar was guilty of faithlessness through his association with Waldrada. Husband and wife may be set apart by law of the Church for two reasons alone: one of guilt, through adultery on his part or on hers; one of innocence, through the desire of both to enter monastic life. Neither of them, once separated for any reason whatsoever, may marry again while the other still lives.

If, however, Theutberga went to her marriage to Lothar with the guilt of incest upon her soul, the marriage was no marriage at all and never has been, for she could not lawfully receive the sacrament of matrimony. In that case, after the fulfilling of due penance for his sin of adultery, Lothar would be free to marry Waldrada at his will.

One of the many questioners asked whether discord might have been brought about between the king and his queen by use of sorcery or witchcraft? In answer Hincmar once again pictured the thought of his time. Certainly, he affirmed, the power of magic is hideous, myriad in its evils. The agents of Satan are constantly resorting to heathen practices for the ruin of men.

His final conclusion and counsel bade that this case of Lothar and Theutberga be tried by a court composed of laymen noble of rank, married men competent to understand the problems involved, and of bishops not only from Lotharingia but from other kingdoms; in short, by a general assembly, comprehensive and therefore trustworthy in its independence, without fear or favor.

Later years were to show that the archbishop of Reims was by no means averse to the thought that, if Lothar, married to the childless Theutberga, died without a son of lawful birth, his kingdom of Lotharingia might fall to France. Among possible heirs, one of his brothers, Louis, king of Italy, was far away, fighting the Saracens; the other, Charles of Provence, was weak and sickly. Of Lothar's two uncles, Charles the Bald had at present the stronger hand. There is, however, as Sdralek observes, no evidence of this ambition in the *De Divortio*, no thought of advancement for Charles the Bald. Hincmar here was dealing honestly with the problem as he saw it through his study of canon law.

9

The years passed on, but things were by no means settled and at peace. The bishops of Lotharingia were clearly not going to listen to the archbishop of Reims in France. In 862 Lothar again decided to act. He knew that his bishops would, for the greater part, support his ever-increasing desire for marriage with Waldrada, and now he called them, on April 29, to a third Synod at Aachen. Before them, Gunther, Theutgaud, Adventius, and their brother bishops of Verdun, Toul, Tongres, Utrecht, and Strasbourg, the king delivered an impassioned appeal:

"To you, who in your sacred dignity are higher than I in my royal estate, to you I make my prayer. You hold in mind what by your own ordering was done when I sent away from me my wife, foul with unspeakable infection, as she herself has confessed. Whatsoever since that time I have done amiss through weakness and necessity, it is now in your power to bid me cease; it is for me to obey your commands.

"You know how I have longed for a son to follow me as king. A concubine is not a wife, and I desire no concubine, but true marriage. Remember, I beseech you, that I am young. What can I do, to whom neither wife nor mistress is allowed? Did not the Apostle himself say, 'He who cannot endure, let him marry?' In all simplicity I tell you and confess that I cannot live without a woman; and I do honestly desire to be free and pure from all sin of the flesh.

"So, beloved, I implore you, for the love of Him Who redeemed us, refuse not, at the peril of my body and soul, for the good of holy Church and of the kingdom committed to me, refuse not to aid me in my need."

The bishops of Lotharingia considered, discussed, and then voted, six against two, to issue, wrapped in much theological argument, the decision which, they had known, would be theirs:

"We believe that Theutberga was as wife neither fitting nor lawful, nor destined by God for marriage with our glorious king. Wherefore in all affection for him and thought for his crown, since not only we, but all canonical authority must forbid marriage to those of incestuous stain, we do not deny him the rightful wedlock allowed to him by God, and by His Apostle, who himself said, 'It is better to marry than to burn.'"

At once Lothar wrote to Pope Nicholas to inform him of this synodal and episcopal consent, and to pray permission from Rome for his marriage with Waldrada. His impatience, however, was so urgent that he did not wait for a reply. What he did do is described by Hincmar in his *Annals of Saint-Bertin* against this year of 862:

"Lothar, demented, as report declared, by spell of evil craft, enticed by blind adoration of that concubine for whose sake he had cast from him his wife Theutberga, supported by two of his special followers, Liudfrid, his uncle, and Walthar, and—a crime even to speak of it—by the consent of some of his bishops, took Waldrada in a so-called 'marriage' and crowned her as his queen, to the grief of the friends who tried to prevent him." The ceremony took place about the end of the summer.

In his king, Charles the Bald, the archbishop of Reims found, as he knew he would find, a wrath equal to his own. It was Hincmar, doubtless, who put into formal words the rebuke of Charles publicly addressed to his nephew, when, with King Louis the German, they met at Savonnières the following November. "The Apostolic See," declared Charles, "forbids anyone to receive a man such as the king of Lotharingia into his home or to bid him Godspeed, lest he become partner in his evil doings."

Some three weeks later everyone knew that Pope Nicholas had taken the matter in hand. The exiled Theutberga had appealed to him again and again. Now those two legates of whom we have already heard, Rodoald of Porto and John of Cervia, were told to hasten, first to Soissons to induce King Charles the Bald to accept the marriage between his daughter and Count Baldwin, and then to Metz, to attend a Synod which the Pope by his order was calling to meet there for judgment concerning Lothar and his rejected wife. Papal letters went to Germany, to France, and to Provence, commanding that two bishops from each of these realms should be present. So also were ordered two bishops from Italy, with the bishops of Lotharingia, together with Lothar the king and the unhappy Theutberga.

On November 23, 862, Nicholas sent out his orders to these bishops and archbishops:

"We are much concerned about this matter," he wrote. "Theutberga has repeatedly declared to us that she is innocent. Will you please work together with our legates for its deciding under Apostolic authority, without craft, malice, or hatred; with no regard for princes or for terrors which arise upon occasion and belong only to the time. Be quite sure in your minds that we shall take prompt action, be you bishops or Papal legates, should any inducement—God forbid it!—turn you from following the canons and laws of the Church. And you will send us without delay account of the proceedings of this Synod."

The spring of 863 had arrived at Rome when the two legates, Rodoald and John, left for France. At this time the Pope had not yet heard that Lothar had taken Waldrada as wife. When he did, in his anger he wrote to his legates. He wrote, also, to all the archbishops of France and Germany. Without fail, he again ordered, they were to be present at the Synod of Metz to pass canonical judgment on Lothar. "Should he not appear there, should he not submit to penance for his crime, we shall banish him from communion with the Church."

Among other hindrances the Synod was also delayed by the death, in January 863, of Lothar's brother, Charles, king of Provence. For long his uncle, Charles the Bald, had cast covetous eyes upon Provence. Already in 861 he had made an attempt to seize its lands, to the deep vexation of Hincmar. The archbishop of Reims, as Schrörs points out, at this time was very ambitious for his king, but in a way in accordance with his shrewd sense of policy. Charles must win the favor of the Holy See at Rome by his championship of moral good. Had he not already received in his kingdom that innocent victim, Theutberga? Had he not roundly condemned her adulterous husband? If Lothar should in the end be excommunicated by the Pope, who knew what destiny might await Charles, king of France, in Lotharingia?

Lotharingia, lying between France and Germany, was of high importance to them both, far more important than Provence.

In 861, however, Charles had been forced to retreat from Provence. Nor did he gain it now, although he hurried there and did all he could to win it. The kingdom went to the two brothers of its late ruler: part, including Provence itself, to Louis, Emperor and king of Italy, the remainder to Lothar of Lotharingia.

Not until mid-June of 863 did the Synod of Metz convene. Everything possible had been done by Lothar and his friends to defeat Hincmar and Pope Nicholas. The Papal legates, well bribed, carried out none of the instructions given them. The letters from the Pope were mysteriously missing; the legates declared that they had been stolen by the agents of Lothar and wrote back to Nicholas to complain and to ask for new credentials. Very probably they had been hidden from sight by the legates themselves.

An interesting bit of correspondence, which illuminates the intrigue of the times, has come down to us from the pen of Adventius, bishop of Metz and enemy of Theutberga. It is addressed to Theutgaud, archbishop of Trier: "For God's sake let no one see this; read it and throw it in the fire. But you must be very, very careful to say nothing to upset Lothar before that meeting at Metz. As you know well, he is going to follow the path pointed out to him by his bishops." Adventius also tried to prove, in a document which he made public, that Waldrada had actually been married in lawful wedding to Lothar when he was a very young man, at the wish of his father, the Emperor Lothar I. Then, so Adventius maintained, after the Emperor had died, Hubert, brother of Theutberga, had forced his sister into unholy union with the young king of Lotharingia, threatening and using coercion upon them both. But Theutberga had never been rightly either wife or queen. The story was farfetched indeed; yet it had its influence with those who wanted support.

Unfortunately we do not possess the Acts of this Synod of Metz. But we can learn much from Hincmar's *Annals;* from the annals of Fulda; from the chronicle of Regino, abbot of Prüm late in this ninth century; and, above all, from the letters of Pope Nicholas.

No bishops appeared on the scene except those of Lotharingia; King Lothar had seen to that. Lotharingia was represented
by all its prelates except the bishop of Utrecht, who was ill. The
letter summoning Hincmar to Metz had arrived too late for a
journey there; and this had doubtless purposely happened in
many other cases. Theutberga, already once acquitted and twice
found guilty, was also absent. Lothar had not been willing to
guarantee her safety, and she was in terror of her enemies.

The proceedings of the Synod may, however, easily be imagined. The story of Adventius, in whose see the meeting sat, was
carefully reproduced; Lothar declared that he was following the
counsel of his bishops; Waldrada was pronounced true wife of
Lothar; Theutberga was again rejected. Finally, Gunther, archbishop of Cologne, and Theutgaud, archbishop of Trier, led the
assembly in signing its records, and, as Hincmar was to write soon
afterward, "Hagano, a man of crafty skill and the most ambitious
bishop in Frankish Italy, persuaded the Synod to send these
Mother Goose rhymes (*neniae*) to the Apostolic See at Rome for
their judgment by the Pope."

Gunther and Theutgaud, accordingly, in this same year carried to Rome and solemnly offered to Nicholas, seated in the midst
of his ministers, the official *libellus*, the sheet on which the records
were inscribed. The Pope ordered its words to be read aloud. At
the end he asked the archbishops to vouch for their truth, and
was told in reply that the document itself was proof enough. They
were then sent back to their lodging, where they waited some
weeks in growing impatience. At last they were again summoned
to the Pope's presence, where they found a Council of bishops
awaiting them. Then and there they heard the Acts of the Synod
of Metz, 863, firmly disallowed and themselves deposed forever
from their episcopal and priestly function and their metropolitan
seats.

The wrath of Pope Nicholas at the deceit, at the unjust cruelty
of the leaders at Aachen and at Metz, blazes in fury through many
of his letters. To Hincmar and the other bishops of France he
wrote declaring that "the crime of King Lothar, if indeed by
reason of his lust he may truly be called a king," in the case of
Theutberga and Waldrada was clear to all. All at Rome, however,

knew, and men outside Rome were writing to tell him, that Gunther and Theutgaud were its authors and contrivers. It was beyond belief, he stormed, that archbishops could act in this way, that they could attempt to ensnare even the Holy Apostolic See in a web of lies. Never again should they hold office in the Church. This, indeed, was not the first time that they had disobeyed its sacred canons and done dishonor to Rome. There was more evidence against them; and here the Pope recalled the aid and shelter allowed by their authority in Lotharingia to the adulteress Ingeltrud, who had deserted for a lover her husband, a count of Italy, and for years had refused all entreaty, all command to return to him: a loose and evil woman, rightly banished, said the Pope, by Papal decree from the altars of the Church.

As for the Synod of Metz, he wrote, it was "a gathering of robbers like that of Ephesus"; it was a "brothel of putrid deeds, fostering adultery"; it was rife with injustice. Had it not condemned Theutberga in her absence, one who already in 858 had been tried and found innocent? No! he answered the bishops of Germany, praying him to relent, to restore Gunther and Theutgaud. "The Holy See does not change its mind," he retorted. "Let these men carry their shame."

Yet Pope Nicholas, as we have observed, was quick to show mercy to the penitent. The bishops of Lotharingia who hurried to acknowledge error and cowardice on their part were allowed to retain their sees. The same leniency was shown even to Adventius of Metz, who pleaded old age, constant pain, and deference to the decision of his superiors. After all, these offenders were not of metropolitan dignity.

It was at Rome itself that the deposing of the two archbishops brought in 864 an outbreak of violence. The Emperor Louis, king of Italy, furious at this humiliation of his brother Lothar's friends, rushed to the Holy City to force from the Pope a canceling of the sentence. Nicholas answered by an order for a general fast and chanting of litanies. While these were going on, a procession of clergy and people was attacked by the Emperor's soldiers in the streets of Rome; some of the devout were injured, and crosses and banners were broken. The Pope kept fast for two days and nights in St. Peter's. Then Louis caught a fever, and his Empress, a woman of quick brain and great energy, talked for him with Nicholas at the Lateran. Under this pressure peace was at last made, and Gunther and Theutgaud were sent back from Italy to Lotharingia. In their bitter resentment they wrote to the Pope words of rabid insult, against "that accursed deposing, alien to fatherly dignity, alien to brotherly goodwill, contrary to canon law, a condemnation which we scorn and reject." "With you, Lord Pope Nicholas," they declared, "we desire no communion or fellowship."

Theutgaud eventually accepted his fate and lived quietly as a layman. Gunther, on the contrary, aroused much talk by daring to celebrate mass, to bless the holy oils for chrism, "as a man without God," Hincmar said. Both men continued to hope for restoration through the aid of the Emperor Louis. Gunther even begged Hincmar to intercede for him, but to no end.

In 864 the evil Hubert was killed in a sudden assault. His sister, Theutberga, continued to live under the protection of Charles the Bald; and the Pope continued to work in her behalf. In 864 and 865 he summoned bishops of France and Germany to Rome for action against Lothar; but they did not come. Nicholas was demanding too much, they had decided; his Papal hand bore down too heavily. Besides, pirates were making the journey too dangerous.

The Lotharingian crown was still without an heir; and on February 19, 865, Charles the Bald and Louis the German met in conference at Tusey on the Meuse. Hincmar's report of this has some interest: "They sent word to their nephew Lothar that, if he meant to go to Rome, and he was always saying this, he had better prepare for his visit by repenting of his sin against the Church, as the Pope and they, his uncles, had told him to do. Lothar thought long and hard over this message and decided that what his two uncles really wanted was to seize his kingdom and divide it between them. He thereupon sent off a request to his brother Louis in Italy: "Would he entreat the Pope to stop them from doing Lotharingia this harm?"

In the summer, as there seemed no prospect of a council in Rome, Nicholas ordered his intimate counselor, Arsenius, bishop of Orta in northern Italy, to France, telling him that the matter of Lothar must speedily be settled. In the name of the Pope and in the Pope's own words Arsenius was to warn this rebel king that the Holy See was about to do what it had threatened again and again: to declare him banished from the Church and all Christian society.

Lothar decided at last to yield; and in August Arsenius warned Charles the Bald to turn away his mind from any thought of invasion. He then escorted Theutberga from France to Lotharingia. At Vendresse in the Ardennes a solemn ceremony was carried out. Six counts and six knights, in the presence of the Papal legate, of the archbishops, the bishops, the nobles, and humbler men from various kingdoms swore a great oath that their lord, Lothar, must and would now take and accept Theutberga as his own lawful wife, as his queen, for now and for the time to come. Thus had the Pope commanded, and thus it was done.

The same day, with fearful warning, Arsenius reunited Theutberga with Lothar in due order and honor. In the autumn he left to fulfill the last part of his mission; for Nicholas had insisted that he bring Waldrada back with him to Rome. They reached Pavia, and there, by the aid of agents of Lothar, she managed to escape. As the Pope described it, "she hurried to join Satan" in Lotharingia. On February 2, 866, he pronounced sentence of excommunication against her.

Life went on as before for Theutberga in her husband's Court. Lothar showed her no more respect there than he had shown her before. In January 867 Nicholas wrote an answer to her petition to him that she might be allowed to "confess" the evil of which men held her guilty, and so win her release to a cloister: "I knew you would ask this of me. We all recognize that you are enduring trouble and tyranny too great for you to bear. But do not talk nonsense. Remember that you are a queen. We hear that Lothar still clings to his filth, to the harm of the Holy Church of God. As for the story, that Waldrada was his wife in lawful marriage, leave it alone. If he ever takes that prostitute again to himself, he will not escape our wrath."

Also in January 867, stinging censure went from the Pope to Lothar for his treatment of his wife; to the bishops of Lotharingia, fierce accusation of their sloth in allowing Waldrada to remain in Lothar's kingdom; to Charles the Bald, prayer that he would help the lawful queen in any way he could. In March Nicholas was asking Louis of Germany also to come forward in her behalf. At the end of October he wrote again to say he was "astonished" that the German king should think it worth his while to ask for restitution for Gunther and Theutgaud. Never!

10

We have seen how Pope Nicholas I held and acted upon a conception of the Holy and Apostolic See as supreme in its authority, in its pastoral charge, and in its responsibility for the souls of men on this earth. In France and Germany the ninth century saw also a rising into great power of the rulers of metropolitan dioceses such as, in the realm of Charles the Bald, that of Sens, of Rouen, of Tours, and, especially, of Reims under Hincmar. For Hincmar, as did his fellow metropolitans, worked hard to raise and to magnify the office of archbishop, as held by one, whether at Reims or Sens or Rouen, who was very high in honor, well skilled in organization, able to command the reverent submission of his layfolk, priests, and bishops alike—able, indeed, with due respect to argue a matter with Pope Nicholas himself. More than once we shall find this archbishop of Reims striving with all his resources to maintain his own case against the action of this man whom he acknowledged as vicar of Christ on earth.

The bishops under his authority as metropolitan, and there were nine of them—of Châlons-sur-Marne, of Senlis, of Soissons, of Laon, of Noyon, of Beauvais, of Amiens, of Cambrai, and of Thérouanne—were not slow to realize his growing power, won by his enormous energy, his political activities, his influence with King Charles the Bald. Most of them followed his leadership with devoted admiration; but some of them had ambitions of their own. These quite naturally began to resent Hincmar's demand of strict conformity with his own point of view, his requiring of exact attention to detail, his firm supervision, his frequent interference, as they held it, with their control of their own diocesan affairs.

As it happened, the ninth century itself gave its rebel clergy support for resistance. They found this support in the publication, some time between 847 and 852, of the famous *Forged Decretals.* By this name is now known a collection, made with marked skill and learning, of "Papal" letters and decrees, of decisions contained in the "Acts" of Councils of the Church, a collection in which genuine matter from past centuries was interwoven with much that was new, forged, and fictitious. So able was the craft which had compiled it that for centuries it was accepted by churchmen as reliable and authentic: a book of reference for all who needed reassurance on some point of canon law. It came from the hand of some cleric—or band of clerics—who wrote under the pseudonym of "Isidore Mercator," a name which recalled to memory St. Isidore of Seville and which was doubtless due to the fact that the old Spanish collection of canon law, the *Hispana,* was used as its basis. Scholars have differed in regard to its place of origin. Some have held that it was compiled in the ecclesiastical province of Tours, since they have connected it with the schism which we have seen dividing the Churches of Tours and Brittany during the fight of Nominoë for independence against Charles the Bald. Many, however, have preferred the province of Reims; perhaps, it has been suggested, the original plan of this support for rebellion sprang from the resistance of Ebbo, or of the clerics of Ebbo, against Hincmar himself.

In any case, one of the chief aims of the author or authors of these false *Decretals* was to support diocesan bishops who came into conflict with their metropolitans. In these letters and decrees, genuine and forged, the bishop was directed to appeal, if he saw fit occasion, from the orders of the head of his province to the supreme authority of the Pope, for in the *Decretals* the supremacy of the Apostolic See of Rome was maintained with all force.

Pope Nicholas scanned the pages of this collection and used it. He felt no great need of it. Did he not know very well that the Papal See was the fountainhead of decision by the Church? He welcomed appeals by troubled bishops. His advisers used it when this was convenient. Hincmar read it, and did not concern himself very much with it. He knew his canon law, and he felt entirely competent to sustain his authority as metropolitan through his own

knowledge of Popes and Councils and their decrees. It was a
learned work, and we have no proof that he discerned in it deliber-
ate forgery. At the same time, Hincmar was prompt in the use of
documents for his own ends; and he seized readily enough upon
those useful for his argument, spurious or genuine, suspicious or
reliable.

History has laid before us three great struggles between
Hincmar and the clergy under his rule, struggles sustained by the
latter with the aid of these *Decretals*. The combatants in these
struggles were the archbishop of Reims, determined to uphold his
authority; bishops, priests, and deacons under his power; and the
Pope to whom they appealed, ever eager to hear and to judge
the case of the distressed.

The first of these bitter controversies concerned one named
Rothad. In 832, more than twelve years before Hincmar became
ruler of the Archdiocese of Reims, Rothad had been consecrated
bishop of Soissons, one of its sees. He had heard the sentence
which banished his archbishop, Ebbo, in 835; he had witnessed
Ebbo's restoration at Reims in 840; he had done as he willed
during the nine years of lack of episcopal rule in the province,
from 835 to 840, from 841 to 845. Then, in 845, this Archbishop
Hincmar had come to watch over what was done at Soissons.

At first Rothad had tried, at least outwardly, to live at peace
with the new régime. He had taken part in the election and the
consecration of this new Head. But soon trouble had started. To
Hincmar Rothad had appeared to be no upholder of strict Church
discipline and tradition, even of the Catholic faith itself. He was
"a lover of novelty," attracted by the arguments of that heretic,
Gottschalk. Letters of criticism, one after another, went from
Reims to Soissons: its bishop, Hincmar claimed, was irregular in
his attendance at important meetings; he did not visit his monasteries as he should; he was arrogant in his conferences with his
priests; he was careless of Church buildings and properties. This
last negligence drew from Hincmar, in 857–58, a monograph de-
fining the correct governing by a bishop of the houses of God in
his diocese. But Rothad's worst sin in his archbishop's eyes was
that he had deposed from office a priest for immoral indulgence,

and had flatly refused Hincmar's request that he restore the offender after due penance had been done.

At last Hincmar's patience—never too great—gave out entirely. In 861, before a Council of bishops gathered in the church of Saints Crispin and Crispinian on the outskirts of Soissons, he declared Rothad excommunicate "until he should decide to obey the rules" of his calling.

Rothad, inspired by the *Forged Decretals,* announced before another Council, which met in 862 at Pîtres, where the river Andelle meets the Seine, that he was going to appeal to the Pope. The Council after some discussion gave its consent. Just as he was preparing to start for Rome, however, Hincmar—so Rothad openly said—encouraged by King Charles the Bald, intercepted a letter written by the bishop of Soissons, and gathered from its words, rightly or wrongly, that Rothad, instead of appealing to Rome, was now about to ask for a new trial in France before twelve judges, appointed by himself.

The archbishop rose in quick wrath. He placed Rothad under arrest, forbade him to go to Rome, declared that he should have his judges, and brought him before a Synod of bishops in a suburb of Soissons in the autumn of 862. There by a court of twelve selected from the Synod he was deposed from his see as "a man of singular folly": in Hincmar's words, "a new Pharaoh, hardened in heart; a man changed to very monster, obstinate and incorrigible in his extravagant, disobedient deeds." Not only was he deposed, and his deposing confirmed by the Synod; he was held imprisoned in a monastery. There he vehemently denied that he had ever thought of giving up his appeal to the Holy See.

Not long afterward, news of these doings reached Nicholas at Rome, brought there by Odo, bishop of Beauvais, once abbot of Corbie and friend of Lupus of Ferrières. Early in 863 a letter from Nicholas was sent off to Hincmar at Reims; and in it the Pope's anger descended fiercely upon the archbishop.

"This is a crime!" he wrote. "Where is your well-known reverence for us? You have attacked and even deposed our brother and fellow bishop, who in proper and traditional custom was appealing to our authority! You have cast him into prison, a man who is old and has deserved reward for his labours, his services to his Church and his land. We are astonished, we are horrified that so dense a cloud should so suddenly have shut off the light within you, that you have thus belittled the rights of this Apostolic seat and broken the canons of the Fathers! This disrespect we will not suffer! If you desire to remain within our communion, within thirty days of the receipt of this letter you will either restore Rothad to his former honour of office, or, if you think that you have acted justly, you will see that he starts at once for Rome, with you or with some person proper to plead your case before us. Should you disobey this order we herewith decree and declare that your *celebret* be taken from you. And tell your fellow bishops who condemned Rothad that the same penalty awaits them if they do not also obey our command."

In April Nicholas wrote yet again, refusing Papal approval of the Acts of the Synod of 862 which had deposed Rothad. By this time another bishop had been appointed to Rothad's see. Further rebuke went to the bishops concerned, and deep reproach to Hincmar: "You ask us, and we are granting your petition, to confirm your rights at Reims as declared at Soissons in 853, when you yourself are doing all that you can to weaken those of Rome! How will your rights be able to stand firm if those of the See which is their source be injured?"

To Rothad the Pope sent kind encouragement: "The bishops who were at Soissons in 862 have asked Rome to confirm their action. This we will not do now; we want to judge your case ourselves. We have told them to take you out of that monastery and to allow you to come here, with some of them as your accusers, or with such persons as may fitly present their case. Dear brother, we cannot acquit you without due examination, lest we seem to be prejudiced in your favour. Nor will we allow you to be judged without our presence, lest you suffer wrong. Do not cease, with all boldness, all force, all means, to persist in your endeavour to come to Rome."

Another letter followed in October 863: "Hincmar has written us that he never received our letter condemning him; and the bishops have sent very many excuses for their judgment against you. We hear that King Charles has ordered you to be removed from the monastery and delivered into charge of some prelate, a friend of yours.

"Now, our brother, listen to us. If your conscience is worrying you and if by any chance you have consented to that sentence passed against you, do not worry. Should the bishops follow our advice and restore you, as we wrote them to do, well and good. If, on the other hand, they delay to do this, do you come to Rome without fear, trusting in the mercy of God. You know quite well that we will not cease to work until justice shall be done and until things now hidden shall be revealed."

Nicholas was evidently well aware of Hincmar's dominating power and influence. At this time, however, he was not at all sure whether in further trial Rothad's condemning at Soissons might not prove to be justified, at least in part. For he wrote in this same October to Hincmar himself: "Perhaps Rothad will realize that he has sinned and will acquiesce in your judgment. If so, you must make King Charles give him abbeys and other holdings which will allow him to live with dignity."

The main concern here, as always in the mind of Nicholas the Great, was that, criminal or not, one who appealed to Papal judgment should indeed be judged before him at Rome.

On October 25, 863, at a Council held in the palace of Verberie-sur-Oise, it was decided that Rothad should leave for Italy, escorted by representatives both of the bishops of France and of King Charles the Bald. Early in 864 they started. At the frontier all were stopped by the order of Louis, king of Italy, and told that they could go no further. The envoys sent word to Nicholas, then turned back to travel home. Rothad retreated to Besançon in Switzerland, declaring that he was too ill to make the journey with them. There he stayed until Louis relented and he could reach Rome.

By this time it was June 864 and Rothad found the Pope in wrathful exasperation. "So often we have warned you," he had written to Hincmar a month before, "three, no, even four times, and you deliberately disregard our commands. At least you could have explained to us why Rothad was hindered from arriving in Rome. Now take notice! Never, Heaven permitting, shall we leave this matter undecided."

Already, however, the archbishop had earnestly tried to explain, and soon his letter was in the hands of Nicholas. "Indeed," he pleaded, "Rothad did deserve to be deposed. I have warned him again and again; and all he has done is to complain that I am forever arguing.

"Many have rebuked me for keeping under my rule a man useless for the sacred ministry. But I have been patient and restrained, as a bishop should be, even while he cared nothing for the souls committed to his charge. After he was deposed, I obtained for him an abbey rich in revenue, that he who had always lived daintily might not be broken by want. But (so men are saying) the Lotharingian bishops who don't like me because of Waldrada, and the German bishops who are angry because their king, Louis the German, was driven out of France in 859 have persuaded him to continue to rebel.

"You have asked me to restore him to Soissons; but I truly could not call another Council to consider this. We who are bishops are all too busy, and I have been far away from Reims on service for the king. And if I were to suggest his restoring, the bishops who know him would think me completely insane. He has done such incredible things; he has even given away valuable property of the Church, property left by the faithful as legacy.

"Indeed, I know that we as bishops are subject to the Pope of Rome. But Papal tradition has consistently held that bishops, assembled in Synod, have authority to decide the matter of a province of the Church. If it shall be your pleasure to restore Rothad, I will submit quietly to your will. Yet I should think that, wise and keen as you are, you would not fail to discern contempt and obstinacy shown by subjects to those placed over them. I would travel to Rome if I could; but for my sins I suffer much in the flesh. I will, however, so endeavour to live henceforth that I may not again receive from you these warnings and threats of excommunication, so often received by me of late and so rare in Papal history."

Six months Rothad stayed in Rome, and no one appeared from France to lay accusation against him. In December 864 he delivered to the Pope a document—*Libellus Proclamationis*—in which he described his own view of the years past. In this document Hincmar was pictured as "lord of all he surveyed, working with all his rushing force to hurl condemnation against his victim," who was calling in terror to the Holy See for rescue. "I call God to witness," declared Rothad, "that not even in thought did I dream of abandoning my appeal to Rome, of turning to any other method of trial. My Archbishop did all he could to stop me from coming here. At one and the same moment he was accuser, witness, and judge. He blamed me in my absence freely, of his own will; and among all his lies the greatest was that I unjustly deposed that priest of mine at Soissons. Without a word to me, Hincmar restored him to the ministry. The priest whom I had appointed in his place Hincmar brought by force to Reims, sentenced him to excommunication, inflicted vital injury on his body, and sent him back, maimed and an outcast, to my diocese. As an Emperor triumphant in battle, as a Chief Pontiff of the Church issuing his decrees, so did my Archbishop send forth his word for my punishment.

"Holy Father, to you, the Pope himself, as is meet and right, I cry for help. There is no one here who accuses me. With that wisdom given you by Heaven finish in mercy what you have begun."

On Christmas Eve the clergy and the people of Rome listened in the church of Sancta Maria Maggiore to the Pope describing Rothad as one "who has escaped to sure refuge as a Jonah from the belly of the whale and a Daniel from the den of lions." His archbishop, Hincmar of Reims, Nicholas said, had long been trying to ensnare him by craft, but by grace of God he had never been caught. Rightly had Rothad removed that impious priest from office. But Hincmar had asked the king of France to call a Council for Rothad's trial; and Rothad had found the bishops of that Council obsessed by fear of the king's majesty and by anxiety to win favor from Hincmar. He had therefore appealed to Rome. It was completely ridiculous to say that he had changed his mind and had wanted to substitute a trial before judges in place of his journey to plead before the Holy See. He had now at last appeared in Rome for trial, and no one had come forward to prosecute him. What was the opinion of those present? Should he or should he not be restored to his bishopric of Soissons?

Consent was at once given. On January 21, 865, the Feast of St. Agnes, and in her church outside the walls of Rome, the *Libellus* of Rothad was received with solemn ceremony, and on the next day his restitution was declared by Pope Nicholas in a Synod at Rome.

July saw the bishop of Soissons on his way, escorted by Arsenius, to his home in France. Nicholas, with one more cannonade against the "presumptuous and prevaricating, disobedient and evasive, contumacious and tyrannical" Archbishop of Reims, warned him to receive Rothad with all honor and to continue to treat him thus. Hincmar obeyed; but he still held firmly his own opinion. Rothad, he said, had been restored by Papal power; but not by right of canon law.

11

This was, nevertheless, a bitter blow to Hincmar's pride. Not only had he incurred the deep displeasure of Nicholas, but relations had considerably cooled between himself and King Charles the Bald. Charles had no desire to be on bad terms with the Apostolic See, or to assert warmly his adherence to one of whom the Pope had written to him himself: "The Archbishop of Reims has treated a multitude of my orders as so much rubbish."

Before long, however, a second struggle, and one far more formidable, was disturbing the peace between Hincmar and both the Pope and the king. This arose from Wulfad, one of Ebbo's clerics who by Hincmar's own working had been deposed from office at Soissons in 853. Since that time through his keen intellect and his power of organization Wulfad had gained the friendship of King Charles, and over the years that friendship had increased. In 858 the king had made him abbot of Saint-Médard at Soissons. The king had also chosen him as tutor for his son Carloman: to him John the Scot had dedicated his *De Divisione Naturae*, "both begun and ended by the encouragement and skill of this fellow-worker in the search for wisdom." From him, too, Lupus of Ferrières had sought word concerning the acts of Charles the Bald, as from one at home in the royal Court. Now, in 866, Charles was thinking that he had found exactly the right place for this distinguished abbot, the archbishopric of Bourges in Aquitaine. Its head, Rudolf, was sick and likely at any moment to die.

The news struck Hincmar with dismay. He was already fiercely jealous of this new friend of Charles at Court, so intimately concerned with the royal doings and the royal plans from one day to another. This was bad enough. But the thought that Wulfad, a clerk ordained by Ebbo and deposed by a Council of the Church in 853, might actually obtain an archbishopric, and an archbishopric comparable in importance in the lands of Charles with his own, aroused all his fears anew. Would those ordinations by Ebbo, after all, be held lawful? Would his own tenure of Reims during those six years while Ebbo still lived be held un-lawful? There were also the horrid realizations that the see of Bourges was in Aquitaine; that Aquitaine was causing Charles the Bald much anxiety; and that the archbishop of Bourges would be a counselor of high importance to the king.

Nicholas the Great was now in a difficult position. He had talked long with Rothad in 865, and in the same year with his own legate, Arsenius, after the return of Arsenius from France. It would be pleasant and useful, thought the Pope, to have an archbishop in France of the intellectual stature of Wulfad; no doubt this might curb the ambition, the arrogance, of Archbishop Hincmar of Reims. There was, however, for the Papal ruler his own problem, caused by his own action. Had he not himself given his assent to the words and the formula of Pope Benedict III in confirming the acts of the Council of 853 which had deposed Wulfad and his companions? Had he not written to Hincmar in 863, three years ago, to announce this fact? It would now be necessary for him to work circumspectly and with care. All must be legal and correct. Still, there were always Anastasius and Arsenius at his side to aid him; and they knew as much about canon law as Hincmar himself.

Accordingly, in April 866 he wrote carefully to the archbishop of Reims: "From many parts of France we have heard, most reverend brother, that you cast out from their function certain of the clergy ordained by Ebbo, once ruler of your diocese. No special thought of privilege for them is prompting us now to write to you; but the care of the afflicted is always our concern, and rightly. So we have thought it worthwhile to look into the archives of this holy see of Rome, and there to study the Acts of the Council of Soissons held in 853. From our reading of its records, which you yourself sent us, it does not seem clear that these clerics were regularly and in proper form deposed. Please do not think that we are stating hastily that they were right and that you were wrong. But we must not close our ears to the cry of the distressed, or leave a question of judgment in any doubt.

"Will you therefore, in all kindness and peace, summon Wulfad and his fellow clerics to your presence and go over the whole matter of their deposing at Soissons with a heart inclined to mercy? If, then, you should decide in your own conscience that their prompt restoration by your authority would be the more acceptable course in the sight of God, please act promptly on your own account. If, however, your conscience forbids you this, then we order you to assemble Archbishops and bishops of France, together with yourself and your own clergy, in Council at Soissons on the eighteenth of August, and to call to this Council Wulfad and his colleagues. There the evidence will be reviewed as a whole and in detail; decision will be made either to restore them forthwith or, if agreement cannot be reached and the clerics appeal to us, to send them at once to our presence. And see to it, our reverend brother, that no feeling of resentment on your part hinder them from the road.

"If, as we have no doubt, you will at once say that the Acts of that Council of Soissons of 853 have received Papal confirmation, will you please look again at your copy of its records? You will find, if you read carefully, that all the acts carried out in or concerning that Council, including their confirmation by Rome, were 'reserved to the will and power of the Apostolic See.' Kindly send us a report upon the proceedings of this Council."

Shortly before the sessions of this Council opened, King Charles the Bald wrote to the Pope: "I have done as you asked, and have tried my best to get Archbishop Hincmar to cooperate in the matter of these deposed clerics. He has been most affable in his words: but I don't know what lies hidden underneath the honey. Rudolf of Bourges has died, and his Church needs very badly an able, strong ruler. The people of Aquitaine are frivolous and fickle, and all the clergy of the diocese are keen to have Wulfad as a leader over them. I have given the kingdom of Aquitaine over to the rule of my son, Charles; he is young in years and is very frail in health. Could you allow us, now that the see of Bourges is vacant, to have Wulfad ordained as priest (he is now only a deacon) and to entrust the administration of its diocese to him?"

The Pope replied that he was indeed glad to hear that the king was working with him for the relief of the clerics, but that all action in regard to Wulfad must wait until August and the Council's meetings.

Hincmar faced the Council with his usual calm; but this calm covered deep misgivings. The two men who influenced his life, the Pope and the king, Nicholas and Charles the Bald, were now both working together against him. It was a critical hour for him. On August 18, 866, in the presence of the king, archbishops, bishops, and nobles, he opened proceedings at Soissons with three very carefully composed addresses.

In the first, he declared that he himself had not condemned the clerics in 853; he had not been sitting among their judges nor had he signed the official report of what had been done; he had merely forwarded the report to Rome. The Acts of the Council of 853, he told his audience, had been confirmed by two Popes, Benedict and Nicholas, and anathema had been pronounced against any who should gainsay them. He, the archbishop of Reims, was ready to obey the Pope and to abide by the decision of this present Council. He bore no malice against the clerics; he had desired, and he still desired, their restoration to office; their deposing had cost no one more than himself. As the Pope had foreseen, his conscience had not allowed him to restore them by his own act. He had not deposed them, and he could not, therefore, undo what he had not done. It was for this great Council to undo, if it willed, what had been declared just and right in 853. It would seem, however, that as Pope Nicholas had marked the Acts of 853 as "reserved to the will and power of the Apostolic See," surely, if he now saw fit to change, to destroy, the double Papal confirmation and to dispose of the anathema attached to it, it would be best for him himself to do so by his own special and singular authority!

The second address told of Ebbo: that he had been condemned, that he had never been restored to office by right of canon law, and that his ministry as bishop of Hildesheim had been brought about by craft of the Devil and was contrary to all proper ruling. As for Hincmar's own consecration to Reims, that was now outside controversy, for Ebbo was dead. Nevertheless, let all present remember that that consecration had been approved by the bishops, the priests and the people of the diocese of Reims, that it had been confirmed not only through the consent of King Charles but through bestowal of the pallium by Pope Leo IV.

The third address warned the Council of the danger of allowing clergy irregularly ordained or deprived of their functioning to minister among the people: "a licence by which all the constitution and vigour of the Church will not only be shaken, but will be thrown into utter confusion."

There was yet a fourth address which the archbishop had prepared for delivery here. It was never read because friends of Wulfad rose up to suppress it. We have, however, its text. In it Hincmar declared that, unwilling as he was to disclose its evidence, he had not dared to conceal it. Wulfad, a deacon condemned in 853 by prelates of five provinces, had actually presumed afterward to come forward as candidate for episcopal consecration to the see of Langres, and had only been recalled from this audacity by a Council of bishops at Quierzy in 857. The Council had elected one Isaac for Langres, and had exacted from Wulfad a written promise that never again and nowhere would he thus unlawfully disturb the peace.

(We may note here that Hincmar had vigorously approved the election of Isaac to Langres.)

The Council of Soissons did not venture on its own authority to restore Wulfad, and in restoring him to restore his colleagues. Instead, it expressed its willingness to obey the Pope, if the Pope decided to show mercy in this case. Nicholas decreed restoration for all; already, in September 866, before the express permission of Nicholas had been received, Wulfad became archbishop of Bourges. It was well for Aquitaine. Its king, that youthful son

of Charles the Bald, had been seriously injured some time before
in a drunken melée while returning at night from hunting wild
game, and he died within a few days of Wulfad's consecration.

Hincmar's account of this Council and its result, as given
in his *Annals*, is characteristic:

"The king and certain others were exceedingly keen for
Wulfad's restoration. But since the sacred canons could not be
plucked apart, and schism and scandal could not otherwise be
prevented, a way of indulgence was found by recourse to the
decrees of Nicaea. It was decided accordingly that, if it pleased
Pope Nicholas to change the sentence which he had confirmed,
the clerics condemned by the bishops of five provinces should
by his will be reinstated. In this way the Synod broke up without
any quarrelling. Its only aim had been to find some way in which
Wulfad might be made a bishop; better this, men thought, than
an outcry from Charles the king. But it was all contrary to the
laws of the Church, and Wulfad was clothed with malediction
in this conferring of episcopal honour. The man who desecrated
rather than consecrated him was Aldo, bishop of Limoges. Aldo
was seized by an attack of fever during the ceremony and died
shortly afterwards."

There was more to come, however, before the matter was
ended. Hincmar sent off to Rome his report of the proceedings
at Soissons; he also explained, or rather, tried to explain, to the
Pope why he had not by his own act renewed the ministry of
the priests and deacons concerned. The bearer of this report was
Egilo, now archbishop of Sens, and two letters from Hincmar
instructed him to walk warily in his important mission. He was
to learn by heart the contents of the documents he carried:
"Those men—you know whom I mean—may try their arguments
on you, and you had better have your answers ready"—a reference, of course to the Papal advisers, Arsenius and Anastasius.

"It would be well, too," continued Hincmar to Egilo, "not
to show the Holy Father or his ministers those addresses which
I brought to the Synod. They might suspect some quarrel among
us concerning the restoration of Wulfad. Be sure you say that *I*
did not depose him and the other clergy in 853. Let us be quite
simple and straightforward about the business. But, if you do

get a chance, you should pass on to our Apostolic Ruler what many people are now saying: that, if the Acts of 853 do not hold good, though the See of Rome confirmed them, then these Acts of 866 will not hold good. In that case, *nothing* decreed by bishops and by the Apostolic See is destined to last in permanence. May the Lord send His angel to guard your ways before you."

On December 6, 866, a sudden storm burst forth from the Lateran in Rome, traveling across the Alps in two letters, one to the archbishops and bishops who had met at Soissons in 866, the other especially directed against Hincmar.

In his letter to the bishops Nicholas began quietly. He was delighted, he said, by their unanimous will to restore the clerics of Ebbo. Nevertheless, in his anxiety to obtain the whole truth before making his decision, he had turned back to examine once again, word for word, that report sent him by Hincmar of the proceedings at Soissons in 853. This second reading had changed his delight into fury against the archbishop of Reims.

"A mass of misdemeanours!" he now wrote to Hincmar. "If I tried to describe them all, not words but paper would fail me! Right at the very beginning you start your lies! You say here that the clerics were pressing upon the doors of the church to enter that synod of 853, when everyone knows that they were forced to attend. You put down Wulfad's name among those petitioning, when he was not there at all, as he was sick in bed. During the Council you, the Archbishop and President, now laid aside your authority and sat among the audience, now you resumed the chair; now you acted as one accused, now you were the accuser, now you came forward as judge; constantly you changed your mind, like that creature which is always changing its colour!"

For long Nicholas dwelt upon Hincmar's repeated effort to obtain Papal confirmation of the proceedings of 853, and then he brought out his sharpest accusation: "By cutting out words, by adding words, you deliberately altered the Acts of the Council of 853 in the copy which you forwarded to us for our reading in Rome, and you did this that you might drive these clerics to despair, in keeping them from appeal to Rome! Of course it is quite absurd for you to say that you neither judged them nor acted for their deposing! The Acts of the Council of 853 state that you did. You did it by your silence, by your written record, by the witness of Pope Benedict himself.

"No, brother, you did *not* desire the restoration of these men. You desired their fall. By our authority they will stand restored. Nevertheless, that you may have full opportunity to follow up all your malicious charges, we allow you one year in which to work. If at the end of a year from now you have brought no just complaint against them to us, on any ground of guilt or irregularity or merited condemnation, you will henceforth hold them as permanently restored."

The Pope informed Wulfad and his companions of what he had done. Let them bear Hincmar no ill-will for their suspension, he wrote. At the same time they would do well to be on their guard!

King Charles the Bald hurried off to Nicholas an apology for the consecrating of Wulfad to Bourges before permission had been received from Rome: "The assault by the pagans rages fiercely in Aquitaine, and there is revolt far and wide there among bad Christians. Our bishops were anxious to quiet things down and to avoid worse troubles. You realize, I am sure, that Bourges is the chief see of that country."

Hincmar, for his part, reported in his *Annals* of 867 that Charles had read into the Pope's letters "many things against him, Hincmar, which clearly were not true." To the Pope he sent a long argument, presented with quiet and even submissive dignity, against his wrathful denunciation:

"I am sure that my Creator must see rust of evil deeply engrained upon my soul, or He would not expose it so often to this purgatorial fire from the seat of Apostolic authority. I know that in other ways I am a sinner; but I have ever been a faithful and a devoted subject of the Holy See and its rulers. With all contrition and with all the humility within me, I beg you not to believe any man who shall tell you that in this I lie. Ever since I received your letter, I have not had a thought of withstanding in any way the decision made at Soissons in 866 and confirmed by you. As to any addition, change, or excision in a Papal text by me, how could I have dared this when I knew that you had a copy in the Papal records to compare with what I wrote?

"You say, too, that for my pride I wear my Archbishop's pallium more often than I should. Of a truth, my occupations, the calls upon me, are so many that I seldom have a chance to wear it in my Cathedral; and when I am there, I rarely do so, even on high Feast days. In any case, to me the pallium is not a mark of honour for the Archbishop himself, but for his metropolitan seat. If a man would win eternal life, he does not need to be a bishop; he needs true faith and good works done in the grace of God. If I could now choose, I would not hold a bishop's office. I have lived long; I am burdened with many infirmities, and the time of my going hence is not far away."

Clergy from the diocese of Reims "dressed as pilgrims, to escape the snares of enemies," as Hincmar writes, carried this letter in July 867 across the Alps to Rome. On October 25, 867, a Council of bishops, from Reims, Rouen, Tours, Sens, Bordeaux, and Bourges, met at Troyes. It approved the resolution reached at Soissons in 866 and asked that the honor of the pallium might be conferred by the Pope upon Wulfad.

Once again the archbishop of Reims wrote in his *Annals* his own account of the proceedings:

"At this Synod the usual thing happened. Certain bishops who were keen to support Wulfad and to please King Charles began to make assertions against Hincmar that were contrary both to truth and to the canons of the Church. But with reasoned argument and sure knowledge he defeated their attempts. Finally, a report was drawn up and given for delivery to the Pope at Rome into the hands of Actard, bishop of Nantes. It was in the form of a letter, and its content declared what Hincmar had written in his letter of July. On his way Actard visited the king, as Charles had told him to do. Then, heedless of the loyalty and the labours of Hincmar now these many years for the Crown, Charles ordered Actard to hand over to him that letter of the bishops. Directly he held it he broke its seal and read the Acts of the meeting at Troyes. After this, because Hincmar had not been put to confusion in the Synod, as Charles had hoped, the king wrote a letter in his own name to Pope Nicholas, a letter directed against Hincmar, and sent it off to Rome."

The two letters, from the Synod and the king of France, never reached Nicholas. That remarkable man and Pope had died on November 13, before Actard arrived. To the last he was fighting for what he held right. But before he died, he had received the letter which Hincmar had sent off by "pilgrims" in July, and he had written back to say that "in all things he was satisfied."

12

Nicholas the Great was succeeded in December 867 by Hadrian II, a Pope who was at times bold in action, but who was apt to yield in the face of attack. History, moreover, has not forgotten the tragedy of his private life, a tragedy described by Hincmar, as chronicler of these years.

Hadrian had been married before he was ordained priest, and his wife and daughter were still living in Rome when he became Pope. A few months later, during Lent of 868, Eleutherius, son of Arsenius, the Papal counselor, carried off this daughter of Hadrian, although she was betrothed to another man, and forced her into marriage. The Pope was beset by horror and distress; but worse was to follow. Arsenius hurried to ask the Emperor Louis, king of Italy, to protect his son in this crisis. The Emperor was at Beneventum in the south, absorbed, as usual, by the peril of Saracen assault. Arsenius arrived there, fell sick in mind and in body, and, as Hincmar wrote, "with talk to devils on his lips (so men said)" speedily departed this life. Eleutherius was left without hope or help. Hearing that he was to be brought to trial before the envoys of the Emperor, in his panic he again lost his wits. He murdered both the wife of the Pope and that daughter whom he had seized for his pleasure, and then he was himself killed by the imperial ministers.

Such repeated tragedy could hardly allow Hadrian to meet with any due calm the daily burden of Papal responsibility. Much of his thought, too, was centered on his constant appeals to King Louis, his only defense at hand against the Saracens, who were now threatening the Holy See itself and its possessions.

Under Hadrian, the third round of wrestling of Hincmar's clergy against his rule was fought, this time by his own nephew, inheritor of his name. The younger Hincmar had been trained and taught at Reims by his uncle, who was proud of his intellectual promise and did all in his power to promote his career. He took him to the Court of Charles the Bald, where the king showed him much kindness and employed him on various missions of importance. Finally, in 858, by the same influence of the king, he was consecrated bishop of Laon, in the province of Reims.

After a while, like Rothad of Soissons, this successful young prelate began to resent his archbishop's firm hand of control, and all the more because in many ways his own forceful character was very similar to that of the uncle who demanded his obedience. He grew careless, conceited, and disobedient, bent on his own will. Far more abundantly than to Rothad, because he was far more quick in mind than Rothad, the *Forged Decretals* gave him aid in his aim of independence of his metropolitan. He was, however, far too independent in character to follow the *Decretals* unless this suited his purpose.

In 868 he fell into serious trouble, through a dispute with Charles the Bald himself, concerning a matter of property; and the king called him to appear before lay judges for trial. Young Hincmar refused; it was not proper for bishops, he declared, to stand trial in a secular court. Charles promptly cut off the revenues of his bishopric and summoned him to a Council of prelates of his own rank and order. At this news, his archbishop and uncle hastened to support him; Hincmar of Reims himself did not approve the hauling of bishops before laymen. At the Council, held at Pîtres in August of this year, he delivered in defense of the bishop of Laon four learned "Expositions" on the freedom of the Church. To some extent they were successful. His revenues, at least, were returned to the bishop of Laon; but the quarrel continued. At last the younger Hincmar appealed to Rome, and Pope Hadrian supported him, as Nicholas had supported Rothad. A very sharp reprimand went from the Pope to the royal Court; and in intense indignation Charles the Bald retorted that never "in all record to be found, had a Pope of Rome written thus to a king of the Franks."

It would be tedious to trace step by step this third history of clerical rebellion. Council again followed Council. In his anger Hincmar of Laon ordered all the priests of his diocese to cease their ministry should he be thrown into prison. In prison he soon found himself; and his clergy in their anguish wrote to his uncle, their archbishop, asking him what they should do? Were the children to remain unbaptized, the penitent unabsolved, the sick to die without the sacraments? Certainly not, Hincmar the elder answered. He told them to continue their work in the churches and homes of Laon. Letter after letter passed between uncle and nephew. And not only letters. Hincmar of Reims wrote fifty-five chapters of expostulation; Hincmar of Laon sent to Reims a mass of extracts from Papal decrees and decisions of Councils. In contempt his uncle wrote back: "These I knew long before you were ever thought of!"

At the Synod of Douzy, near Sedan, in August 871, King Charles charged the younger Hincmar with disobedience and disloyalty to the throne; and the archbishop of Reims charged his subordinate with stubborn refusal to fulfill the duties of a bishop to his people, his king, his metropolitan, his Church. Whereupon the attending prelates declared him guilty, and Hincmar of Reims himself pronounced sentence against his sister's son: that the bishop of Laon be deprived of all episcopal function, honor, office, and dignity, subject only to the authority of the Pope.

With the acts of the Council a letter from the deposed bishop's uncle traveled to Hadrian at Rome. "Would that I had never seen him, far less consecrated him as bishop!" he wrote. "A man through whom so great scandal has arisen in our churches and our land! Not without reason might I say, 'Good were it for him had he never been born!' Many years I have lived in fear and in grief through his unworthy ways; man to man I have borne his insolence!"

The Pope, however, refused to confirm the Acts without further trial. Hincmar of Laon had appealed to the Holy See; before its tribunal the verdict must therefore be decided. No protest, no remonstrance (and bold remonstrance there was, from both the king and the archbishop of Reims) could move him. The matter was still undecided, and the see of Laon was still vacant, when Pope Hadrian II died toward the end of 872.

Pope Hadrian, as Nicholas would surely have done, had sent the pallium to Wulfad as Archbishop of Bourges. He had released

Waldrada from the ban of excommunication imposed upon her by Nicholas, under one condition, "that she have nothing to do with King Lothar." He had done his best—and it was a failure, in the spirit, if not in the letter—to keep that king and his wife, Theutberga, together in marriage. Lothar was faithless to his queen until his death; and he had died three years before Hadrian, in August 869. His death and that of Hadrian marked both an ending and a beginning of trouble for Archbishop Hincmar of Reims and for his king, Charles the Bald.

13

Enough of canon law. The upheavals in Carolingian politics which came upon Hincmar after King Lothar's death now lie before us. But before we enter upon these, we should look for a few moments at the conflict, this time in theology, which lasted from 849 until at least 866 and which perhaps cost Hincmar's conscience more debating than any other of his numerous battles: the long duel with Gottschalk, his prisoner of Hautvillers.

Hincmar was not primarily a theologian. In matters of the Church he was an organizer on the active side, a canonist on the intellectual. Gottschalk, however, had been committed to his keeping. He was his to guard, and, if possible, to convert; and the archbishop of Reims never neglected anything which his office and his official duty laid upon him.

We have already seen Gottschalk twice condemned for heresy: at Mainz in 848, at Quierzy in 849. Since that time he had been held in the monastery of Hautvillers, near Épernay. The archbishop was truly anxious that he should turn from his views to those of the Church, concerning Divine predestination, redemption, and human free will. In 849 he sent to him a statement of Catholic doctrine in the hope that it might change his stubborn mind. Its substance ran, in brief form:

1. God wills the final salvation of all souls, to be attained by the redemption offered to all by Christ in His Passion, and by the Divine gift of grace offered to all during their lives on earth.
2. God has also given to all souls the gift of free will. He has known from all eternity what will be the final state of each in the life to come; but he compels none to co-operate with His grace. The soul that chooses

to reject Him, God will not, and cannot, compel to accept Him, or that Vision of Himself which will be the joy of the life hereafter.

Gottschalk wrote back that he would not assent to this teaching; and to emphasize his firmness he sent a detailed "Confession" of his own belief. With him agreed, more or less, Ratramn of Corbie, the monk so keen on theological argument; Lupus, abbot of Ferrières; Prudentius, bishop of Troyes; and certain scholars connected with the Church of Lyons. On the side of Hincmar, upholding the doctrine of free will, stood Hraban Maur, archbishop of Mainz, and Pardulus, predecessor of the younger Hincmar in the bishopric of Laon.

Further action soon appeared necessary. Gottschalk had been condemned to silence; he was allowed no visitors from the outside world. It seemed impossible, however, to stop him from smuggling out letters, since some of the monks of Hautvillers secretly sympathized with his views. Hincmar again took up his pen. Now in 849–50 he wrote his first long work on predestination, addressed to the "humble and simple" clergy and laity of his diocese, those, so he thought, who might easily get hold of the letters of Gottschalk and be led astray. "You know well this man," wrote the archbishop of Reims, "by name and face and conversation. We know him as a false prophet, a servant of the Devil, long held in foul report for the abomination of his perverse words. He has poured virulent poison into your ears and hearts, confusing God's foreknowledge with predestination. He has also, I hear, dared to try to probe the mystery of the Beatific Vision of God, thinking rather of how he is to see God than of how he may merit this grace." For good measure Hincmar repeated word for word the sentence pronounced against Gottschalk at Quierzy in 849, and ended: "Let the simple folk of this diocese of Reims beware of a like damnation, here and in the Judgment to come."

His learned opponents did not let this pass in silence. Hardly was this open letter published, before Ratramn of Corbie sent out a long list of errors which, so he declared, he had found in its quotations from the Fathers of the Church. Unfortunately Hincmar was not proof against such errors, for often he had no time to check his sources.

He was, of course, much upset by this criticism. He was also worried about his prisoner. Gottschalk was sick, and was daily asking for the communion of the altar from which he had long been barred. Suppose he were to die without the last sacraments? The archbishop in his perplexity wrote to consult Hraban, who in two letters said that in his opinion Gottschalk should be held excommunicate until he saw fit to repent.

Someone of high authority and learning, thought Hincmar, must certainly refute the views still making their way from this heretic's cell. He consulted Pardulus of Laon, a bishop of his own province, and together they decided to call upon the philosopher John the Scot, at this time director of the Palace School of King Charles the Bald. Would John use his great knowledge in writing a work to crush Gottschalk for all time?

John was delighted. "I cannot say," he wrote, "how grateful I am to you who have deigned to call to me for the defence of the Catholic faith. I will do my very best, busy as I am. Truly at the moment I feel like a ship tossed upon the heavy seas which now rage around the realm of our Lord King Charles."

Doubtless he did do his best; but it was a failure. His book, published in 851, drew upon John a violent attack from the theologians who supported Gottschalk. Prudentius of Troyes wrote to Wenilo, archbishop of Sens: "In your zeal of brotherhood, Father, you sent me some nineteen chapters from a book by a certain Scot, asking for my opinion on them. I will tell you. They are full of error: the poison of Pelagius, the madness of Origen, the ravings of Collyrian heretics. I felt panic coming over me, yes, panic, when I found that the old evils, so long fast asleep, were once more rising up in these days of ours."

Then the Church of Lyons joined battle. About 852 two works appeared. One was directed against the "erroneous definitions" of John the Scot, very possibly by that deacon, Florus, whom we found so savage in assault upon Amalar of Metz. The other, the *Liber de tribus epistulis,* a dissertation dealing in bitter scorn with letters written by Hincmar of Reims, Pardulus of Laon, and Hraban Maur, was anonymous. Perhaps it came from Remigius, elected in 852 archbishop of Lyons; perhaps from Ebbo, nephew of Hincmar's predecessor at Reims, a young man connected with Lyons and destined from 854 to be bishop of Grenoble; or perhaps we may see here once again the hand of Florus.

All was disappointing enough; but Hincmar only worked the harder. In 853, with some members of the Council of Soissons —that Council which had deposed the clerics of Reims—he went on to a conference at Quierzy and there presided over the drawing up of four brief but definite statements of the faith held by him and his supporters.

For nearly two years the conflict simmered in private. Then, in January 855, bishops of Lyons, Vienne, and Arles, at a meeting in Valence, south of Lyons, issued a report flatly contradicting the statements sent out from Quierzy. It was drawn up by Ebbo, now bishop of Grenoble, and it was answered in 856–57 by Hincmar in his second treatise on predestination: an "immense volume" of retort against the friends of Gottschalk and against those critics "who have declared that we live and fight on Scottish porridge": a reference, of course, to John the Scot. This treatise is lost; we have only its letter of dedication to Charles the Bald.

At long last a hope of relaxation appeared. In 859 the opponents of Hincmar presented sixteen canons, previously composed by them, for consideration in the General Council of Savonnières, near Toul. Opinions were still divided, but the archbishop of Reims pleaded with so great vigor for his views that the members of the Council resolved to meet again some time in the future, after the return to France of peace from rebels and raiders. Then, it was thought, "more wholesome theories" might unanimously be adopted.

Hincmar again toiled in his cell at Reims; and the winter of 859–60 produced his third work on predestination. Fast and strenuously he wrote, and with some misgivings both concerning his haste and his labors. "In hurry and hustle," he says, "I have put together my words. The reader will grow weary, I fear; but he will forgive me. The Catholic faith is herein for him to find."

Not only Hincmar's readers, but all men were growing tired of this unending war of debate. Beneath the joy of argument, behind the flood of quotations from the Scriptures, from patristic tomes, the soul, if not the body, of the thought on both sides was essentially the same. No man, not even Gottschalk himself, was resigned to an eternity in hell; or loved a Lord who had designed this end as an inevitable certainty for "a mass" of men, doomed from the day of their birth in time.

In the end, then, Hincmar conquered in this struggle. At Tusey, also near Toul, the final meeting was held, in October 860, and there he recorded agreement that "God wills *all* to be saved and none to perish"; that "if men of their own free will could neither avoid evil nor do good, they would be like to stones, to lifeless matter without feeling or reason, rather than to beings made in the image of God."

Not even now, however, was there an end of controversy; Gottschalk persisted in his theological arguing. Nor could Hincmar be silent. In 860–61, as Perels, editor of Hincmar's Letters, dates it, there appeared from the pen of this archbishop of Reims another lengthy work, on the Holy Trinity. For long, so he wrote in his weary determination, Gottschalk had been defending the words *trina deitas,* "threefold Deity," taken from the line of a hymn:

Te trina deitas unaque poscimus,

as being in accordance with the Catholic faith. Hincmar took the opposite view. "This pseudo-monk of Orbais," he declared, "partly through ill-feeling against me, for he had heard that I had forbidden those words *trina deitas* to be sung in church, and partly through his customary love of the new and the unusual, of teachings contrary to orthodox belief, has already written much on this matter and has sent his writings to all whom he could reach; this he has done at first secretly and then openly, so far as he could manage. Recently a pamphlet of his on this subject came into my hands, containing his pestilential and deadly poison, and I think it well to answer it."

So, to the people and clergy of the Archdiocese of Reims, Hincmar sent out his answer to Gottschalk on the Holy Trinity. It is especially interesting in that he inserted in its pages the little treatise of Gottschalk mentioned above. This pamphlet, and other writings of Gottschalk, discovered and edited within recent years, have greatly increased our knowledge of his mind and its working.

But the center of all this strife, Gottschalk himself, was still in his monastic prison, and men were crying out in anger. Hincmar, as the years went on, wrote to Pope Nicholas in his own defense. "Wild in mind," he described his captive, "impatient of quiet, delighting in new, strange ideas, singularly harmful to other men—foolish, half-educated men—who are attracted by his quick, mobile spirit, his claim of knowledge, his desire of leadership. I take no pleasure," the archbishop went on, "in this stubborn endurance of imprisonment, and I grieve at this obdurate refusal to yield."

He took other precaution as well. When, in September 866, Archbishop Egilo of Sens left France for Rome as envoy to Pope Nicholas, he not only carried with him instructions in the matter of Wulfad, but also in this matter of Gottschalk.

"Word has come," Hincmar instructed Egilo, "that one of Gottschalk's friends, a monk at Hautvillers and a very bad one, has escaped from the monastery. He may go to Rome and present an appeal from Gottschalk to the Pope. You must be careful, and I will tell you why. Gottschalk has had many supporters, and among them Prudentius, once bishop of Troyes. Do you know what Prudentius wrote in his *Annals?* He actually declared, against the year 859, that Nicholas, Pope of Rome, believed in a double predestination! I never heard that said about the Pope by any one else, or in any other place. But those *Annals* are read by many people, and so you had better suggest to our Apostolic ruler that there must be no scandal in the Church. And there would be if—God forbid!—it were thought that he agreed with Gottschalk's beliefs. Please, I beseech you, be also careful concerning me. I hear that many people have been writing things far from pleasant to the Pope about me, and the rumour no doubt is true. I don't want to be blamed for no fault of mine.

"Mind you, if any one asks you about Gottschalk's imprisonment, you can answer quite truthfully. He has just the same to eat and to drink as the monks of Hautvillers, and it is served to him with all regularity. Clothing is also offered him, and enough of it, if he will take it, and wood for a fire, and, too, hot water for baths. But since he has been in the monastery, he has refused even to wash his face. He was filthy enough when he came, and he is firmly determined to stay so. There will be a terrific upset in the Church if he is set free from prison or ordered before a Synod. That matters nothing to me; I don't care for myself, only for others. But, mark me, I know what I am saying."

His words were never put to the proof. Shortly after 866 Gottschalk died. Hincmar had written to the brethren of Hautvillers that if he "should come to his senses" before his last hours, they were to be kind to him, body and soul. If he repented and acknowledged his error, he was to receive viaticum, and after his death the monks were to chant for him the Office of the Dead with all its psalms and hymns. Should he remain obstinate to the end, no such chanting was to be allowed, and his body was not to be laid in the burial ground of the brethren, but in a separate place, by itself. Even this burial, Hincmar added, was to be granted only for humanity's sake.

After word reached him that Gottschalk had died unrepentant, the archbishop wrote for him an obituary in words which long before had been written of the traitor Judas: "He ended his unworthy life by a death in keeping with it, and went to his own place."

Chapter VIII

THE LAST YEARS OF THE CAROLINGIAN EMPIRE

1

The shadow of that barrier raised between Charles the Bald and Hincmar, his archbishop and prime statesman, through the king's warm support of Wulfad and through the censure of Hincmar by the Pope in regard to him, was to last in greater or lesser degree during the rest of the reign of Charles. Confidence between them had been broken, never to be fully restored, even though at times their collaboration resumed something of its former energy. The only really marked revival of this collaboration was brought about by the death of Lothar, king of Lotharingia, in 869.

In 868, King Lothar, distressed as ever by the tie which bound him to his wife, Theutberga, and by his desire for Waldrada, always hovering near, decided that the only course open to him was to go to Rome and plead his cause in person before the Pope, Hadrian II. Long before he actually started on his way, fear of the consequence rose high. What might his two uncles, Charles the Bald and Louis the German, whose kingdoms touched Lotharingia on either side, what might they not attempt in his absence? To both went warnings from the Pope that they do no harm to Lotharingia. In the eyes of Hadrian the only rightful heir of that realm was Lothar's brother, Louis, king of Italy and Emperor. Louis meant everything to Rome. Was not he her only support at hand against the Saracen menace? Lothar himself in 869 sent envoys to both kings for the assuring of his country's safety. "From Charles," Hincmar reported, "he received no guarantee; but, so it was said, Louis gave his word," and Lothar went toward Rome.

In Rome he presented splendid gifts to Hadrian; yet all he received in answer to his appeal was the Papal decision that bishops from the realms of Charles the Bald, of Louis the German, and of Lothar, the appellant, were to journey to Rome for the debating of the matter in a general Synod. With this he was forced to be content, and he started home, troubled by an attack of fever which grew steadily worse. At last he reached Piacenza, where on August 8, 869, he died.

The messenger bearing the news found Charles the Bald in France at Senlis. Immediately he hurried to his palace at Attigny, where envoys of leading men of Lotharingia presented to him a petition that he would do nothing until he could consult with his brother, Louis of Germany, at that moment engaged in fighting Slavic raiders upon his land. The two could then, the envoys said, discuss a division of Lotharingia between them.

But in far greater force came what Hincmar called "saner counsel," encouraging his king's desire to gain Lotharingia, and Charles again hastened on his march, joined as he went by many nobles and their armed followers. On September 5 he was at Metz. On the ninth he was anointed and crowned there as king of Lotharingia, in its cathedral of St. Stephen, and by Hincmar himself. To Hincmar this was a day of rejoicing, and not only for the sake of Charles. From this time forward his own position as archbishop would be far more comfortable. His province of Reims would be subject only to one king, and that his own, when both France and Lotharingia were under the rule of Charles the Bald.

In his *Annals* Hincmar gave a detailed account of the ceremonies at Metz. Eloquent addresses were delivered before the great congregation of bishops, lords, and people of humbler station gathered there, by Adventius, bishop of Metz, by Charles himself, and by Hincmar. He was speaking at the express request, he was careful to say, of various bishops from the province of Reims and elsewhere. Did anyone, he asked, feel that his presence in Metz, that the presence of these bishops of his, was an intrusion upon the rights of Lotharingia? Let him who would protest remember that the metropolitan sees of Reims, in France, and of Trier, in the kingdom of Lotharingia, for long had been connected by the bond of fellowship. Let all men look upon this presence of bishops from a sister province as a sign of that unity of the One Church—that unity which is the will of God.

To this all assented. The archbishop proceeded to declare

that it was also the will of Heaven that the king of France, who ruled, and had ruled, well and beneficially over his own people, should now extend his rule to this kingdom of Lotharingia. Truly, he continued, God had revealed this fact to the congregation which had gathered at Metz to witness the coronation of King Charles. Not only between the provinces of Reims and Trier, but between the cities of Reims and Metz, the bond of history had long been sealed. Had not the father of Charles, Louis the Pious, been crowned as Emperor by Pope Stephen before our Lady's altar at Reims? And after he had been stripped of his imperial crown, had it not been restored to him in this very cathedral of St. Stephen at Metz? "I myself was here and saw it," Hincmar added. "In days of old," he went on, "rulers crowned themselves by their own hands. Was it not well that this king be crowned here, that here he be anointed, by the hands of the bishops of the Church?"

All again cried assent. Hincmar administered the benediction and the anointing with holy oil; and each bishop present in the sanctuary laid his hands upon the crown as it was placed upon the head of Charles.

Doubtless Charles felt happy; doubtless the anxieties of Hincmar faded out for the moment. They both conveniently forgot that in this same city of Metz not long before, in 867 or 868, Charles, king of France, and Louis, king of Germany, in the presence of Hincmar had each solemnly made pact with one another in these words: "If God give us land from our nephew Lothar's realm, in gaining and in dividing that land, without craft or deception, with you, my brother, I will sincerely and justly co-operate." It was also perhaps convenient that by the will of Heaven Irmintrud, queen of Charles, died just a month later. As another marriage could not be entered upon at once, the king hastened to take as his mistress one Richilde, a most desirable choice as the daughter of a noble Lotharingian family. Thus encouraged, he hurried to Aachen, seat of government in Lotharingia, in the hope that men from Provence and upper Burgundy would join him.

In this he was disappointed, and in November he went on to the palace of Gondreville, on the Moselle near Toul. Here envoys were waiting to deliver messages from Pope Hadrian, who, still ignorant of what had actually happened, again warned all and everyone to keep hands off the realm of Lotharingia. Charles paid little attention. Early in 870 at Aachen he married Richilde. Then he received another message, sent from a different quarter and given in words which he did not expect. It came from his brother, the king of Germany: "If you do not straightway leave Aachen and the realm once held by Lothar, I shall promptly march against you in war."

Before Easter of 870 Charles the Bald and Louis of Germany at Aachen had each again made solemn oath to divide Lotharingia with one another; and on August 8 near Meersen the exact boundaries of the division were defined, stated, and accepted on both sides. On October 9 of this same year Charles was at the abbey of Saint-Denis, keeping its Patronal Feast. From its chapel and from solemn high mass he was called out to receive a "terrible"— the word is Hincmar's—letter from the Pope. Similar outpouring of Hadrian's wrath went to Hincmar: "If you kept in mind the blessings which you have received through this Holy See, and if you cared for the troubles of other men as you do for your own, then indeed either the love of God or the fear of hell would rouse you from your sleep of sloth to carry out the duties of your pastoral charge! Who knew better than you that the sons of Louis the Pious had sworn never to invade a kinsman's lands? Now King Charles in contempt of this oath has seized the rightful inheritance of Louis of Italy, brother of the late king of Lotharingia and nephew of Charles himself! But you, who kept silence while this was done and never rose to rebuke, even mildly rebuke, this crime, you are not only partner in it—No! Worse still, you appear as its author and instigator!

"Insist, we command you, that Charles withdraw from this realm of our son, Louis! And take care for yourself. In honour and dignity, it is true, you stand higher than any bishop of France. But not for that reason will we allow you to condone the evil done by your king!"

The archbishop of Reims wrote a spirited answer: "Did not our lord kings, Charles and Louis the German, take upon themselves in due division the rule of this land of Lotharingia? Otherwise, revolt, as many men are saying, would have broken out among its people; battles and insurrection would have destroyed lives, as once before when Louis the Pious was dead. May I also humbly remind your Reverence that Lotharingia was given long ago to this same Charles, now our king, by his father, that Emperor Louis the Pious himself, with the consent of his bishops and nobles?"

2

Charles the Bald pursued his ambition still further; and in the course of time this pursuit brought about serious difference between himself and Hincmar. In 871, while on his way to enjoy some days of hunting near Orville in the region of the Aisne, the king had been met by envoys from "very many" in Italy. Would he, they were asking, come at once to Italy, because his nephew, the Emperor Louis, its king, had been killed in fighting rebels of the south? The rumor proved untrue, but the invitation lingered in memory. Then, in a letter of 872, a letter intended to allay sore feelings caused by previous Papal communications, Pope Hadrian wrote to Charles: "We love and respect you with all devotion as a righteous man worthy of praise. Truly, loyal as we are to our present Emperor, Louis, king of Italy, we declare that if you should survive him and we should still be living at the time of his death, not for any amount of gold would we want to see or to receive any other as king of Italy and Emperor but you yourself."

It was Hadrian's last letter to Charles. He died toward the end of the year, and by December 872 an archdeacon of Rome, old in years but remarkable in energy, was ruling the Apostolic See under the name of John VIII.

On August 12, 875, Louis did depart this life, worn out by wars against disloyal subjects and pirate Saracens. Now Charles seized his chance. From Douzy in the Ardennes, where he heard the news and was assured of its truth, he went to Ponthion, from Ponthion to Langres, gathering military forces, provisions, and supplies day by day. On the first of September he left France; through the Great St. Bernard Pass he and his army marched to enter Italy.

Hincmar heard that he had gone and judged him bitterly as foolish and irresponsible. That the king should leave his own country exposed to the terror of pirates, that he should leave his kingdom a prey to outlaws bent on destruction, to nobles seeking nothing but their own ends, was bad enough. France was in danger; and Charles was now seeking to add Italy to its burden of defense, an Italy already face to face with its own disaster. But to this archbishop and statesman it was even harder to realize that the king of France had deserted the ideal which Hincmar had always held before him: of a Frankish state at unity in itself, standing secure in its laws, guided by the Church, administered by the controlling power of its king, happy in the happiness of its people. Nothing now seemed to concern this king but the increase of his own rule and sovereignty. Not long before, Hincmar had written—perhaps, as Schrörs has suggested, in 873—his treatise *On the Character of a King and his Royal Ministry*. In it he had declared: "By necessity alone are good men to be called to wage war and to enlarge a kingdom," and his words had been addressed to Charles the Bald. The possession of Lotharingian territory was, it might, of course, be claimed, quite a different matter. On its western side Lotharingia touched France, and their union made for safety.

In Italy King Charles succeeded in defeating two attempts by sons of Louis of Germany to stop his march, and he duly arrived in Rome. The Pope did not agree with Hincmar. He had lost the protection given to Italy and the Holy See by Italy's King Louis, the Emperor; here was another royal Carolingian, also familiar with the horror of barbarian assault. If sufficient inducement were offered him, he, too, would render aid in these perilous times. This was the will of Heaven, thought Pope John, and an immense relief! With all magnificence John VIII received Charles in St. Peter's; with all splendor of ritual he crowned him Emperor on Christmas Day of this same year, 875: a timely reminder of the imperial coronation on Christmas Day, 800, of that grandfather of his, Charles the Great, whose name his mother Judith in such high hope had given him.

Three weeks were spent in Rome in talking with the Pope, and then this new Emperor left for Pavia, capital city of Lombardy. Nobles, spiritual and lay, gathered there in great number to hail him "unanimously as protector, lord, defender of them all, and king of the realm of Italy." There, early in 876, Charles held a general assembly and issued from a written roll his orders, made with the consent and counsel of Ansbert, Archbishop of Milan, for the honor and defense of the Church in his new Italian land.

3

Meanwhile the subjects of Charles in France were facing a totally different scene. Once again Louis, king of Germany, had seized his chance to invade. In the palace of Charles at Attigny he kept his Christmas with triumph of success. All seemed to be going well. The nobles of France were again flocking to his side; in company with German troops they were overrunning and ravaging the neighboring fields and roads.

Already once more Hincmar had risen for the defense of his country and its absent king. Charles to him was a fool and a deserter; but France was France. From Reims had already gone out an appeal, a command, to the bishops and magnates of the province. Had not this same Louis come from Germany as invader in 858, eighteen years ago, and had he not been driven out, a fugitive fleeing home?

"Our Lord Charles," Hincmar wrote to the sees and the castles of his great diocese, "our Lord Charles of his own will has left us and our kingdom. Now, so men say, Louis the German is coming a second time to seize it. But our queen and her son are here, and they have men and their leaders to defend us until our ruler has gained the kingdom he wills to receive in Italy and has returned to us, as we pray, in peace. It is for us meanwhile, the bishops of France, to inspire and encourage the ministers of our State in this evil hour. We stand between the hammer and the anvil, between these two brother kings, held fast in their strife.

"Shepherds of our people we are, not hirelings. We have not forsaken our king; he has forsaken us, left us to face an invading power. If we yield, death awaits us. No! We will stand as those having authority, to guide and to counsel with calm courage until victory brings these troubles to an end."

Victory came. Pope John fiercely rebuked the leaders of both France and Germany. A wave of loyalty filled again all the land; and Easter 876 found the invasion past and Louis back in his own palace at Frankfurt. Charles returned home, but only to draw still deeper division between himself and the archbishop who had defended his crown.

4

On June 21, 876, in his palace of Ponthion, near Châlons-sur-Marne, the king assembled a great Council for the recognition of his new imperial honor. Two Papal legates had come from Italy to give their presence and authority. At the opening session Charles appeared in Frankish dress, such as Charles the Great, king-Emperor, had worn, radiant with gold. Prayer was offered, and then the senior legate read aloud a letter from the Pope, announcing that he had appointed Ansegis, archbishop of Sens, as his vicar apostolic, his representative throughout France and Germany.

The fact was known by many, for Pope John VIII had already written of his decision to the bishops of those kingdoms; yet the knowledge did not lessen the feeling aroused in the Council, and in no man more than in Hincmar of Reims. Not many years had passed since Ansegis, abbot of Saint-Michel in the diocese of Beauvais, had humbly obeyed his authority as head of the province in which Beauvais lay. Now Ansegis was to be preferred before him, and, of course, by act of Charles himself. He had asked this of the Pope when he was at Rome.

Nor was this merely a personal matter. Once, as we saw in 851, Hincmar would have welcomed for himself this honor. But since that time his stature as upholder of right and rule had greatly increased. Both he and his fellow archbishops were now determined that no one of them should hold authority over the rest; that all, so far as office went, had equal rights; that the only seniority which could justly be claimed by any one of them rose from length of tenure. Had not Drogo, archbishop of Metz, been granted this same preferment by Pope Sergius in 844? And had it not come to nothing?

With one exception, all the heads of provinces present replied that they would obey the Pope in general, but that in regard to this matter the rights and privileges of each of them must be respected and observed. Nothing could move them from this stand; and when Charles the Bald ordered the chair of Ansegis to be placed before those of all the other metropolitans, next to that of the Papal legate who was sitting on his own right hand, Hincmar rose to his feet and declared in the hearing of all that this was contrary to sacred ordinance. Ansegis took his seat for the moment; but his Vicariate, like that of Drogo, never attained reality of power. While the Council was still in session there came from Hincmar, who must have worked all night on it, a vigorous statement, *On the Law relating to Archbishops*. Drogo, he reminded its members, had accepted the inevitable, the independence of each ruler of an ecclesiastical province. Let them all follow his example, and give to the Emperor the things of Emperors, to bishops the rights of bishops. His advice was followed.

5

Two months later, in August 876, Charles moved further. His longtime rival in rule, his brother Louis, king of Germany, now died. The king-Emperor did not hesitate; he marched in September to Aachen and on to Cologne, bent on seizing that part of Lotharingia which had been given to Germany in the division of 870.

Enemies, however, had been left to him in the sons of Louis the German. They were three: Carloman, king of Bavaria; Louis the Younger, king of the eastern Franks; and Charles, known as Charles the Fat, king of Alemannia. Of these Louis the Younger offered negotiation, which entirely failed. Charles marched to battle, and with his army, tired out by a nightlong march and soaked with rain, came upon Louis encamped at Andernach, on the Rhine north of Coblenz. It was October 8; the men of Louis were full of energy after their rest and rushed to meet the attack. In mid-battle Charles, completely defeated, turned to flee with a small following; prisoners and plunder in quantity fell to Louis and his army. Hincmar made caustic comment: "Then was fulfilled the saying of the prophet: *Thou who spoilest, shalt not thou thyself also be spoiled?*"

And now there descended on the head of this king of France the bitter harvest of his crowning by the Pope. In letter after letter John VIII implored his aid, his presence in Italy, for the warding off of imminent peril to the Holy See. In November 876 he wrote: "All the timber of all the trees in the forest, were it made into living tongues that speak, could not tell what I suffer from the Saracens! Cities, fortresses, estates, are deserted, lying in ruins; bishops are scattered here and there." In February of 877: "Everything outside our walls lies in one sheer waste of solitude and desolation. Nothing now remains for us except—God avert it!—the destruction of our City." In May: "The Church of Rome beseeches you to come to her rescue. We have no hope, no refuge, save in you."

Charles had been very ill through an attack of pleurisy. The pirate raids upon his shores were increasing. Nevertheless, he felt obliged to go, and in this same month he turned to prepare himself and his kingdom. At Compiègne he sent out command that bishops of dioceses and abbots of monasteries should all and each contribute a stated quota toward the sum—and it was huge—which was to be paid to the pirates on the Seine as an inducement to retreat. At Quierzy, in mid-June, he appointed his young heir, Louis the Stammerer, as ruler during his absence; counselors were chosen for his guidance. But not the archbishop of Reims! He was merely to take care of the royal charities and the royal treasure of books.

Then the king went off once more across the Alps. Pope John embraced him fervently at Vercelli and traveled with him to Pavia, where they heard that Carloman, king of Bavaria, was advancing against Charles with a vast army. On they hurried to Tortona, where Charles expected the leaders among his nobles to meet him: Hugh, his cousin, abbot of Saint-Martin of Tours and count of Anjou; Boso, his brother-in-law, whom he himself had made count of Vienne, duke of Lombardy, and chancellor of his Court; and Bernard, count of Auvergne.

They did not come. Anger had again risen in France. Rebellion would not allow these nobles to follow a ruler who would not stay at home to defend his land, but went on campaign to fight the Saracens. Charles waited a while. At last Carloman was almost upon him. The Pope in despair fled back to St. Peter's, and the king turned more slowly, for he was still suffering from pleurisy, to the road of retreat to France.

His sickness grew steadily worse. He was carried in a litter through the Pass of Mont-Cenis; and a short distance beyond it, in a shepherd's hut, he died among the mountains. It was October 6, 877. Hincmar reported a story which told that the direct cause of the king's death was a draught of poison, given him by his Jewish doctor Zedekiah, "a man whom he loved too well," in an ignorant attempt to free him from his fever.

6

There is another story, also recorded as coming from Hincmar himself, of a vision seen by one Bernold of the diocese of Reims in his last hours on earth. To him, he told the priest by his bedside, it had been given to behold in the other world men whom he had known in this life, now enduring torment for their sins. Among them was King Charles the Bald, a gaunt and wasted figure, lying in filth and devoured by vermin. "Go to Hincmar, the bishop," implored this unhappy soul, "and tell him that I suffer these pains here because on earth I did not listen to him and to others of my faithful counselors. Tell him that I always had faith in him; and beg him to help me now that I may be delivered from this punishment. Gladly would I go yonder to the place of the saints who walk in Paradise."

Bernold hastened back to earth—as it seemed to him in the vision—and there he found Hincmar with his clergy ready and vested at the altar for mass. Quickly he told the archbishop of his king's petition. Then, as his story went: "I journeyed once more to the place where the Lord Charles had been lying, and I found him in the place of light, whole and sound of body and clothed in royal state. 'See you,' said he to Bernold, 'what your mission has done for me!' "

The story would have made pleasant hearing for Hincmar. At the same time, when we come down to earth, it would be foolish to believe that the news of his king's departing was altogether tragic to him at this moment. Charles the Bald of late years had failed him. It had now become his duty to try to teach the son and heir of Charles to do his utmost for his country. On December 8, 877, he crowned him king at Compiègne. Once more the archbishop of Reims was a man of high power in the Court of his king.

We still have the instructions which he wrote for this Louis the Stammerer. He proposed to the new ruler a hard and indeed impossible task: to redeem a land exhausted by ravages and raids, its treasures squandered, its justice and judgment withered and dead, its boldness lost both in will and in word.

Louis did obey his archbishop's bidding to stay at home and to think upon home problems. When we find him engaged in business of another country, it is for the Pope. John VIII had long tried in every way, possible or impossible, to stem the advance of the Saracens. He had launched sentence of excommunication against two Italian nobles who had been treacherously working with the enemy. He had accepted the unwelcome proposal of young Carloman of Bavaria, already in October 877 acclaimed at Pavia ruler over Italy, that he receive coronation at the Pope's hands in Rome as Emperor in succession to his uncle, Charles the Bald. He had been eagerly anticipating aid from Carloman in return for this promised grace. But to no purpose had he hoped. Word had come that the young king of Bavaria was seriously ill and had been obliged to return home to Germany, neither crowned Emperor nor rescuer of the Holy See.

As a last measure of hope John VIII set out for France. Perhaps by his own presence he might compel the son of Charles the Bald to follow his father's example and to journey to Rome for Italy's defense.

He gained nothing. Louis the Stammerer also was ill, and Hincmar was with him when, at Troyes in August 878, they joined bishops and nobles of France assembled to hear the Pope. He spoke to no purpose, and finally he went back to Italy as forlorn and desperate as before. Only one person found comfort in this Council, and he, strangely enough, was Hincmar's nephew, once bishop of Laon. Friends brought him before it, and with the Pope's consent it was voted that he should receive part of the revenues of Laon's diocese for his support. Somehow he contrived to deliver before the Pope another ringing accusation of his uncle. No doubt Hincmar the elder forgave him, since he was now in great poverty. He was blind, for an enemy had struck out his eyes; he had lived long in exile, in prison, and there was no question of his restoration to Laon. One Hedenulf had been appointed its bishop in 876, and was unhappy enough in his office. He wanted to enter a monastery; but he asked in vain.

The one deed of benefit to his state which Louis the Stammerer managed to carry out during his brief rule was a meeting for conference at Fouron, near Aachen, on November 1, 878, with his cousin of Germany, Louis the Younger. Here may be seen the force of Hincmar's influence, in this welcome approach to friendship and union. The two kings discussed plans for a peaceful settlement of the problems of Lotharingia and of Italy. So hopeful did this talk seem to them that they decided to meet again, in February 879, and to ask Carloman of Bavaria and Charles the Fat, brothers of Louis the Younger, to share their debate.

Such a conference between the four rulers of France and Germany, Hincmar must have hoped, might bring forth great result. But in February 879, both Carloman of Germany and Louis the Stammerer were too ill to travel, and on April 10, the people of France heard that their king was dead.

Louis the Stammerer had done little enough; but his death gave men cause for thought. Who was to be crowned Emperor at Rome? And who was to reign at Pavia for the protection of that land? Who was to rule and to defend France in this critical year of 879?

Its late king had left two sons: Louis, about sixteen years old, and Carloman, thirteen or fourteen. (It is unfortunate that they hold the same names as their cousins of Germany, but we will try to keep their story clear.) Their father, the Stammerer, had broken his union with their mother and had married another woman; therefore, by many they were declared illegitimate. At once a civil war broke out in regard to the succession. Abbot Hugh of Tours led a strong party of those who, with Archbishop Hincmar, supported the claim of the elder boy, Louis; others seized upon the rumor of illegality or the fact of the heir's youthful years and sent to invite Louis the Younger, king in Germany, to assume rule over France.

He accepted the offer and, as Hincmar recorded, "he invaded the land; his army did more harm to it than even the heathen Danes were doing in their raids." Abbot Hugh sought safety in a bribe. Would the king accept that part of Lotharingia which in 870 had been assigned to France, and would he then return in peace to his own German realm?

Louis the Younger would and did; and the friends of Louis the Stammerer promptly hurried both his young sons to the abbey of Ferrières-en-Gâtinais, once ruled by Abbot Lupus. In its church Ansegis, archbishop of Sens, crowned them both joint kings of France, with the titles of Louis III and Carloman. So far, so good, men said. But to Hincmar's mind it was hard that the share of Lotharingia which he had aided their grandfather, Charles the Bald, to gain, should now be torn from France to make a German borderland.

It was not the last tearing apart. In this same year, 879, that Duke Boso whom Pope John so greatly admired and trusted, whom Charles the Bald as his brother-in-law had so highly honored, proved himself a traitor and a usurper. On October 15, at Mantaille near Vienne, he was elected king of Provence by archbishops, bishops, and nobles of southern France. Hincmar in his *Annals* made dry comment: "Boso's wife said that she could not bear to live if she, a daughter of the Emperor Louis, once king of Italy, could not see her husband gain a throne. As for the bishops who anointed and crowned Boso, they were partly pushed to it by threats, partly drawn by promises of abbeys and estates."

Good, however, came out of evil. Against the dangers which threatened each or all—whether from Scandinavian pirates, or from Slavic barbarians, or from rebels among their own people, or from Duke Boso—the royal Carolingian cousins now decided to work as one united clan. Carloman, king of Bavaria, died in March 880; his brother, Louis the Younger, was sick and forbidden to move by his doctors. But three of them, Louis III and Carloman, of France, and Charles the Fat, of Germany, met in June 880 at

Gondreville, where they agreed to join their forces in the autumn for the besieging of Boso's fortified city of Vienne.

The day arrived. Charles the Fat entered upon the siege with his kinsmen, but he did not stay to see its end. Pope John had been appealing to him, and he had already spent the winter of 879–80 in Rome, talking things over in the Lateran Palace. Now, late in 880, he slipped off again across the Alps. In St. Peter's, early in February 881, the Pope crowned him as Emperor.

For some time Hincmar, in his endeavor to support two very young kings of France, and faced by many other problems, had been directing his thought very earnestly toward this Charles the Fat. Now that a new friendship seemed to be rising between France and Germany, was it not possible that Charles, who was stronger in health and far more energetic in mind than his brother, Louis the Younger, might take the young kings under his care? Perhaps he might even adopt one of them, bring him up as heir of all or part of his rule? He had no son of his own. That would bring the ideal of a united Carolingian state far nearer reality. In 881 the archbishop ventured to write to Charles on the matter.

7

Unfortunately for his hopes, Hincmar was to find deep disappointment in the elder of the two youths, Louis III. Unlike his father, Louis would not listen to serious advice. He liked to talk with those who flattered and made much of him; he liked to choose his own way, in politics and in administration, as in lighter things. For a while the archbishop was patient. Then in 881 matters reached a crisis. Odo, bishop of Beauvais, had died, and it was necessary to elect his successor. As was the rule, the clergy and people of that diocese, which was in Hincmar's own province of Reims, were ordered to name their candidate by free and individual vote. In a Council of bishops of the province of Reims, held at Fismes, near Reims, on April 2, two candidates, thus proposed by the clergy and people of the diocese of Beauvais, were rejected as unworthy. The election now passed, as was also the rule in such case, to bishops of neighboring sees, acting under the leadership of Hincmar. These in due course elected a candidate, who was approved by Hincmar. Promptly his name was sent for confirmation by the king, Louis III. France by this time had been divided between the two royal youths into two spheres of rule, one for Louis, the other for Carloman, and the see of Beauvais was in the realm of Louis. He entirely refused to confirm the election, and at once declared his will that one Odacer be consecrated for Beauvais.

This was placing the authority of a king in matters spiritual before that of the Church, a proceeding entirely opposed to the principle which had been growing in power since the days of Louis the Pious. To Louis III the archbishop of Reims, long past his seventieth year and struggling with many burdens of office and with frequent sickness, now wrote in all the fury of his earlier life: "It is the Spirit of evil, that serpent of Paradise, who has hissed into your ears the name of that man whom you desire, encouraged by those fools and knaves who say soft words to you! Your decree regarding Odacer comes neither from Catholic source nor from Christian king, but is vomited forth from hell. Do men say that the ruling of bishops lies in your power? Their words come straight from Satan! You have written to me that if I submit to your will in this matter, you will honour in all things those near and dear to me. Here is my answer: I elect no one, I recognize no one, I receive no one as bishop, who does not enter upon his ministry through the keys of the Church!"

Odacer finally was excommunicated as an "intruder and aggressor" within the province of Reims; and it was Hincmar who as its head announced the sentence to all concerned.

Without doubt young Louis III resented that dominant will which, after thirty-six years of work at Reims, still burned within Hincmar. The king did not lack courage to defend his own. Ever since he had been crowned, the Danish pirates had been building up, higher and higher, the now uncontrollable terror of their presence in Belgium and the Netherlands. The annalist of Saint-Vaast in Arras has described the scene:

"Everywhere between the Scheldt and the Somme and across the Scheldt monks, canons, nuns, of every age and condition, fled with the relics of their saints. The Danes spared no one and nothing, not even the old and the ancient, but destroyed all by fire and the sword. From their winter camp at Courtrai in 880 they assailed the people of Flanders. In December they burned Cambrai; in February, 881, they were stripping the great abbey of Saint-Riquier near Amiens; then they fell upon Amiens itself and the cloister of Corbie, with no man to stop or stay them."

"Meanwhile," the story continues, "King Louis was sorely distressed, seeing the destruction of his realm. In July he gathered his army and marched to battle. In August he met the Northmen and fought them at Saucourt, near Abbeville. They fled, and he pursued them in a most splendid triumph. Some of the Danes who had escaped carried word of the slaughter of their men to the Danish camp, and from that day the Northmen began to fear the young king." The song, *Das Ludwigslied*, which afterward told of the victory, was known far and wide; it is in print today. But as for Hincmar, he held the success of Louis in contempt.

8

In January of the following year, 882, came the death of Louis the Younger of Germany, and, in August, of Louis III himself, this willful but valiant young king of France. Hincmar told only the bare facts: that he fell ill at Tours while on campaign against the Northmen, that he was carried to the abbey of Saint-Denis, outside Paris, and that he died and was buried there. It was Saint-Vaast again which gave out the story, a story which Hincmar scorned to tell:

"King Louis marched in the direction of the Loire to drive out the Northmen from his realm and to make Haesten, the Danish leader, his friend; and this he did. But because he was young, he rode in pursuit of a girl, daughter of one Germund, and followed her to her father's house, laughing in his sport. As he leaned to catch her, he fell, hitting badly his shoulder against the doorpost and breaking his breastbone upon his horse's saddle."

These two deaths left Charles the Fat Emperor and sole king of Germany; and Carloman, younger brother of Louis III and now about seventeen years old, sole king of France.

With a great effort Hincmar roused his energy to new hope. Would Carloman redeem the losses and failures of the past? The old archbishop searched in his library at Reims and brought out a book which he had always kept, its faded rolls still bearing the lessons taught him by that "old man and wise" when he was a young student in the Court of Aachen. It was the *De Ordine Palatii*, "On the Administration and Order observed in the Palace," compiled by Adalard, abbot of Corbie; and from this Hincmar now pictured an ideal for Carloman, with much of his own thought on the fulfilling of royal function by the king. "Three things," he wrote, "are needful for a king if he will maintain his rule: the fear which he inspires in his subjects; the firm and vigorous control of his administration and governing; the love which his people give to him as their lord. Above all, let the king, guided and taught by the bishops of the Church, by his power and with his protecting lead on his people to fulfill their part, one and all, in the realizing on earth of a truly Christian State."

But the tide of pirate invasion grew in strength and steadily advanced. Already Cologne and Bonn and Trier and the Palace of Aachen had fallen to the Danes. In the royal chapel of Charles the Great their horses had munched their hay. Already Charles the Fat, Emperor and king of Germany, had broken the hope of Hincmar that he might protect his cousin Carloman of France. He had marched to attack the Danish camp Elsloo near the Meuse, northeast of Aachen, and there, as Hincmar told, "his heart failed him," and he made peace with Godfred, their chieftain, who gave his submission to Christian baptism in return for the gift of wide regions in Frisia of the Netherlands.

We come now to the last records in Hincmar's *Annals*, which he wrote until the end of his life. Now the pirates marched into his own province, to Laon, to Soissons, burning and ravaging as always; now, men cried, they were approaching Reims itself. By night the archbishop fled from his city, too old and infirm to walk, but carried in a litter with the relics of his patron Saint, Remigius, and the treasures of his cathedral. His clergy and monks ran for their lives wherever they could. With great difficulty and barely escaping, Hincmar crossed the Marne and reached Épernay, some fifteen miles to the southeast. Reims was saved. History tells that its defense was largely due to the courage of Hugh the Abbot and his king, Carloman. Hincmar believed that it was due to God and His saints, without the work of man, and that his belief reflected more glory on his cathedral seat.

At Épernay he died, according to Flodoard, who in the tenth century wrote a *History of the Church of Reims.* Tradition has given the day of his death as December 21, 882. Even in his last hours he sent out from his refuge one final word of warning and exhortation to the powers in whose hands lay the life of France, its nation, and its Church.

Hincmar of Reims was a great man, although he was not a lovable one. In his letters and his *Annals,* he stands out as cold, never an intimate friend in the human sense of a Walafrid, a Lupus, an Einhard. He could not, like them, forget himself in his thought for his fellow men. At times his honesty lies under shadow, for his statesman's craft was always at work, and often with cunning skill. If he did not love warmly, he hated bitterly, nor did he hesitate to declare his hatred. But none labored as he labored, with unceasing desire and amid every obstacle, for that ideal of law and government which he had learned in the early years of this ninth century.

His death came in a timely hour. He did not hear of the murder of Pope John VIII at Rome in December 882; of the death of his king, Carloman, in December 884; of the long and savage siege of Paris by the Northern pirates in 885–86. Nor did he live to see the Emperor Charles the Fat deposed by his own nobles in 887 and dying, if not murdered as some said, in exile, in January 888.

9

The Frankish Empire built up by Charles the Great had come to an end. A mere shadow lingered for a while, soon to fade away. Against this year, 888, Regino, abbot of Prüm near Trier, mournfully recorded in his *Chronicle* that "the realms of the Franks would have brought forth many princes worthy of rule, had not their fortune, in striving after deeds of glory one against another, armed them for their destruction, one and all."

There were many other reasons for the Empire's fall. There was, as his son, Louis the Pious, well realized, the loss of the controlling power and personality of Charles the Great himself. There was a growth, an expansion, too sudden and spread too widely, to allow due settlement in harmony. There were new nations, only in time to be brought into accord, nations which spoke each its own language and desired each its independence of aliens. Pirate invaders—in France the Scandinavians, in Germany the Slavs, in Italy the Saracens—brought an ever-present problem which no ruler was able to solve. There were the nobles of France and Germany, hungry for wealth and land, even for a throne; there were the peasants, hungry for food. There was the relation, of submission or of authority, that changed again and again during this ninth century between the Church and the state.

Finally, we should not forget the thought of Heinrich Fichtenau ° : "The whole Frankish Empire stands, it is true, as the first great conception of the young Europe, as a draft for the future. In itself it was fated to fall, not only through the hastiness and superficiality of its creation, but still more through the immaturity of the men who made it: men to whom it was not given to combine the necessity of law with liberty."

° Translated from *Das karolingische Imperium*, page 203.

The Carolingian Line

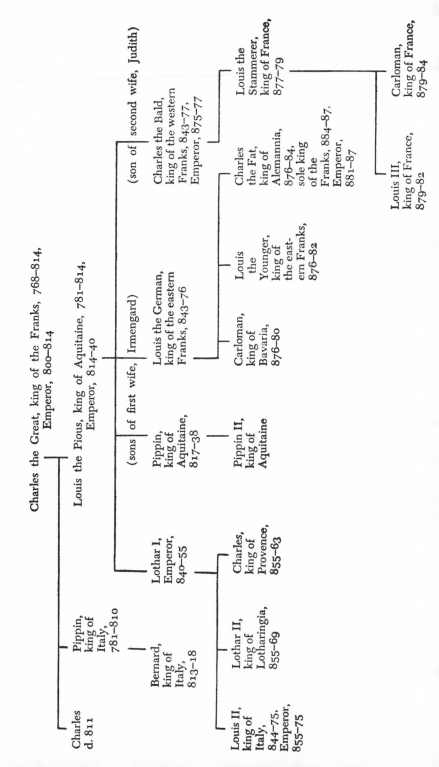

Popes During the Carolingian Empire

795–816	Leo III
816–17	Stephen IV
817–24	Paschal I
824–27	Eugenius II
827–44	Gregory IV
844–47	Sergius II
847–55	Leo IV
855–58	Benedict III
858–67	Nicholas I
867–72	Hadrian II
872–82	John VIII
882–84	Marinus I
884–85	Hadrian III
885–91	Stephen V

Table of Dates

Dates	Events in Frankish history	Einhard	Amalar	Walafrid	Lupus	Hincmar
800	Crowning of Charles the Great as Emperor in the West by Pope Leo III at Rome.		*c.796(?)* Studying under Alcuin.			
806	*Divisio Imperii.*			*c.808–9* Born in Alemannia.	*c.805* Born in northeast France.	*c. 806* Born, probably in northern France.
			c.809–14. Archbishop of Trier.			
812	Constantinople recognizes Charles as Emperor in the West.				*c.812–29* Pupil at abbey of Ferrières.	
813	Charles crowns his son Louis as co-Emperor.		*813–14* Envoy of Charles, the Emperor in the West, to Constantinople.			
814	Death of Charles the Great. Louis the Pious becomes king of the Franks and Emperor in the West.	*815* Receives from Louis the village of Mülinheim (Seligenstadt).	*814–831* Engaged in study of liturgical words and symbolic interpretation.			*c.814–22* Pupil of Hilduin at abbey of Saint-Denis.
		815 onward Rules various monasteries as lay abbot.				
816	Crowning of Louis by Pope Stephen IV. Ebbo becomes archbishop of Reims.			*c.816–26* Pupil at abbey of Reichenau.		*816* Note Ebbo, under *Events.*

Table of Dates (continued)

Dates	Events in Frankish history	Einhard	Amalar	Walafrid	Lupus	Hincmar
817	Ordinatio Imperii.					
817–18	Revolt and death of Bernard, king of Italy. Penitence of Louis at Attigny.					
822						822–c.829 At Court of Aachen, studying under Hilduin and Adalard.
823	Birth of Charles the Bald, son of Louis and his second wife, Judith.		c.823 First edition of his Liber Officialis.			
824	Constitutio Romana.					
		827–28 Quest for relics for his church at Mülinheim (Seligenstadt).		c.826 Writes Vision of Wettin. 826–29 Student at Fulda.	c.828–36 Student at Fulda.	
829	Assembly of Worms causes resentment against Louis the Pious. Synod of Mainz releases Gottschalk from Fulda.			829–38 At Aachen as tutor of Charles the Bald.		
830	Rebellion of sons and subjects of Louis the Pious.	830–40 In retreat at Seligenstadt. c.830–36? Writes his Vita Caroli.			c.830–36 Corresponds from Fulda by letters with Einhard.	830–31 Accompanies Hilduin into exile, but soon returns to Saint-Denis.

Dates	Events in Frankish history	Einhard	Amalar	Walafrid	Lupus	Hincmar
831	*Divisio Imperii.*		831 At Rome as envoy of Louis the Pious.			*c.832–44* In service of the Frankish Church and state.
833–34	Second rebellion of sons and subjects of Louis the Pious.		831–35 Compiling of *Antiphonary* and of 3rd edition of the *Liber Officialis* (831–33).			
833	Second penitence of Louis and his deposition.					
834–35	Restoration of the Emperor Louis the Pious.					
835	Synod of Thionville. Banishment of Ebbo, archbishop of Reims, and of Agobard, archbishop of Lyons.		835 Synod of Thionville accepts his *Liber Officialis* and appoints him acting archbishop of Lyons.			Note Ebbo and Reims, under *Events.*
835–40	See of Reims vacant.	836 Death of his wife, Imma. Corresponds with Lupus. Writes his *On the Adoration of the Cross.*			836–c.862 In residence at Ferrières; occasional journeys and missions of state.	
837	Assembly of Aachen; lands given to Charles the Bald.					

Table of Dates (continued)

Dates	Events in Frankish history	Einhard	Amalar	Walafrid	Lupus	Hincmar
838	Council of Quierzy.		838 Condemned for heresy and dismissed from Lyons. 838–c.850 In retirement.	838 Elected abbot of Reichenau.		
839	Assembly of Worms. Division of Frankish Empire between Lothar I and Charles the Bald.				839 Writes Life of St. Maximin.	
840	Death of Louis the Pious. Lothar I, now Emperor, invades realm of Charles the Bald.	840 Death of Einhard.		840–42 In exile from Reichenau.	840 Elected abbot of Ferrières.	
840–41	840 Ebbo is restored by Lothar I as archbishop of Reims; but abandons Reims in 841. 841–45 See of Reims vacant.					Note Ebbo, under Events.
841	Battle of Fontenoy.					
842	Oaths of Strasbourg.			842 Restored as abbot of Reichenau.		
843	Treaty of Verdun.					

Dates	Events in Frankish history	Amalar	Walafrid	Lupus	Hincmar
844	Conferences of Yütz and of Ver.			844 Captured while with army of Charles the Bald in Aquitaine; freed within a short time. 844–45 Envoy to Burgundy.	845 Elected and consecrated archbishop of Reims. At Council of Meaux (845) suspends clerics ordained by Ebbo at Reims 840–41. 848 Note Gottschalk, under *Events*.
845 847	Synod of Beauvais. Defeat of Charles by Bretons at Ballon. First Conference of Meersen.				
848 848–62	Council of Mainz condemns Gottschalk. Constant raids by Vikings within lands of Charles the Bald.				
849	Charles fighting against Aquitaine and Brittany. Council of Quierzy condemns Gottschalk again.	c.849 Writes in aid of Hincmar against Gottschalk.	849 Death of Walafrid.		849–c.866 Holds Gottschalk prisoner in abbey of Hautvillers. 849 Writes his *Opus I on Predestination* (against Gottschalk).

Table of Dates (continued)

Date	Events in Frankish history	Amalar	Lupus	Hincmar
850	Campaign against Brittany.	c.850 Death of Amalar.	850 Censures Nominoë, Breton chieftain. c.850 Writings on predestination.	
851				851 Death of Ebbo, formerly archbishop of Reims.
853	Council of Soissons.		853–62 Peril of abbey of Ferrières through raids of Viking pirates.	853 Approves at Soissons the deposing of clerics ordained by Ebbo during his restoration to Reims, 840–41. Pope Leo IV refuses to confirm this act.
855				855 Writes for third time to this Pope to ask for the confirmation. The next Pope, Benedict III, confirms the deposition.
856				856 Marries Judith, daughter of Charles the Bald, to Ethelwulf, king of Wessex.
857	857–69 Lothar II of Lotharingia seeks divorce from his wife, Theutberga.			857–65 Contest with Rothad, bishop of Soissons. 857 Opus II on Predestination (against Gottschalk).

Dates	Events in Frankish history	Lupus	Hincmar
858	Invasion of the kingdom of Charles the Bald by Louis the German. Northern Vikings encamped on the Seine.	Ferrières in danger.	858–59 Defies Louis the German and rescues realm of Charles the Bald.
859	Synod of Savonnières.		859–60 *Opus III on Predestination* (against Gottschalk).
860	Treaty of Coblenz. Synods I and II of Aachen discuss question of divorce for Lothar II.		860 Restores by his leadership peace between Carolingian princes.
			860–69 Fights against a divorce for Lothar II.
			860 Writes his *De Divortio*; gains general consent regarding conflict on predestination, at Council of Tusey.
861			861 Begins recording of *Annals of Saint-Bertin*.
862	Synod III of Aachen permits Lothar II to marry Waldrada. He promptly makes her his queen.	*c. 862* Death of Lupus.	862–65 Struggle continues against Rothad, bishop of Soissons.
			862 Rededicates his cathedral of Reims, restored and enlarged.
863	Synod of Metz declares Waldrada lawful wife of Lothar II.		863 Hincmar absent from Synod of Metz.

Table of Dates (continued)

Dates	Events in Frankish history	Hincmar
865	Papal legate, in France, restores Theutberga as wife and queen of Lothar II.	
866	Synod of Soissons.	866–67 Struggle against Wulfad, cleric ordained by Ebbo. c.866 Death of Gottschalk at Hautvillers.
867	Council of Troyes.	
868		868 Writes four "Expositions" in defense of clergy.
869	Death of Lothar II of Lotharingia.	869 Crowns Charles the Bald as king of Lotharingia.
870	Division of Lotharingia between Charles the Bald and Louis the German.	
875	Death of Louis II, king of Italy and Emperor in the West. Charles the Bald is crowned Emperor at Rome by Pope John VIII. Rebellion in France, in realm of Charles.	871 At Douzy deposes Hincmar of Laon from his see. 875 For the second time saves France under invasion by Louis the German.
876	Council of Ponthion. Death of Louis the German. Charles the Bald invades Lotharingian territory of Louis and is defeated at the battle of Andernach.	876 Growing rift between Hincmar and his king, Charles the Bald. He writes *On the Law relating to Archbishops*.
877	Charles the Bald at Council of Quierzy arranges affairs of his kingdom before leaving again for Italy, called to the aid of Pope John VIII against the Saracens. Further rebellion in France. Charles fails in his mission, retreats, and dies while returning home. His son, Louis the Stammerer, succeeds as king of France.	
878	Pope John VIII calls Council at Troyes. Conference of Fouron.	Works hard for support of Louis the Stammerer and for unity between France and Germany and their kings.
879	Death of Louis the Stammerer. His two sons, Louis III and Carloman, succeed him as joint-kings of France. Growing hope for unity between France and Germany.	Endeavors to support the two young kings of France.

Dates	Events in Frankish history	Hincmar
881	Charles the Fat, son of Louis the German, is crowned Emperor at Rome by Pope John VIII.	881 Struggle against his king, Louis III, for freedom of the Church.
881	Council of Fismes.	
881–82	Terror of Viking invasion.	
882	Charles the Fat sole king of Germany. Death of Louis III; Carloman sole king of France.	882 Writes *De Ordine Palatii* for the aid of his king, Carloman. Forced by pirate invasion to flee from Reims to Epernay. From there sends a last word to Carloman. Dies at Epernay.
884	Death of Carloman, king of France.	
887	Deposing of Charles the Fat, king of Germany and Emperor in the West, by his own nobles.	
888	Death of Charles the Fat in exile. End of the Carolingian Empire founded by Charles the Great.	

Sources (Selected), Primary and Secondary

Abbreviations

B E C : *Bibliothèque de l'École des Chartes*
Cap. I–II : *M G H* : *Capitularia Regum Francorum* I, ed. A. Boretius
    (1883); II, ed. A. Boretius and V. Krause (1897).
C E : *Catholic Encyclopedia*
Conc. II : *M G H* : *Concilia* II (*Concilia Aevi Karolini* I), i–ii, ed. A.
    Werminghoff (1906–1908).
D A C L : *Dictionnaire d'archéologie chrètienne et de liturgie*
D H G E : *Dictionnaire d'histoire et de géographie ecclésiastique*
D T C : *Dictionnaire de théologie catholique*
E C : *Enciclopedia cattolica*
Epp. : *M G H* : *Epistolae* III–VIII, i (*Epistolae Karolini Aevi* I–VI),
    ed. E. Dümmler and others.
L M A : *Le Moyen Âge*
M G H : *Monumenta Germaniae Historica*
Neues Archiv : *Neues Archiv der Gesellschaft für ältere Geschichtskunde*
P L : *Patrologia Latina*, ed. Migne
P L A C : *M G H* : *Poetae Latini Aevi Carolini*
R B : *Revue Bénédictine*
R B P H : *Revue belge de philologie et d' histoire*
R H : *Revue historique*
R T A M : *Recherches de théologie ancienne et médiévale*
S R G S : *M G H* : *Scriptores Rerum Germanicarum in usum scholarum*
S S : *M G H* : *Scriptores*, ed. G. H. Pertz and others.
S S R M : *M G H* : *Scriptores Rerum Merovingicarum*

Chapters I and II and General:

Agobard, Archbishop of Lyons. *Cartula de poenitentia ab imperatore acta,*
   833 : *Cap.* II, 56 f.
———. *Epistolae*, ed. E. Dümmler : *Epp.* V, 150 ff.
———. *Libri duo pro filiis et contra Judith uxorem Ludovici Pii*, ed. G.
   Waitz : SS XV, i, 274 ff.
Alcuini Vita, auctor anonymus, ed. W. Arndt : SS XV, i, 182 ff.
Amann, Émile. *L'époque carolingienne* : *Histoire de l'Église*, ed. A. Fliche
   and V. Martin, VI (1947).
Annales Bertiniani, ed. G. Waitz (1883) (*S R G S*).

Annales Fuldenses, ed. F. Kurze (1891) (*S R G S*).

Annales Mettenses primores, ed. B. de Simson (1905) (*S R G S*).

Annales regni Francorum, the "Royal Annals," Versions I and II, ed. F. Kurze (1895) (*S R G S*).

Annales Xantenses et Annales Vedastini, ed. B. de Simson (1909) (*S R G S*).

Ardo, *Vita Benedicti abbatis Anianensis*, ed. G. Waitz : SS XV, i, 198 ff.

Arquillière, H. X. *L'Augustinisme politique* (1934).

"Astronomer, The," *Vita Hludowici Imperatoris* : SS II, 604 ff.;*PL* CIV, 927 ff.; trans. Allen Cabaniss (1961).

Auerbach, Erich. *Literatursprache und Publikum in der lateinischen Spätantike und im Mittelalter* (1958).

Böhmer, J. F., and Mühlbacher, E. *Die Regesten des Kaiserreichs unter den Karolingern*, I, ed. J. Lechner (1908).

Bonnaud Delamare, Roger. *L'idée de paix à l'époque carolingienne* (1939).

Calmette, Joseph. *La Diplomatie carolingienne* (843–877) (1901).

———. *L'Effondrement d'un Empire et la Naissance d'une Europe* (1941).

———. *Charlemagne, Sa vie et son oeuvre* (1945).

Cambridge Medieval History, II, 1913; III (1922).

Cambridge Medieval History, Shorter, I, by C. W. Previté-Orton, ed. Philip Grierson (1952).

Chronicon Moissiacense : SS I, 280 ff.

Codex Carolinus, ed. Ph. Jaffé, *Bibliotheca Rerum Germanicarum*, IV (1867), 1 ff.; ed. W. Gundlach, *Epp.* III, 469 ff.

Daniel-Rops, H. *The Church in the Dark Ages*, trans. A. Butler (1959).

Dawson, Christopher. *The Making of Europe* (1932).

Deanesly, Margaret. *A History of Early Medieval Europe* (476–911) (1956).

Divisio Imperii, 839 : *Cap. II*, 58.

Divisio Regnorum, 806 : *Cap. I*, 126 ff.

Ebbonis Remensis archiepiscopi Resignatio, 835 : *Cap.* II, 57 f.; *Conc.* II, ii, 696 ff.

Ebert, Adolf. *Allgemeine Geschichte der Literatur des Mittelalters im Abendlande*, II (1880).

Eigil. *Vita S. Sturmi abbatis Fuldensis* : SS II, 365 ff.

Episcoporum ad Hludowicum Imperatorem Relatio, 829 : *Cap.* II, 26 ff.

Episcoporum de poenitentia quam Hludowicus Imperator professus est, Relatio Compendiensis, 833 : *Cap.* II, 51 ff.

Ermoldus Nigellus. *In honorem Hludowici Caesaris Augusti Elegiacum Carmen*, ed. E. Dümmler: *P L A C* II, 1 ff.; ed. and trans. (French) E. Faral (1932).

Fichtenau, Heinrich. *Das karolingische Imperium* (1949); English trans. of the greater part by Peter Munz (1957).

Ganshof, François L. "La fin du règne de Charlemagne. Une décomposition" : *Zeitschrift für schweizerische Geschichte*, XXVIII (1948), 433 ff.

────. *The Imperial Coronation of Charlemagne : theories and facts* (1949).

────. "Observations sur l'Ordinatio Imperii de 817" : *Festschrift Guido Kisch* (1955).

────. "Louis the Pious Reconsidered": *History*, XLII (1957), 171 ff.

Halphen, Louis. *La pénitence de Louis le Pieux à Saint-Médard de Soissons* : *Bibliothèque de la Faculté des Lettres de Paris*, fasc. XVIII (1904), 177 ff.

────. *Études critiques sur l'histoire de Charlemagne* (1921);

────. "L'idée d'État sous les Carolingiens" : *R H* CLXXXV (1939), 59 ff.

────. *Charlemagne et l'Empire carolingien* (1947).

────. *A travers l'histoire du Moyen Age* (1950) (containing studies previously published and of value for this period).

Hauck, Albert. *Kirchengeschichte Deutschlands im Mittelalter*, II (neunte, unveränderte Auflage) (1958).

Hefele, J., and Leclercq, H. *Histoire des Conciles*, IV, i–ii (1911).

Himly, Auguste. *Wala et Louis le Débonnaire* (1849).

Kendrick, T. D. *A History of the Vikings* (1930).

Kleinclausz, Arthur. *L'Empire carolingien* (1902).

────. *Charlemagne* (1934).

────. *Alcuin* (1948).

Laistner, M. L. W. *Thought and Letters in Western Europe A.D. 500 to 900* (2d. ed.; 1957).

Levison, Wilhelm. *England and the Continent in the Eighth Century* (1946).

Liber Pontificalis, ed. Louis Duchesne, I–II (1886–92); III (1957).

Liber Traditionum sancti Petri Blandiniensis, ed. A. Fayen (1906).

Lot, Ferdinand, and Ganshof, François L. *Histoire du Moyen Age*, I : *Les Destinées de l'Empire en Occident de 395 à 888* : ii, *De 768 à 888* (1941).

Manitius, Max. *Geschichte der lateinischen Literatur des Mittelalters*, I (1911).

Mansi, G. D. *Sacrorum Conciliorum nova et amplissima Collectio*, XIV–XVII (1769–72).

Moss, H. St. L. B. *The Birth of the Middle Ages, 395–814* (1935).

Nithard. *Historiarum Libri IV* : SS II, 649 ff.; ed. E. Müller (1907) : (*S R G S*); ed. and trans. (French) Ph. Lauer (1926).

Ohnsorge, Werner. *Das Zweikaiserproblem im früheren Mittelalter* (1947).

Ordinatio Imperii, 817 : *Cap.* I, 270 ff.

Ostrogorsky, George. *History of the Byzantine State*, trans. Joan Hussey (1956).

Painter, Sidney. *A History of the Middle Ages* (1953).

Paschasius Radbert. *Vita Adalhardi abbatis Corbeiensis*, ed. (excerpts) : SS II, 524 ff.

————. *Vita Walae* (*Epitaphium Arsenii*), ed. *PL* CXX, 1557 ff.; SS II (excerpts), 533 ff.

Regino Prumiensis. *Chronicon*, ed. F. Kurze (1890) (*S R G S*).
Regni Divisio, 831 : *Cap.* II, 20 ff.

Schieffer, Theodor. "Die Krise des karolingischen Imperiums," *Aus Mittelalter und Neuzeit* (1957), 1 ff.

Schramm, Percy E. "Die Anerkennung Karls des Grossen als Kaiser," *Historische Zeitschrift*, CLXXII (1951), 449 ff.

Simson, Bernhard. *Jahrbücher des fränkischen Reichs unter Ludwig dem Frommen*, I–II (1874–76).

Sullivan, Richard. *Heirs of the Roman Empire* (1960).

Thegan. *Vita Hludowici Imperatoris* : SS II, 585 ff.; *PL* CVI, 405 ff.

Wallace-Hadrill, J. M. *The Barbarian West, 400–1000* (1952).

Wallach, Luitpold. *Alcuin and Charlemagne* : *Studies in Carolingian History and Literature* (1959).

Wattenbach, W. *Deutschlands Geschichtsquellen im Mittelalter;* Heft II, bearbeitet von W. Levison und H. Löwe (1953); Heft III, bearbeitet von H. Löwe, (1957).

Winston, Richard. *Charlemagne* (1954).

Chapter III

Alcuin. *Carmina*, ed. E. Dümmler, Nos. XXVI, XXX, 2 : *P L A C* I, 245 f., 248.

————. *Epistolae*, ed. E. Dümmler, No. 172 : *Epp.* IV, 285.

Annales de Saint-Pierre de Gand et de Saint-Amand, ed. Philip Grierson (1937).

Bondois, Marguerite. *La Translation des saints Marcellin et Pierre* : *Étude sur Einhard et sa vie politique de 827 à 834* (1907).

Buchner, Max. *Einhard als Künstler* (1919).

Dronke. *Codex diplomaticus Fuldensis* (1850).

Einhard. *Epistolae*, ed. K. Hampe : *Epp.* V, 105 ff.

————. *Quaestio de adoranda cruce* : *ibid.* 146 ff.

————. *Translatio et Miracula SS. Marcellini et Petri*, ed. G. Waitz : SS XV, i, 238 ff. (cf. *ibid.* 329; 391 ff.).

————. *Vita Karoli Magni Imperatoris* : ed. O. Holder-Egger (1911) (*S R G S*); ed. H. W. Garrod and R. B. Mowat (1915); ed. and trans. (French) Louis Halphen (1923).

————. *Early Lives of Charlemagne, by Eginhard and the Monk of St. Gall*, trans. (English) A. J. Grant (1922).

————. *The History of the Translation of the Blessed Martyrs of Christ, Marcellinus and Peter*, trans. (English) Barrett Wendell (1926).

————. *Einhardi omnia quae exstant Opera*, ed. and trans. (French) A. Teulet, I–II (1840–43).

————. *Les Oeuvres d'Éginhard*, trans. (French) A. Teulet (1856).

Fichtenau, Heinrich. *Zum Reliquienwesen im früheren Mittelalter* : *Mit-*

CAROLINGIAN PORTRAITS

teilungen des Instituts für österreichische Geschichtsforschung, LX
(1952), 60 ff.

Folz, R. *L'idée d'empire en Occident du Ve au XIVe siècle* (1953).

Ganshof, François L. "Notes critiques sur Éginhard, biographe de Charlemagne" : *R B P H* III (1924–25), 725 ff.

———. "Éginhard à Gand" : *Bulletin de la Société d'histoire et d'archéologie de Gand* (1926);

———. "Éginhard, biographe de Charlemagne" : *Bibliothèque d'Humanisme et Renaissance*, XIII (1951), 217 ff.

Gesta abbatum Fontanellensium. ed. S. Löwenfeld (1886) (*S R G S*).

Grierson, Philip. "The Early Abbots of St. Peter's of Ghent" : *R B* XLVIII (1936), 129 ff.

Halphen, Louis. "Einhard, historien de Charlemagne" : *Études critiques* (1921), 60 ff. (See L. Levillain, *L M A* XXIV, 1922, 183 ff.)

Hampe, Karl. "Zur Lebensgeschichte Einhards" : *Neues Archiv*, XXI (1896), 599 ff.

Hinks, Roger. *Carolingian Art* (1935; Ann Arbor Paperback, 1962).

Hraban Maur. *Carmina*, ed. E. Dümmler, *Epitaphium Einhardi* : *P L A C* II, 237 ff.

Kleinclausz, Arthur. *Éginhard* (1942).

Lintzel, Martin. *Die Zeit der Entstehung von Einhards Vita Karoli* : *Historische Studien*, Heft 238 (1933), 22 ff.

Walafrid Strabo. *Carmina*, No. XXIII : *P L A C* II, 377.

Chapter IV

Adémar de Chabannes. *Chronique*, ed. Jules Chavanon (1897).

Agobard of Lyons. *Opera* : *PL* CIV, 29 ff.

———. *Epistolae*, ed. E. Dümmler: *Epp.* V, 150 ff.

Amalarius of Metz. *Opera liturgica omnia*, ed. J. M. Hanssens, S.J., I–III (1948–50) (*Studi e Testi*, 138–40).

———. *Opera* : *PL* CV, 985 ff.

———. *Epistolae*, ed. E. Dümmler: *Epp.* V, 240 ff.

———. *Versus Marini* : *P L A C* I, 426 ff. (cf. *P L A C* II, 694).

Apel, Willi. *Gregorian Chant* (1958).

Beeson, M. "Agobard" : *D H G E* I, 998 ff.

———. "Amalaire" : *ibid.* II, 922 f.

Bishop, Edmund. *Liturgica Historica* (1918).

Braun, Joseph, S.J. *Die liturgische Gewandung im Occident und Orient nach Ursprung und Entwicklung, Verwendung und Symbolik* (1907).

Cabaniss, J. Allen. "The Personality of Amalarius" : *Church History*, XX (1951), 34 ff.

——. "Agobard of Lyons" : *Speculum*, XXVI (1951), 50 ff.

—. "The Literary Style of Amalarius" : *Philological Quarterly*, XXXI ?), 423 ff.

————. *Amalarius of Metz* (1954).

————. *Florus of Lyons* : *Classica et Mediaevalia*, XIX (1958), 212 ff.

Chadwick, Owen. Review of Hanssens, ed. Amalarius : *Journal of Theological Studies*, New Series, II (1951), 211 ff.

Debroise, E. "Agobard" : *D A C L* I (1924), 971 ff.

————. "Amalaire" : *ibid.* 1323 ff.

Duchesne, Louis. *Christian Worship* (5th English ed.; 1919).

Ellard, Gerald, S.J. *Master Alcuin, Liturgist* (1956).

Florus of Lyons. *Opera* : *PL* CXIX, 71 ff.

————. *Epistolae*, ed. E. Dümmler: *Epp.* V, 206 ff., 267 ff. See also Hanssens, ed. *Amalarius*, II, 567 ff.

Franz, A. *Die Messe im deutschen Mittelalter* (1902).

Jungmann, Joseph. *The Mass of the Roman Rite*, trans. F. A. Brunner, revised by C. K. Riepe (1959).

Liber de Tribus Epistulis : *PL* CXXI, 985 ff.

Mönchemeier, R. *Amalar von Metz* (1893).

Moreau, E. de, S.J. "Les Explications allégoriques des Cérémonies de la Sainte Messe au Moyen Age" : *Nouvelle Revue Théologique*, XLVIII (1921), 123 ff.

Morin, Dom Germain. *R B* VII (1890), 65 f., 300 ff.; VIII (1891), 433 ff.; IX (1892), 337 ff.; XI (1894), 231 ff.; XVI (1899), 419 ff.; *D T C* I, 933 f.

Sahre, Rudolf. *Der liturgiker Amalarius* (1893).

Wilmart, Dom André. "Un lecteur ennemi d'Amalaire" : *R B* XXXVI (1924), 317 ff.

Young, Karl. *The Drama of the Medieval Church*, I–II (1933).

Note : Since 1612, when Père J. Sirmond, S.J. wrote his letter *De duobus Amalariis* (published in his *Opera Varia*, 1696, IV, 641–47), there has been argument on the question whether the history of Amalar belongs to one man or should be divided between two of this name: Amalar, of Metz or of Soissons, and Amalar, Archbishop of Trier. For a theory of two Amalars, see Mönchemeier, Sahre (who inclines toward Soissons), Franz, and Hauck. Scholars, however, in spite of difficulties of tradition, are now inclining toward a view of one Amalar; on this view see Morin, Hanssens, Manitius, Dümmler, Debroise, Cabaniss, and Laistner. It is this second view which I have followed here.

Chapter V

Anderson, A. O. *Early Sources of Scottish History*, I (1922), 263 ff.

Beyerle, Konrad (ed.). *Die Kultur der Abtei Reichenau*, I–II (1925).

Ghellinck, J. de, S.J. *Littérature latine au Moyen Age*, I (1939).

————. "Le développement du dogme d'après Walafrid Strabon à propos du baptême des enfants" : *Recherches de science religieuse*, XXIX (1939), 481 ff.

Gottschalk. *Carmina*, ed. L. Traube : *P L A C* III, 2, 707 ff.; ed. K. Strecker, *P L A C* IV, 2, ii, 934 ff.; ed. N. Fickermann, *P L A C* VI, i, 86 ff.

————. *Confessio* : *PL* CXXI, 347 ff.

————. *Confessio Prolixior* : *PL* CXXI, 349 ff. (See also Dom. C. Lambot and Dom. G. Morin among the writers listed under Chapters VII and VIII.

Lambert, R. S. (English trans.). *Hortulus or The Little Garden* (1923).

Leclerc, Henri. (French trans.). *Le Petit Jardin* (1933).

Madeja, E. "Aus Walafrid Strabos Lehrjahren" : *Studien und Mitteilungen zur Geschichte des Benediktinerordens*, XL (1919–20), 251 ff.

Nober, P. *Valafrido* : *E C* XII (1954), 961 ff.

Plath, Konrad. "Zur Enstehungsgeschichte der Visio Wettini des Walahfrid" : *Neues Archiv*, XVII (1892), 261 ff.

Raby, F. J. E. *A History of Christian-Latin Poetry* (2d ed.; 1953).

Sudhoff, K., Marzell, H., and Weil, E. Walahfrid, *Hortulus*, after the first edition of 1510, with commentaries (1926).

Walafrid Strabo. *Ad Karoli Magni Vitam Prologus* : ed. L. Halphen, *Éginhard, Vie de Charlemagne* (1923), 104 ff.

————. *Ad Thegani Vitam Hludowici Imperatoris Praefatio* : SS II, 589 f.

————. *Carmina*, ed. E. Dümmler : *P L A C* II, 259 ff.

————. *Commentaries on Exodus and Leviticus* (Abridgments of those by Hraban Maur), *Prefaces to* : *Epp.* V, 515 f.

————. *Libellus de exordiis et incrementis quarundam in observationibus ecclesiasticis rerum*, ed. V. Krause : *M G H Cap.* II, 473 ff.

————. *Vita S. Galli* (rewriting) : *Vita S. Galli Confessoris Triplex*, ed. B. Krusch : *S S R M* IV, 280 ff.; trans. Maud Joynt (1927).

————. *Vita S. Otmari abbatis Sangallensis* (rewriting) : SS II, 40 ff.

Note : Walafrid Strabo is no longer held by scholars as the author of the *Glossa Ordinaria*, a twelfth-century compilation, although some of his work may have been used in the compiling. On the *Glossa* see J. de Blic : *R T A M* XVI (1949), 5 ff.; H. H. Glunz, *History of the Vulgate in England from Alcuin to Roger Bacon* (1933), 103 ff.; H. Peltier, *D T C* XV, 2, 3498 ff.; B. Smalley, *R T A M* VII (1935), 235 ff.; VIII (1936), 24 ff.; IX (1937), 365 ff.; *Cambridge Historical Journal*, VI (1938), 103 ff.; *The Study of the Bible in the Middle Ages*, ed. 2 (1952), 56 ff.

Zeumer, Karl (ed.). *Formulae Augienses* : *Collectio C*, Nos. 8, 11, 25 (?) : *M G H Legum Sectio* V, 368–69 f., 376.

Chapter VI

Amann, É. "Loup Servat, abbé de Ferrières" : *D T C* IX, i (1926), 963 ff.

Beeson, C. H. *Lupus of Ferrières as a Scribe and Text Critic* : Medieval Academy of America, Publications No. 4 (1930).

Fontanellensis Chronici Fragmentum, 841–859 : SS II, 301 ff.

Halphen, Louis, and Lot, Ferdinand. *Le Règne de Charles le Chauve*, I, (840–51) (1909).

Hildegar, bishop of Meaux. *Vita S. Faronis*, ed. B. Krusch : *S S R M* V, 171 ff.

Levillain, L. "Étude sur les Lettres de Loup de Ferrières" : *B E C* : LXII (1901), 445 ff.; LXIII (1902), 69 ff., 289 ff., 537 ff.; LXIV (1903), 259 ff.

Levison, Wilhelm. "Eine Predigt des Lupus von Ferrières," *Aus rheinischer und fränkischer Frühzeit* (1948), 557 ff.

Lot, Ferdinand. "Une Année du Règne de Charles le Chauve : année 866" : *L M A*, 2e série VI (1902), 393 ff.

———. *Mélanges d'Histoire bretonne* (1907), 33 ff., 58 ff.

———. "La grande invasion normande de 856–862" : *B E C* LXIX (1908), 5 ff.

Lupus of Ferrières. *Opera* : *PL* CXIX, 431 ff.

———. *Epistolae*, ed. E. Dümmler : *Epp.* VI, 1 ff.; ed. and trans. L. Levillain, *Les Classiques de l'Histoire de France*, X and XVI (1927–35).

———. *Liber de Tribus Quaestionibus;* and *Collectaneum de Tribus Quaestionibus* : *PL* CXIX, 619 ff., 647 ff.

———. *Vita Maximini episcopi Trevirensis*, ed. B. Krusch : *S S R M* III, 71 ff.

———. *Vita Wigberti abbatis Friteslariensis*, ed. O. Holder-Egger : *SS* XV, 1, 36 ff.

———. *Boetii Philosophiae Consolationis libri quinque*, ed. Rudolf Peiper (1871), xxiv–xxix (text of Lupus : Commentary on the Metra of Boethius).

von Severus, Emmanuel. *Hrabanus Maurus und die Fuldaer Schultradition* : *Fuldaer Geschichtsblätter*, XXXII (1956), 113 ff.

———. *Lupus von Ferrières : Beiträge zur Geschichte des alten Mönchtums und des Benediktinerordens*, XXI (1940).

Chapters VII and VIII

Apologeticum Ebbonis : Mansi, G. D. *Sacrorum Conciliorum nova et amplissa Collectio,* XIV, 775 ff.; *Conc.* II, ii, 794 ff.

Cabaniss, J. Allen. (English trans.) *Liber de Tribus Epistulis* (selections) : *Library of Christian Classics,* IX, ed. George E. McCracken (1957), 148 ff.

Charles the Bald. *Epistolae* : *PL* CXXIV, 861 ff.

Crosby, Sumner McK. *L'abbaye royale de Saint-Denis* (1953).

Demaison, Louis. *La Cathédrale de Reims* (n.d.).

Ebbonis Remensis Restitutio, 840 : *Cap.* II, 111 f.; *Conc.* II, ii, 791 ff.

Epistolae ad Divortium Lotharii II regis pertinentes, ed. E. Dümmler : *Epp.* VI, 207 ff.

Epistolae Pontificum Romanorum

Gregorii IV : *Epp.* V, 228 ff.;

Sergii II : *PL* CVI, 913 ff.;

Leonis IV : ed. P. Ewald : *Neues Archiv* V (1880), 275 ff.; *PL* CXV, 655 ff.;

Benedicti III : *PL* CXV, 689 ff.;

Nicolai I : *Epp.* VI, 257 ff.; *PL* CXIX, 769 ff.;

Hadriani II : *Epp.* VI, 695 ff.; *PL* CXXII, 1259 ff.;

Joannis VIII : *Epp.* VII, 1 ff.; *PL* CXXVI, 651 ff.

Epistolae selectae Sergii II, Leonis IV, Benedicti III, ed. A. de Hirsch-Gereuth : *Epp.* V, 581 ff.

Epistolae variorum inde a saeculo nono medio usque ad mortem Karoli II (Calvi) imperatoris collectae, ed. E. Dümmler : *Epp.* VI, 127 ff.

Epistolarum Fuldensium Fragmenta : *Epp.* V, 517 ff.

Flodoard. *Historia Remensis ecclesiae, Libri II–III*, ed. J. Heller and G. Waitz : SS XIII, 447 ff.

Ganshof, François L. *Le Moyen Âge* (1953).

Godescalc d'Orbais. *Oeuvres théologiques et grammaticales de Godescalc d'Orbais* : *Spicilegium sacrum Lovaniense, Etudes et Documents*, ed. Dom C. Lambot, XX (1945).

Grierson, Philip. *Eudes Ier, Évêque de Beauvais* : *L M A* XLVIII (1935), 161 ff.

Hincmar of Laon. *Epistolae et Opuscula* : *PL* CXXIV, 967 ff.

Hincmar of Reims. *Opera* : *PL* CXXV–CXXVI.

———. *Ad reclusos et simplices dioceseos Remensis*, ed. W. Gundlach, *Zeitschrift für Kirchengeschichte*, X (1889), 258 ff.

———. *De ecclesiis et capellis* : *ibid.* 92 ff.

———. *Carmina*, ed. L. Traube : *P L A C* III, 406 ff.

———. *De Ordine Palatii*, traduit et annoté par Maurice Prou (1884) : *Cap.* II, 517 ff. (see on this L. Halphen : *R H* CLXXXIII [1938], 1 ff.).

———. *Epistolae (Pars Prior)* : *Epp.* VIII, i, 1 ff.

———. *Vita Remigii*, ed. B. Krusch : *S S R M* III, 239 ff.

Hraban Maur : *Epistolae*, ed. E. Dümmler : *Epp.* V, 379 ff.

John the Scot. *De Praedestinatione Liber* : *PL* CXXII, 355 ff. (See also *Epp.* V, 630 ff.)

Jolivet, Jean. *Godescalc d'Orbais et la Trinité* : *la Méthode de la Théologie a l'époque carolingienne* (1958).

Jones, A. H. M., Grierson, P., and Crook, J. A. "The Authenticity of the 'Testamentum S. Remigii' " : *R B P H* XXXV (1957), No. 2.

Lavaud, B. "Prédestination" IV : *D T C* XII, ii, 2901 ff.

———. "Le cas de Godescalc" : *Revue Thomiste*, XV (1932), 71 ff.

Lesne, E. *La hiérarchie épiscopale : provinces, métropolitains, primats, en Gaule et Germania, 742–882* (1905).

———. "Hincmar et l'Empereur Lothaire" : *Revue des questions histori-ques* (1905), 5 ff.

Lothar II, king of Lotharingia. *Epistolae tres* : *PL* CXXI, 371 ff.

Mann, Horace K. *The Lives of the Popes in the Early Middle Ages*, II (1906); III (2d ed.; 1925).

Morin, Dom Germain. "Gottschalk retrouvé" : *R B* XLIII (1931), 303 ff.

Narratio clericorum Remensium : *Conc.* II, 806 ff.

Netzer, H. "Hincmar, archévêque de Reims" : *D T C* VI, ii, 2482 ff.

————. "Hincmar, évêque de Laon" : *ibid.* 2486 f.

Noorden, Carl von. *Hinkmar, Erzbischof von Reims* (1863).

O'Neill, J. D. "False Decretals" : *C E* V, 773 ff.

Parisot, Robert : *Le royaume de Lorraine sous les Carolingiens (843–923)* (1899).

Ratramn, monk of Corbie. *De Predestinatione Dei Libri duo* : *PL* CXXI, 11 ff.

Regesta Pontificum Romanorum, ed. Ph. Jaffé and W. Wattenbach, I (1885).

Rothad of Soissons. *Libellus Proclamationis* : *PL* CXIX, 747 ff.

Schrörs, Heinrich. *Hinkmar, Erzbischof von Reims* (1884).

Sdralek, Max. *Hinkmars von Rheims kanonistisches Gutachten über die Ehescheidung des königs Lothar II* (1881).

Spätling, L. *Incmaro* : *E C* VI (1951), 1769 f.

Sprömberg, H. "Judith, Königin von England, Gräfin von Flandern" : *R B P H* XV (1936), 397 ff., 915 ff.

Turmel, J. "La controverse prédestinatienne au IXe siècle : *Revue d'Histoire et de Littérature religieuses*, X (1905), 47 ff.

Ullmann, Walter. *The Growth of Papal Government in the Middle Ages* (1955).

Villien, A. *Décrétales (Les Fausses)* : *D T C* IV, 212 ff.

INDEX